Philosophical Praxis

PHILOSOPHICAL PRACTICE

Series editor: Lydia Amir, Tufts University

The last decades have witnessed a renewed interest in the power of philosophy to address everyday problems, on both an individual and a social scale. The outcome has been a theoretical and practical field called "philosophical practice," an original approach that highlights the timely and perennial need for philosophy. This series aims to bring to the academic public the best reflections that bear on the relation of philosophy to everyday life and to the contemporary world, as grounded in experience or arguments or both. It honors the founders of this innovative field while calling for new ways of empowering philosophy by demonstrating its relevance to individual and social concerns both inside and outside academia. It thus hopes to strengthen philosophy by bringing its potency to the attention of philosophers and scholars from other disciplines, as well as to students and the general public.

Titles in the Series

Philosophical Praxis: Origin, Relations, and Legacy, by Gerd B. Achenbach, translated by Michael Picard

Philotherapy: An Integration of Psychotherapy, by Aleksandar Fatić

Philosophy in Philosophical Counseling: Unasked Questions, Open Answers, by Ora Gruengard

Wonder, Silence, and Human Flourishing: Toward a Rehumanization of Health, Education, and Welfare, edited by Finn Thorbjørn Hansen, Solveig Eide Botnen, and Carlo Leget

The Philosophy of Practical Affairs: An Introduction, by Joseph Agassi

Philosophical Praxis

Origin, Relations, and Legacy

Gerd B. Achenbach
Translated by Michael Picard

LEXINGTON BOOKS
Lanham • Boulder • New York • London

Published by Lexington Books
An imprint of The Rowman & Littlefield Publishing Group, Inc.
4501 Forbes Boulevard, Suite 200, Lanham, Maryland 20706
www.rowman.com

86-90 Paul Street, London EC2A 4NE

British Library Cataloguing in Publication Information Available

Library of Congress Cataloging-in-Publication Data Available

ISBN: 9781793651136 (cloth)
ISBN: 9781793651143 (ebook)

For Laura

Contents

Acknowledgments

Many are owed much and teeming thanks for all the aid that has been extended to help this book come to be. As translator, and on behalf of the author, I would like to recognize them all here. Though they cannot all be named, there are a few who must not go unmentioned.

Let me save the greatest debt of thanks for last, but to begin, no small thanks are due to Douglas College, where I work, for twice granting education leave (an academic year of half-time teaching duties), without which this project could not have gotten off the ground. Thanks are especially due to Dean Carla Hotel and VP-Academic Thor J. Borgford for supporting these semi-sabbaticals, as well as to the education leave committee for trusting in me twice. Much work accomplished during these two periods will appear in planned future publications, so that advance thanks for that are already in order.

To Jana Hodges-Kluck of Lexington Books we owe thanks for her stellar combination of patience and pressure. Thanks are certainly also due to Lydia Amir, who, although general editor of Lexington's book series in Philosophical Practice, performed something closer to angel-overseer duties.

A squad of Douglas College librarians, seemingly ever-ready to help, tracked down references, located existing English translations, painstakingly sought and got permissions to reprint this or that snippet, beleaguered neighboring universities with interlibrary loan requests, and more than once stayed open late a few minutes so I could get there to borrow a book. The tireless scholarly communications librarian, Gretchen Goertz; at interlibrary loans, the resourceful Christine Fojas; the persistent associate director of learning resources, Katherine E. Shipley; along with others at Douglas College libraries (e.g., Jacquie Ticknor and Rob Leeson-Stotesbury): all are very well aware of how I have overtaxed and overworked them these past few years, and strangely don't seem to mind.

Special thanks are due to the poet Robert Gernhardt for his poem, *Immer*, which appears in translation in chapter 10, and also to his publishers,

S. Fischer Verlag, for permission to publish that translation here, which, though lightly-amended, is due to Johannes Litger, whom we also thank.

For permission to print the chapter epigraphs, we are grateful to:

- The *Revue de Théologie et de Philosophie*, for a translation of a line from an article by Paul Ricœur from "Philosophie après Kierkegaard";
- Standford University Press, for use of Adrian Del Caro's translation of a line by Friedrich Nietzsche;
- Reclam, for a quotation I translated from Odo Marquard's *Der Einzelne. Vorlesungen zur Existenzphilosophie*;
- Christopher Janaway and Cambridge University Press, for a quotation from the translation by Judith Norman, Alistair Welchman, and Christopher Janaway of volume 1 of Arthur Schopenhauer's *The World as Will and Representation*;
- Henry W. Pickford, for permission to quote from his translation of Adorno's *Critical Models: Interventions and Catchwords*;
- Polity Books, for permission to quote from Wieland Hoban's translation of Peter Sloterdijk's *God's Zeal: The Battle of the Three Monotheisms;*
- Frederick Ungar, for a quotation from the Walter D. Morris translation of Thomas Mann's, *Reflections of a Nonpolitical Man*;
- Princeton University Press, for a quotation from the David F. Swenson and Lillian Marvin Swenson translation of volume 1 of Søren Kierkegaard's *Either-Or*.

Efforts—unfortunately unsuccessful—were made over the course of several months to obtain permission to use as chapter epigraph my own translation of a quotation from a publication by Hartmut von Hentig.

Thanks and perhaps an appeal for pardon are due to my family: my beloved wife, Nilu Nemati, and my long-lost and late-returned son, Arya Nemati Zardalo, who bore my extended absences while my head was in a thesaurus. I thank them for their patience and for their presence.

I have left till last the greatest debt of gratitude we owe. No one did more to make this book not only come to be, but come to be as good as it could be, than did Laura V. Adrian. A resourceful go-between for both author and translator, but also a substantial presence in all our meetings and on every resulting page, Laura richly deserves the book's dedication and a share in its fate.

Translator's Note

This project began one night in Mexico City, long after midnight, with a sudden shiver and a dim inchoate realization. A few days earlier I had quite unceremoniously met Gerd B. Achenbach for the first time; I was attending a workshop he held there in German, assisted by two others, one translating into Spanish for the locals, another into English for the international conference-goers. I realized in the event (though I say this without impugning the quality of the live translation) that my rusty German might be of service in putting Achenbach's points in English. My interventions, having met some welcome, later drew a sudden and surprise hearty thanks from Achenbach himself. Later that night, it dawned on me that, with a little study and review, I might offer the larger service of translation, so that this influential yet misunderstood innovator might have his say on his own terms, but in print in English.

To say as much is to confess that I knew very little about Achenbach before I met him. His reputation had of course preceded him and had drawn me to his workshop. By then he existed in English as a scattering of obscure academic articles, plus a few handy slogans, often taken as *reductios.* With all that, I was familiar, but I knew little more. In all selfishness, I was attracted to the adventure. So back home I dashed off a bad translation (my best first attempt) of something short he had written and sent it to him. This led in turn and in time to an invitation for me to speak at the *Gesellschaft für Philosophische Praxis*, which I did in 2019.[1] I arrived in Bergisch Gladbach with a sprawling lecture in English, but over the course of several days, Achenbach, with the indefatigable assistance of Laura V. Adrian, coddled and coaxed me into successfully delivering a short and orderly talk in German, which they had ably translated from my dismembered original. I left there feeling obliged to repay their kindness, their *Aufmerksamkeit*, by bestowing the same individualized energy and attentive care on translating Achenbach's work that they had devoted to mine, insignificant though mine was in comparison.

Those tales seem like distant memories now, as this first book in a two-or-three-book project[2] comes to its overdue completion. I owe a short account of the process by which this translation has come into existence.

Recently, well-meaning friends urged me to bring this long-delayed first book to a close, trying to speed me on by noting that, after the duty-scribe drudgework of translation was finished, I could go on to my own personal creative enterprises. The kind words stunned me. The assumption was that in translating one is doing someone else's work, putting one's own genius aside to play mindless conduit, and be another person's mouth. For my part, I undertook the job out of adventure, an excuse to play with words under intriguing new constraints, and a chance to repay a kindness and a boon. I did it for philosophy, without strategic intent. And yet in my actual experience, it was a free expression of mind and—although I am pleased with the results, recognizing the wordings as my own productions—there is a higher and more distinctive pleasure in giving it all away, in fact in never having properly claimed any of it to begin with, and for the world to say that they are someone else's words and thoughts. For are they not? And who, after all, can possess the truth?

It remains for me to describe the process and draw attention to a few salient features of the translation. On and off for years we met weekly in video conference calls to review successive draft translations; indeed, this book would not have been possible without Zoom and its predecessors. Another technological prerequisite, or at least great aid, has been translation software, with outputs that served as clumsy first drafts, which, though crude, were often very helpful, especially getting started on a fresh text. Too, the hypertext thesaurus function was a great convenience (though ultimately it has only driven me closer to my weathered *Roget*'s). Helpful as such software is, neither semantic nuance nor philosophical subtlety survive current algorithms.

Laura V. Adrian attended *all* the video conferences; a few times, especially as we approached completion of the book, it was just the two of us. Her role as a sort of linguistic go-between would have been impossible without her subtle appreciation of language and profound understanding of Achenbach, which constantly kept me on track. For Achenbach's participation throughout almost all of our meetings I am warmly and enormously grateful. It was often only through his generous erudition and the zestful, even bouncy humor he demonstrated in these sessions that I came to appreciate the meanings that dance playfully around his prose. No less important, it provides the reader with some assurance that this translation has been 'authorized' (in a literal and active sense of the word), and that the results, even the discrepancies with the original German text, are faithful to the author. He is so much the jester that he more than once joked that my English was going to sound better than his German. That I doubt. But, in all sincerity, for me personally the journey has been a wonderfully edifying tour of regions of philosophy that were scantly known to me beforehand. I got all the adventure I imagined and more, and look forward to the next trek.

A word, perhaps, about the mentioned discrepancies. The German book upon which this translation is based[3] is a selection of key texts, mostly lectures, written and delivered over the decades since the founding of Philosophical Praxis in 1981. Though most have been previously published, the collection itself is only to be published in German this year and will appear more or less at the same time as this translation. Due to last minute changes in the German edition, it will include some texts that are not translated here. Furthermore, on close inspection of the common texts, attentive readers will find innumerable minor and plenty of not-so-minor differences in content and wording that distinguish the two. For the most part, these changes earned the approval of Achenbach, and indeed he shared the current translation in draft with scholars undertaking a Korean translation. It nevertheless falls to the translator to accept responsibility for the infelicities that remain in the destination language.

Yet I can hardly be blamed if I fall only a little short. I could never have guessed when I began my adventure at the magnitude of the literary challenge I would face. This is not scientific discourse, not analytic finagling with words to formulate precise definitions to be clung to throughout. There is a non-accidental literary dimension to Achenbach's prose. Even explicit distinctions that take some effort to set out are let slide in subsequent paragraphs, as if to caution against too much logical consistency. There is no edifice-building going on here, not even statuary, for nothing is carved in stone. Something more is going on that taxes the translator to a greater extent than if the aim were to produce a strictly literal rendition. I have already mentioned the innumerable and ubiquitous allusions to other philosophical texts, artistic creations and cultural realities. In tone, at times, the language of fairy tales is evoked, or a mock scientific attitude will suddenly be displayed, with critical and ironic undertones. Or a Biblical style will be struck, followed shortly thereafter with ruthless yet oblique critique. In such literary antics and agility Achenbach often embeds his irony and humor. Of one notorious for impugning method, readers have a right to ask—why all this? Why such play? Why seek to irritate and frustrate the usual way of speaking and . . . *thinking*? But now the question has answered itself—it is in order to think differently, to think further, to think onward; in short, to stimulate, provoke and persuade. As author of *How to Play Philosophy*,[4] and thoroughly guilty of related sins against linguistic and even logical expectation, I have early, often, and increasingly during this project felt that I was after all very well suited, by proclivity and inclination, to undertake it, despite its adventitious beginning. My mischievous joy in language, deployed to philosophical ends, so clearly put to work in that recent book, at last found its match in the task of translating Achenbach. Notwithstanding that, it is impossible to deny, and therefore easy to excuse, my inevitable failure to render Achenbach with full justice. Yet I must and do accept full responsibility for all infelicities and errors of translation.

Footnotes in the German original have become endnotes, marked with an indication that they are translations of Achenbach's comments, but this is only done for notes with significant content, not for simple citations. For the latter, German references have been replaced by English translations where available; although in some cases I have had to, or preferred to, use my own translations. The endnotes are often also an opportunity to explicate cultural and philosophical context, which was generally flushed out in elucidation Achenbach provided during meetings. I do not hesitate to use first person in these notes, so it is perhaps prudent to state upfront that all endnotes not attributed to Achenbach originate with the translator.

I have had to depart from the Lexington style guide by giving a distinct use to single vs. double quotation marks. Double quotation marks are used to indicate words quoted from others, and references are given. Single quotation marks are used to mention words or common phrases, also when they are to be taken in a received, dubious or unusual sense, and also for words used in imaginary or summarized dialogue; in general, when no reference is needed. Occasionally, instead of single quotation marks, I also mention words by placing them in *italics* instead, but this is done only for individual words and when ambiguity does not ensue. Italics are also used for emphasis, in most cases reflecting Achenbach's emphasis in the original.

In many instances I would have preferred gender neutral language, at least when it could be innocuously introduced. But this is not always possible (e.g., plurals can detract from the immediate individuality of issues at stake in a given context; and 'he or she' cannot be used repeatedly in long sentences without considerable inelegance). On this issue I have mostly deferred to Achenbach's original; nor did it seem right to impose fashions of speech, however laudable, on what, despite their timely quality, are historical texts.

A few words should be devoted to individual German terms the translation of which has caused particular difficulty, and sometimes fruitful or contentious discussion. These come in three non-exclusive orders. First, there are of course regular philosophically relevant German terms, like *Aufklärung*, *Begriff*, *Bildung*, *Geist*, *Gestalt*, *Klug*, etc., that are notoriously difficult to render consistently, and present terrible or vexed choices to all translators. When it has seemed important, the German is given in endnotes, along with explanatory comments if necessary; but I have sometimes kept the German word in the text [in square brackets] immediately after the translation, when it has seemed helpful and not intrusive. Square brackets are also used in the text to indicate words inserted editorially into (maybe also cut from) quotations to fit them to the immediate grammatical or semantic context.

On a second level are German terms that have a special or outsized role in Achenbach's own thinking; these include: *anerkennen* (recognize, respect, accede); *Aufmerksamkeit* (careful attentiveness; often rendered as 'hearkening'); *Zuhörender* (as 'hearkener,' active and attentive listener); *Zumutung* (instigation, imposition; a respectful overburdening or worthwhile bother); *besinnen*/*Besonnenheit* (assimilated to the Greek, *sophrosyne*, 'moderation' or 'self-control'; here often 'judiciousness,' sometimes 'levelheadedness'); *nachdenken* ('rethink,' rarely merely 'reflect'); *nachdenklich* (thoughtful, rethoughtful, perhaps circumpsect); *weiterdenken* ('think further' or 'think through and beyond'); *Haltung* (bearing, attitude, though not merely mental); etc. Readers will be well repaid for their attention to these terms, so I have tried to keep translations consistent, or at least to indicate the relatedness [using square brackets] of underlying cognates. But context trumps, and consistency often needs to be sacrificed.

On yet another level altogether are Achenbach's own coinages, such as *Kopfwerk*, *Gesonnenheit*, and *Weltgetriebe*, but including most notably *Lebenskönnerschaft* and *Eingelassenheit.* We have left the latter two words untranslated, which, to a translator, is an open admission of failure. (I will add defiance; let others try who will.) Notwithstanding, it was, in both cases, Achenbach's decision. If I have any face-saving defense, it is that the contexts of their respective introductions are rich enough to set adequate parameters for interpretative debate. For instance, in the case of *Lebenskönnerschaft*, it is presented in pointed opposition to *Lebenskunst* (the more familiar 'art of life') and is clearly bound up in an intimate way with a notion or implicit theory of virtue. The word *Eingelassenheit* is taken apart and assembled with sufficient granularity not only to make it tolerably clear, but also to show that no single English translation could possibly bear similar treatment or be made to grind so many axes at once. (If the word in a given immediate context is indeed translatable, the particular context is often decidedly untranslatable.) It is amusing that emulating in English the freedom one has in German to assemble novel compound nouns mostly produces unutterable word-monsters, even when the German original seems deft or poignant.

A final word on the importance of translating Achenbach. It is a curiosity that if an author underlines their own importance, they tend to come off as vain, whereas a translator can speak highly of the importance of the work lying before the reader without necessarily seeming to put on airs or peddle copies. I shall say only this. I can report numberless occasions thinking, during this work, that when these ideas, some of them as much as forty years old, arrive in English and land in the still-quite-small pond of philosopher-practitioners, they will make a sizable and somewhat uncomfortable splash.

They are unlike anything else out there. Though I make no predictions about ripples or waves that might ensue in larger ponds and in the broader cultural ocean, I do feel confident that we here launch a sea-worthy vessel on a long and adventuresome *Fortleben*.

Michael Picard, MSc, PhD

NOTES

1. Michael Picard, *Bewusstsein Und Realität: Die Frage Des Idealismus in Der frühen Indischen Philosophie* [Consciousness and Reality: The Question of Idealism in the Early Indian Philosophy]. *Gesellschaft für Philosophische Praxis* (GPP), 2019. The talk is available online in print at https://dc.arcabc.ca/.

2. Also expected and underway: *On Right in Wrong* (forthcoming in this series from Lexington Books). It is a translation of *Vom Richtigen im Falschen: Auf Wegen philosophisch inspirierter Lebenskönnerschaft* (Freiburg: Herder, 2003; Köln: Dinter, 2014). A variety of other texts of diverse character are also being prepared for a planned Special Issue of the US academic journal, *Philosophical Practice*.

3. Gerd B. Achenbach, *Philosophie der Philosophische Praxis. Einführung* (Baden Baden: Alber Verlag and Nomos Verlag, 2023). A Spanish translation with again a slightly different line-up of chapters also exists. There is a 1984 book by Achenbach and others, *Philosophische Praxis* (Köln: Verlag für Philosophie/Dinter, 1984, 2nd ed., 1987), but it is unrelated to the present book, despite the similar title. Note that many of the chapters below also appeared in Gerd B. Achenbach, *Zur Einführung der Philosophischen Praxis* (Köln: Dinter, 2010).

4. Michael Picard, *How to Play Philosophy* (Lanham, MD: Hamilton, 2022).

Preface

To 'Upper America'—as I would like to call the northern half of the American continent—belongs the honor in the last century of having originated, within the wide, perhaps over-extended terrain of the schools of psychotherapy, certain essential inspirations and innovations which were later taken up in Europe and adapted to the old European way. This is not to deny that Vienna (above all) and Switzerland are the birthplace of the original forms of all later therapies—Freud's psychoanalysis, C. G. Jung's analytical psychology, and Adler's individual psychology. Significant further developments from this triple root then spread to North America; it is enough to recall the innumerable variants of so-called "humanistic psychology."

And now it looks as if this back-and-forth inter-continental movement is swinging back again. This time it is the renewal of the practice of philosophy, which in 1981 I called into being as *Philosophical Praxis*[1] in Germany, but which very quickly gained a foothold in the neighboring European countries—first of all in Austria and the Netherlands—and then very soon spread from the old continent across the pond into the 'New World.' There it gained attention and recognition in its own right, first in Vancouver, Canada (where in 1994 the First International Congress for Philosophical Practice[2] took place at the University of British Columbia), and then shortly thereafter in New York by Lou Marinoff,[3] who in 1999 wrote *Plato, Not Prozac! Applying Philosophy to Everyday Problems*. Thanks in no small part to English being the current *lingua franca*, this in turn bolstered the presence of Philosophical Praxis worldwide.

It is therefore all the more urgent to make a small selection of writings available in the language now advanced to a near universal idiom—texts that, while founding Philosophical Praxis, initiated a revival of the oldest philosophical impulses. The significance of this latest rebirth of philosophy out of the spirit of its original endeavor to create an exemplary form of life—as understood in antiquity and made contemporary by Pierre Hadot[4] and Michel Foucault[5]—is by no means limited to a mere return in practical terms to the original mission and aspiration of philosophy. Rather, the proper task of this new configuration of philosophy is to establish itself as the first real alternative to 'therapy-culture.' Those who might hitherto have gone into therapy will more and more turn to the philosopher-practitioner in their distress. Thus, the practice of philosophy, for the first time ever, opens up the possibility of establishing itself as a proper profession.

From amongst my publications[6] devoted to this rebirth of philosophy, or intellectually paving the way for it, I have endeavored to select pieces that would offer philosophically interested people in the Anglo-American world some insight into this pioneering project. And now I am sending these texts, accompanied by friendly greetings, to the Western continent, from which the call to Philosophical Praxis may go out to all parts of the world.

However, I must not hand over the typescript of this book without expressly thanking three people.

First and foremost, to my friend—and companion since we met at the International Congress of Philosophical Praxis in Mexico—Michael Picard, the philosophical practitioner and professor of philosophy at Douglas College in Vancouver, who devoted himself with never-flagging love and veritably angelic patience to the extraordinarily daunting task of translating the texts collected here into subtly tempered English of equal rank. This required not only an extremely sensitive knowledge of the language, but at the same time also confronted him as translator with the almost insurmountable task of bridging—if at all possible, even partially overcoming—the peculiar gulf that separates Anglo-American cultural space and understanding from that of continental Europe. Such a task could hardly be accomplished by even a Hermes.

Secondly—and in the same breath, so to speak—my heartfelt thanks go to my wife, Laura V. Adrian, who has been equally tireless in her support of Michael during this months-long translation marathon. In countless meetings, most of which lasted many hours, they jointly wrangled to determine the best rendering in each case. Thanks to her extraordinary expertise in Philosophical Praxis, as well as her truly sublime sense of language, she was called upon to do this as no one else could have.

Last but not least, we would all like to thank our American-Israeli colleague Professor Lydia Amir, both generally for her unparalleled contributions to Philosophical Practice—with worldwide impact—but also particularly for her editorship of this Lexington Books series in Philosophical Practice, which this book, but for unavoidable delays, was to inaugurate.

Gerd B. Achenbach

NOTES

1. Odo Marquard, "Praxis, Philosophische." In the *Historischen Wörterbuch der Philosophie*, ed. Joachim Ritter et al., Vol. VII (Basel, 1989), 1307f. Also accessible online at www.achenbach-pp.de/.

2. The first international congress for philosophical practice took place at the University of British Columbia in Vancouver in 1994, almost exactly forty years ago.

3. Lou Marinoff, *Plato, Not Prozac! Applying Philosophy to Everyday Problems* (New York, 1999).

4. Pierre Hadot, *Exercices spirituels et philosophie antique* (Paris: Etudes augustiniennes, 1981). Several of Hadot's books have appeared in English, most notably (translated by Michael Chase): *Philosophy as a Way of Life* (Oxford: Blackwell, 1995); *The Inner Citadel: the Meditations of Marcus Aurelius* (Harvard University Press, 1998); *What is Ancient Philosophy?* (Harvard University Press, 2002). See the bibliography for full details and other works.

5. Michel Foucault, *Histoire de la sexualité*, vol. 1: *La volonté de savoir*, 1976, vol. 2: *L'usage des plaisirs*, 1984, and especially vol. 3: *Le souci de soi*, 1984. These volumes appeared respectively in English (translated by Robert Hurley) as: *The History of Sexuality* (New York: Vintage, 1980); *The Use of Pleasure* (Vintage, 1985); *Care of the Self* (Vintage, 1986). See the bibliography for full details.

6. Gerd B. Achenbach, *Philosophische Praxis* (Köln: Verlag für Philosophie/Dinter, 1984, 2nd ed., 1987); with T. H. Macho, *Das Prinzip Heilung* (Köln: Verlag für Philosophie/Dinter, 1985); *Das kleine Buch der inneren Ruhe* (Freiburg: Herder, 2000; rev. and exp., 2016); *Lebenskönnerschaft* (Freiburg: Herder, 2001; Köln: Dinter, 2010); *Vom Richtigen im Falschen* (Freiburg: Herder, 2003; Köln: Dinter, 2014); *Zur Einführung der Philosophischen Praxis* (Köln: Dinter, 2010); *On Right in Wrong*. Trans. by Michael Picard (Lanham, MD: Lexington Books, forthcoming). See the bibliography for full details.

Prelude

With dubious persistence, voices here and there are raised calling for a 'theory of Philosophical Praxis.' And I have made a habit of ignoring such voices with equal and opposite persistence. For what should we say to them, if pre-educated people—*nota bene*: their pre-education is their problem[1]—if scientifically trained people think that they cannot know what Philosophical Praxis is until they are in possession of a 'theory' of it? These unfortunate friends of theory are like those who find themselves in a most beautiful landscape, take a look around, then declare that they see nothing because they possess no map of it.

Perhaps we do yet better to construe such persistence as the contemporary rule over our minds of the algorithm, if indeed its reign has not already been instituted *within* them. Thereunder it holds true: one 'understands' only in knowing the schema according to which processes run. We can do no better than the telling analogy of *process engineering.*

Yet I feel like asking those askers: have any of you who demand a 'theory' of Philosophical Praxis ever heard tell of a 'theory of philosophy'? Unlikely, I should think. Still, it *is* possible—after all, one does read all sorts of things! In that case, the one who poses the question (and—*even more so*—the one who is subjected to it) would do us all a favor by leaving such 'contributions to research' on the dusty library shelves where they may be abandoned without causing any harm.

No—in the spheres of philosophy the contrary has always held true: the philosopher thinks and at the same time bethinks his thinking and even, within *his* thinking, the very possibility of thinking *as such*. Thus not only has he no need of the well-worn rut that keeps the theory-driven man in his predetermined path; on the contrary, such constraints would lie upon him as a yoke, and he would feel as if bound in fetters by the head and limbs. Let us not shy away from one of the *leading ideas* of the philosophical tradition: whereas others fancy themselves safe and secure at the end of the leash of a chosen theory, the philosopher suffers from the loss of that *freedom*, without which thinking wastes itself away in mere correctness until it degenerates at last into dull routine, and finally dies.

In order to forestall a widespread misunderstanding: the responsibility of the philosopher is not only, possibly not even primarily, to what he 'thinks' but instead to *rethink*, to *become thoughtful*, or—to resort to quaint old terms—to become judicious. Under *this* mandate, wherever possible, he rescues thoughts trapped under rubble, and pries open new springs of dried-up thinking, that they may once again begin to flow.

What's more: taken in its widest scope, such thinking is not a ring-fenced nature park in which the philosopher would let himself be confined. On the contrary: he feels; senses; looks; detects; suspects; sees coming; distrusts and believes; fears, trembles and hopes; remembers the forgotten; calls attention to the overlooked; insists where others are 'already further along'; irritates the questions whose answers are already known; keeps calm when the armies march; makes a fuss where others look aside—in sum: he *lives*, and it does not elude him *that*, or *how*, he lives. That is his base, that is where he gathers experiences. But here I break off, though clearly enough this list could be extended *ad libitum*.

Only one more point to be noted at this juncture: the domain of philosophy is no longer that of 'knowledge' [*Wissens*]—or, as one would say today to preserve generality, 'putative' knowledge. It is this that accounts for why it no longer misconceives itself as sister to the sciences, but rather is to be found in the neighborhood of the arts, of music, and of a literature that in its own way aspires to be knowledge [*Erkenntnis*].

So, instead of glorying in conquests within the narrow, stipulatory quarters of Knowledge,[2] a philosophy that must stand the test of practice, in which the figure of the philosopher-practitioner attends to the cares and needs of the people who turn to us—such a philosophy at least comes down to deliberate *bearing*, learned kindness,[3] and a self-wrought *constitution*; in other words: to being granted entry into the realm of *education* where we can come to be at home, as well in the *here-and-now* as in *past ages*.

What this means in relation to the guest in our practice is that we are challenged to do what the typical academically refined seminar graduate is least able to do. Even as Orpheus once followed his Eurydice, so too the philosophical practitioner must find his way to, and then within, the world in which his guest has entangled himself, or has been entangled, and in which he endures, hoping for a way out.

There we find him and take him with us to where doors are open to him, if he dares to go with us and is able to do so. So we ourselves become for him what, according to Schopenhauer's deeply thought image, *Death* is to every rigorous, non-indulgent philosophizing: namely, Apollo Musagetes, Apollo as Leader of the Muses. He, however, does not lead us down into the lightless realm of shadows, but awakens us as one and guides us up into the well-woven vivifying spirit realm, which awaits and now warmly welcomes and receives the philosophers.

What, finally, will I then say, if there continues to be a demand for a 'theory of Philosophical Praxis,' as can be assumed with sad certainty?

I will say: The reply must be efforts toward a *philosophy of Philosophical Praxis*, the pieces of which are nothing but *essays* (in the literal sense) put together to form a polyphonic fugue.

It may also be said, however, that the essays I gather here are harvest bounty, as they certainly did not fall by chance *to one* who over a period of forty years labored to harrow, sow, and reap, which has been both an honor and a limitation. The individual—to speak exactly, the *unique*—preconditions that I as a particular being bring forward have bathed the newly opened terrain in a light, the color of which is completely tempered personally. This rules out that any training in theory could suffice for a subordinate practice, or for the creation of application-oriented methods as a helping hand to zealous 'practitioners.'

At the same time, the texts in this book are so many contributions to a conversation that has already been going on for decades, first in the form of a series of colloquia organized with international participation by the *Gesellschaft für Philosophische Praxis* founded in 1982 in Bergisch Gladbach;[4] but then above all in the ever-expanding context of the (so far) seventeen international congresses on Philosophical Praxis.[5]

It was to be expected that straight away—as per usual: as soon as academics meet on the public scene—'trends' emerged, in the worst case even so-called 'schools,' which may offer a certain identity-insurance to those who find shelter there, even if a truly independent, self-responsible, especially philosophically imbued thinking has always eschewed such comforts.[6]

With fitting seriousness, however, it ought at least to be noted that Philosophical Praxis is attracting attention in seemingly philosophically distant but practically engaged, scientifically ambitious circles; for instance, when it comes to providing a 'philosophical foundation' for the 'counseling professions'[7] or entering into conversation with psychotherapeutically oriented practitioners.[8]

Most significantly, however, the importance of Philosophical Praxis is now increasingly being perceived in medical circles, where doubts about the 'scientific turn' that occurred in the nineteenth century are emerging and, in the wake of this, a renewed insistent interest in philosophy in practical terms is emerging.[9]

It remains to be seen to what extent Philosophical Praxis will succeed in being taken up with prestige at high schools—as is already the case at numerous universities worldwide,[10] though so far not yet in its 'home country.'

The conviction may even be argued for: however much Philosophical Praxis has to learn from academic philosophy, there is very likely far more that university-established philosophy has to learn to its own benefit from the experiences in Philosophical Praxis, if only it opens itself to them. Undoubtedly there are already plenty of confidence-building examples. For it suffices only to recall Montaigne, Pascal, Spinoza, Schopenhauer, Kierkegaard, and Nietzsche, to show that the fire of philosophy often first blazed outside the walled-in academy before advancing as a revitalizing force into the well-kept fortress of higher learning.

And it is the spirit that scales all walls.

From Vienna, May 2023

NOTES

1. Pre-education—*Vorbildung*; pre-educated—*vorgebildete*. This mocking concept ought to be understood over against the central role in Achenbach (and in this book) of *Bildung* (education, culture, self-formation); see especially chapter 8, notes 3, 8 and 30–33. The notion may also be profitably juxtaposed with *Vorbild*, the paragon, standard-bearer or role model, the existence of which for the philosophical practitioner Achenbach denies (as for example in the very title of chapter 2).

2. Narrow, stipulatory quarters of Knowledge—*ausbedungenen Wissensquartieren*.

3. Kindness—*Gesonnenheit.* An Achenbach construction derived from the expression, "wohl gesonnnen," meaning well-disposed. It is a benevolent solicitude *toward* a situated individual. "Self-wrought constitution" is "erlangte Verfassung."

4. See the documentation of the early years in the *Kleine Chronik der Philosophische Praxis, 1981–1995*, which is available online at https://www.achenbach-pp.de.

5. In Vancouver (1994), Leusden/Netherlands (1996), New York (1997), Bergisch Gladbach (1998), Oxford (1999), Oslo (2001), Copenhagen (2004), Seville (2006), Carloforte/Italy (2008), Leusden (2010), Chuncheon/Korea (2012), Athens (2013), Belgrade (2014), Bern (2016), Mexico City (1018), Petersburg (2021), and Timisoara/Romania (2023); see the website at https://icpp.site/.

6. Donata Domizi, Philosophische Praxis. Eine Standortbestimmung, *Information Philosophie*, Heft 4 (2019), 86–94.

7. See, for example: Luitgard Brem-Gräser, *Handbuch der Beratung für helfende Berufe*, 3 vols. (Munich-Basel: 1993), most notably volume 1, pages 121–131.

8. See *psycho-logik. Jahrbuch für Psychotherapie, Philosophie und Kultur*. Published since 2006 in Freiburg-München by Karl Alber Verlag.

9. A representative selection: Klaus Dörner, *Der gute Arzt. Lehrbuch der ärztlichen Grundhaltung*, 2nd ed. (Stuttgart: Schattauer, 2003), therein especially: Sorge um mich selbst. / Das gute Leben / Medizin als Philosophie / Philosophische

Grundhaltung des Arztes. But see also the volumes edited by Giovanni Maio, *Auf den Menschen hören. Für eine Kultur der Aufmerksamkeit in der Medizin* (Freiburg-Basel-Vienna: Herder, 2017) and *Vertrauen in der Medizin. Annäherungen an ein Grundphänomen menschlicher Existenz* (Freiburg-Basel-Vienna: Herder, 2023). One may also consult G. B. Achenbach, "Aussichten auf ein Ende des kalten Krieges im Reich der Medizin. Philosophisches Plädoyer für eine praktische Weisheit, die den Streit der Theorien schlichtet," in *Patientenorientierung und Professionalität*, edited by Peter F. Matthiessen, 2nd expanded ed. (Bad Homburg: Verlag Akademishe Schriften, 2011); and G. B. Achenbach, "Der Patient und sein Arzt," *in Ärztekammer Nordrhein: Kommunikation*, 117. Deutscher Ärztetag (Düsseldorf: 2014), 67–92.

10. Thus, among others, in the University of Tokyo, Kyungpool National University, Korea Counseling Graduate University, Catholic University of Portugal, Ca'Foscari University for Venice, University of Roma 3, Université de Liège, University of Vienna, Timisoara University/Romania, Institute of Psycoanalysis/Russia, Milkwaukee School of Engineering/USA, Universidad Vasco de Quiroga/Mexico, National University of Buenos Aires, Universidad de Chile, and University of the State of Rio de Janeiro. (List incomplete.)

Chapter 1

Short Answer to the Question: What Is Philosophical Praxis?

One must make something new to see anything new.

—Lichtenberg[1]

I started the world's first *Philosophical Praxis* in 1981,[2] and coined the term that same year.[3] In 1982 the Society for Philosophical Praxis was instituted in Bergisch Gladbach near Cologne; later it became the international umbrella organization for numerous national societies. So much for the institutional part. Now for the question: What, in short, is Philosophical Praxis?

The philosophical life-counseling that takes place in Philosophical Praxis establishes itself as an alternative to psychotherapies. It is an adaptation for those who, tormented by their sorrows or problems, and unable to 'come to terms' with their lives, find themselves somehow 'stuck.' Philosophical Praxis is for people beset by life-questions that they can neither solve nor get rid of, or for those who are able to prove themselves equal to everyday life, but nevertheless feel 'under-burdened,' perhaps because they suspect that their reality does not correspond to their potential. Others turn to Philosophical Praxis when they are not satisfied merely to exist or muddle through, but demand instead *to examine their life*, to see clearly its contours, its whence and why and whither-to.

Their need is often simply to reflect on the unique circumstances, the peculiar entanglements, and the often oddly ambiguous course of our lives. Briefly put, people seek out practicing philosophers because they want to understand and to be understood. They almost never arrive with the Kantian question "What ought I do?"[4] but rather with the question of Montaigne, which runs: "What am I doing?"[5] Perhaps in the background, operative as an insight, lurks that most ancient philosophical wisdom—namely the maxim of Socrates, that only the examined life is worth living. It may make its presence felt as a shadowy fear that a life so 'lifeless' is hardly even lived at all, and instead somehow 'wasted,' 'forfeit,' 'squandered'—a life about to undo itself. Schopenhauer:

> Most people, when they look back at the end, find that they have lived their whole life through provisionally, and are amazed to see that what they allowed to pass by so unappreciated and unenjoyed was their very life, the very thing in whose expectation they lived. And so the course of one's life, as a rule, is such that, made a fool of by hope, one dances into the arms of death.[6]

Whoever has shared this terrifying prospect may through philosophical reflection find the burden of life appear like a promise [*Verheißung*]; for the philosophical attitude to life is in fact—like a promise—a respectful overburdening that lends gravity to our existence, a sense to our being here, and a meaning to our present.

Usually there are distinctive occasions which bring the guest to the decision to consult the philosophical practitioner. Commonly they involve disappointments, unforeseen or at least unexpected experiences, clashes with other people, strokes of fate, the experiences of failure, importunate or just plain blah life-outcomes. In such circumstances, one assumes (however unclearly) the task of Philosophical Praxis, as outlined by Sir Karl Popper before the practice even existed:

> We all have our philosophies, whether or not we are aware of this fact, and our philosophies are not worth very much. But the impact of our philosophies upon our actions and our lives is often devastating. This makes it necessary to try to improve our philosophies by criticism. This is the only apology for the continued existence of philosophy which I am able to offer.[7]

If we are to be concise here, we must ask: in what way do practicing philosophers help their visitors along? The usual way to frame the question is confusing: 'what method do practical philosophers follow?' To speak correctly, philosophy works not *with*, but at best *upon* methods. Obedience to method is the pride of the sciences, not the point of philosophy. Philosophical thinking does not move along ready-made paths; it looks anew in each case for the 'right way.' Rather than deploy well-worn thought-routines, it sabotages them to clarify itself.

It is not a matter of leading guests of Philosophical Praxis on a philosophically predetermined course, but rather of helping them along their own way. Incidentally, this presupposes on the part of the philosopher the ability to appreciate others without necessarily agreeing with them; indeed, as Goethe said, in a way that "neither approves nor censures."[8]

Philosophy cannot simply be 'applied,' as if the concerns brought by the guest could be 'treated' with a dose of Plato, or Hegel or whomever else. Philosophical readings are not remedies to be prescribed. Does the patient go to the doctor to take in a medical lecture? Nor should the visitor to Philosophical Praxis be taught by the philosopher, still less deceived by clever words, and certainly not served up with theories. The question is whether the philosopher, through their own reading, has become wise and understanding and attentive, whether they have acquired in this way a sensitivity for the otherwise well-overlooked, and learned to become at home in wayward and offbeat thinking, feeling, and judgment. For only as co-thinker and sympathizer can one liberate visitors from their loneliness—or forlornness—and thus perhaps to move them to other appraisals of life and its circumstances.

Isn't it the same for psychologists and psychotherapists? For the pastor, too? The question inevitably arises—a sign of our *yet blooming* therapeutic culture—as to the boundary between Philosophical Praxis and psychotherapies. The psychologist and psychotherapist are specialists, specially trained to perceive the specific in a special way, specifically psychogenic or psychologically conditioned disorders. Where they are not specialists, they are dilettantes. Paradoxically, the philosopher is a specialist in the non-special, both the general and the plain (as well as in the rich tradition of reasoned thought), but also in the contradictory and the deviant, with particular emphasis on the individual and the unique.

In this way, the philosopher in practice takes visitors seriously: not in the grips of any theory (that is, not through schematic understanding) and not as a mere 'instance of a rule,' but as *this very one*. No value scale is held over above the visitor, not even that of health. The question is whether visitors are living up to themselves or, to paraphrase Nietzsche's famous words, whether they have become who they are.

It should be added that Philosophical Praxis by no means only takes the form of individualized consultations. It also supports companies, organizations and associations in their attempts to find their mission, sound principles and orienting guidelines.

NOTES

1. Georg Christoph Lichtenberg, *Sudelbücher*, Heft J, 1756–1770, No. 1770. Picard Translation.

2. See Odo Marquard, "Praxis, Philosophische." In the *Historischen Wörterbuch der Philosophie*, ed. Joachim Ritter et al., Vol. VII (Basel, 1989), 1307f.

3. This chapter was previously translated by Dr. Patrick Neubauer. That translation was consulted but little used and not relied upon.

4. "1) What can I know? 2) What should I do? And 3) What may I hope?" Immanuel Kant, *The Critique of Pure Reason*. Trans. by Paul Guyer and Allen W. Wood. (CUP, 1998), A805/B833.

5. What Achenbach calls "the question of Montaigne" is not the question "Que sçais-je?" or, "What do I know?" that Montaigne took "as a motto, inscribed over a pair of scales" (Apology for Raymond Sebond, in *The Complete Essays of Montaigne,* Donald Frame translation [Standford University Press, 1958], 392–393), and which is often called '*the* question of Montaigne.' *That* question, as Montaigne tells us, expresses his dalliance with "the Pyrrhonian philosophers." But the question Achenbach considers to be far more characteristic of Montaigne than even his motto arises often enough in the *Essays*, and is decidedly less epistemic; it asks after self-understanding in action: 'What am I actually doing?' ("Was tue ich eigentlich?"). Montaigne: "I do not make it my business to tell the world what it should do—enough others do that—but what I do in it." *Essays*, I, 142. Look also to "On some verses of Virgil," *Essays*, III for illustration: "My philosophy is in action, in natural and present practice, little in fancy" (639–640); or "I am hungry to make myself known, and I care not to how many, provided it be truly" (643); and "I owe a complete portrait of myself to the public. The wisdom of my lesson is wholly in truth, in freedom, in reality; disdaining, in the list of its real duties, those petty, feigned, customary, provincial rules, altogether natural, constant, and universal; of which propriety and ceremony are daughters, but bastard daughters" (677).

6. Arthur Schopenhauer, On the doctrine of the nothingness of existence, §145. In *Parerga and Paralipomena: Short Philosophical Essays*, 2. Trans. by Adrian Del Caro and Christopher Janaway (CUP: 2014), 304.

7. Karl Popper, *Objective Knowledge: An evolutionary Approach* (Clarendon, 1972), 33. The passage, Popper's "excuse" for doing philosophy, is preserved in the Revised edition of 1979, reprinted 1994. Achenbach cites the German translation, *Objektive Erkenntnis. Ein evolutionärer Entwurf* (Hamburg: Hoffmann Und Campe Verlag, 1973), 44.

8. Achenbach Note: With regard to his novel, *Die Leiden des jungen Werther*, which some of his contemporaries had expected to display a "didactic purpose," Goethe notes: "the true work of art has none. It neither approves nor censures, but instead develops sentiments and actions in sequence, and thereby illuminates and instructs." Goethe, *From My Life: Poetry and Truth*, Part 3. Vol. 4 of *Goethe: Collected Works* (Princeton, NJ: Princeton University Press, 1994), 433. Thus does Goethe describe what is also the mission of Philosophical Praxis.

Chapter 2

Philosophical Praxis Boasts a Long Tradition, but No Paragon

> As long as philosophy retains the faintest trace of the title of a book published by an old Kantian more than thirty years ago, *From the Philosophy Corner*, it will remain nothing more than the fun its detractors make of it.
>
> —Theodor W. Adorno[1]

Philosophical Praxis boasts a long tradition—but no paragon, no standard-bearer.[2] Any number of well-known forebears are to be named, with Socrates at their head as original ancestor and progenitor. And there exists a legacy handed down from very long ago. But this accumulated wealth is like a sack of old coins with no market value, alluring and compelling keepsakes, though without currency, no longer valid tender.

Thus was minted that maieutic-elenctic art of the prickly Socrates himself, who with unprecedented determination honored the *logos*—honored it indeed too much—thereby initiating the tradition of philosophico-medical arts. Thus issued too the philosophical praxis, set up very early on, of Antiphon (480–411 BCE), the Attic sophist and philosophical Asclepiad. Plutarch reports of him that, "he composed a manual for the avoidance of troubles, on the analogy of the treatment of the sick by doctors; and getting himself a room near the marketplace at Corinth, he advertised that he had the power of curing by means of speech those that were in trouble."[3] To these coiners we may add the excessively clever life-husbandry and happiness-economy of Epicurus. Plus Stoicism, with its more clearly fathomed depths and an already highly sophisticated knowledge of soul [*Seelenkunde*], counseling the supervision of drives and monitoring of emotions, and offering the "tranquility of the soul"[4] as a picture of the fulfillment of life that is, at the very least, not fatuous.

As is well-known, it was above all certain Stoics who lent greater significance to the Socratic turn away from grand doctrine and cosmic speculation to philosophy as a thought-through way of being, as *habitus*, and they did so by developing further the Socratic motif of a *medicina mentis*. Whereas Socrates had already used a medical metaphor, referring to dialectical philosophy as a "*katharticon*" (i.e., a laxative that through "blows of speech" rids us of blockages of thought[5]—an idea, by the way, that lucidly aligns the lower purgations with the upper purification of the head through the work of thought); for certain Stoics, reason already shifts to the bodily center; i.e., the passions and the desires of the soul were no longer offside, not hidden in the shadows cast by brilliant philosophical thought. For instance, Chrysippus (280–208 BCE), who, after completing a three volume work on the passions, wrote one called *Therapeutikos*. With anticipatory ingenuity, he recognized "a side of reason" itself in the "Other of Reason," which further bifurcated into "soma" and "psyche." An uncut philosophy sets itself the task of becoming not only a *scientific medicine of the soul*, but even more a *science of the logos* to be realized not in the head only, but in its own way in the body (or soma) as well.

Something else arose with the Stoics, which perhaps only today is rightly understood: a clear individualism. For instance, Panaetius of Cos/Rhodes (c. 185–109 BCE) presented astonishingly modern thoughts; let me insert one here in quotation:

> The diversity of individual natures goes so far that, sometimes, in the same situation, it falls to one person to give himself death, but not to the other. Odysseus, in order to achieve his goal, endured every abuse, to which Aias would have preferred death a thousand times. Let each one keep this in mind and examine what he carries within himself, and let him follow that and not try out what is foreign to him. For the most appropriate thing for everyone is what flows from his personal being.[6]

Of course, here as elsewhere it is not the past that teaches us in the present, but rather the present that sheds light for us on the past—just as the gallery of forebears of Philosophical Praxis does not show us the way, but (quite the opposite) Philosophical Praxis extends itself backwards and with new and other interests revives perspectives on philosophical prehistory. Naturally such reading-for-traces leads straight away to antiquity, and not only out of respect for chronological order, but because in antiquity—as Hegel quite approvingly remarked—"philosophy was regarded generally as concern for life, and for the whole of life, not as it is by one who hurries through lectures on philosophy in order to hasten on to something else."[7] So weighty an aim was shared even by the training in moral consciousness offered by the philosophizing pedagogues and self-educators of later Rome—a garden, as it were, in which more ripened than odious fruits like the emperor, Nero.[8] Today, of course, such advice-spewing philosophy would be a ridiculous embarrassment, at least if it sought to present itself in the high-pitched tone in which Seneca, for instance, announced it. Here I quote:

> Philosophy . . . is not carried on with the object of passing the day in an entertaining sort of way and taking boredom out of leisure. It molds and builds the personality, orders one's life, regulates one's conduct, shows one what one should do and what one should leave undone, sits at the helm and keeps one on the correct course as one is tossed about in perilous seas. Without it no one can lead a life free of fear or worry. Every hour of the day countless situations arise that call for advice, and for that advice we have to look to philosophy.[9]

One problem here is that any such hourly advice-dispensing philosophy runs the risk of getting lost in sixty-minute intervals. Another more alarming problem with this sort of philosophical paternalism is the violence inherent within it, through which it tries to force life to fit its plan and render it docile, a trait consistently associated with philosophical hubris and self-glorification. It even appears as a threatening gesture in the otherwise rather gentle and quite sensitively instructive Epictetus:

> Whatever rules of conduct are set for you, hold to them as if they were laws, as if it would be an impiety for you to transgress them; as to what anyone says about you, pay no heed to it, since in the end that is not your concern. . . . You've acquired knowledge of the philosophical principles that you ought to accept, and have accepted them. What kind of teacher, then, are you still waiting for, that you should delay any effort to reform yourself till he appears?[10]

This is pure normativity in action, the mind set against the mindless; and in the imperative gesture he conceals his actual impotence. Here we distinctly detect the tone in which, somewhat later, divine commands will be issued, softened only slightly by the promise of unmeritable grace, shaking those ensnared in sin, and converting those even goodwill could not reach.

However remote from us today such religious inspiration and celestial lures may be, they possessed in their day (chronicled philosophically first and foremost by Augustine) a life-redeeming potency, that has meanwhile become foreign to us—unless of course the hope announced then has been perverted into the contemporary faith in salvation which therapy brings to market. One has a right to wonder whether the new yoke (which ranges richly from the gentle inquiry of the 'empathic' therapist to compulsory drugging by institutional psychiatry) is indeed the lighter of the two, or perhaps just the sweet poison of the inconsolable, rendering them forgetful of the imitative character of contemporary personal-change techniques.

Be that as it may, Philosophical Praxis survived in the Middle Ages, and not only in the succession of Augustine, whose biographical philosophizing originated in his own depression and illness. Even as he disdained the guidance available from the Hippocratics, Platonists and the Stoics (in comparison with the help of the "Savior"—"for this disease Thou alone curest"[11]), so faith in the Christian God becomes the true *medicina mentis*, and philosophy—at least in terms of practice—accordingly becomes *ancilla theologiae*. But, remarkably, philosophy remained *medicina mentis* in *De consolatione philosophiae*, the neoplatonic solace-text of Boethius, which was still read in late scholasticism with pleasure and 'with edifying intent.'

Distinct from this, Philosophical Praxis also survived in the form of meditative practice, above all in monasteries and under the guise of mysticism. Thus the principle of individuation was not completely lost in the compulsory orientation to the universal, but lived on below the metaphysical ceiling of the Cathedral of the Scholastic Spirit, finding an inconspicuous refuge in the *unio mystica* of the seekers (and finders) of God. Eckhart's teaching on souls; the encouragement of practical exercises; the search for "inner serenity"[12] proposed by Eckhart's pupil, Seuse, as a fundamental element of Christian life; the sermons of Tauler in which one is directed to enter "simple-mindedly . . . into one's inner ground"[13]—all these preserved those traditions threatened with extinction by the opulent high scholasticism of *Summa Theologica.*

In sum: the religiously delimited special milieu (ideally a monastic enclosure or piety-soaked hermitage) in which the fundamentally practical spirit of philosophy spent its long internal emigration, was not after all an adverse climate for the practice of philosophy. And yet such eccentricity vouchsafed by heaven invited a philosophical life that, for all its approbation of the everyday, and despite its occasionally succumbing to '*amor fati*,' drew its impetus not least from experiences of distance that underpin the status of chosenness and exalt the spirit as exceptional. In the colder but also more hotly agitated air of the outside world, philosophy—especially that within it which ill fits the world, its esotericism—would have long since disappeared or, under the pressures of conformity, degenerated into utter irrelevance.

And yet, after having been freed from strict adherence to the Christian monopoly on salvation, a philosophy emerged that ranks as a precursor to Philosophical Praxis. Here I refer to the skeptical intelligence of Montaigne, and his self-reflective refinement of life. Here philosophy is wholly resettled: rather than going on ahead as a kind of commander on our life's way (ordering us onto the right path by barking back all manner of orders, rules and unshirkable duties, with no less a prospect than perfection as a destination point), philosophy for Montaigne instead follows along behind, usually quietly and unobtrusively. Seldom does the man even seek it out, and then only in order to try with its help to clarify life *post factum*. "My mores (*moeurs*) are natural,"[14] Montaigne writes in the 'Apology for Raymond Sebond':

> I have not called in the assistance of any discipline to erect them; but, weak as they are, when it came into my head to lay them open to the world's view, and when to expose them to the light in a little more decent garb I went to adorn them with reasons and examples, it was a wonder to myself accidentally to find them conformable to so many philosophical discourses and examples. I never knew what regimen my life was of till it was near worn out and spent; a new figure—an unpremeditated and accidental philosopher.[15]

This "new phenomenon" of a philosopher—"in the rough and without a model"[16]—first laid down roots in France, where the moralists, with sharpened psychological insight and educated wit, launched highly astute reflections on social life.

The ambition of this light-footed philosophy was not to provide a foundation to praxis, but to explore it, and with sufficient integrity both to give primacy to the concrete, and to strip away its semblance of self-evidence.

Despite its breezy tone and its disinterest in the systematic organization of knowledge, this deadly serious skepticism was far above so-called 'popular philosophy,'[17] which in Germany at that time fancied itself charged with enlightening the better classes and urging them to live a reasonable life. These German treatises, with their life-counsel, would become involuntary comical caricatures of themselves. Yet the same thing in the hands of Spinoza demands great respect and recognition. With Spinoza—according to Bloch's effusive testimony—"arose the most consequential figure of wisdom so far, and the most exemplary,"[18] one who took philosophy once again to be "*medicina mentis*, [acting] quite simply as healthy clarity, and against the confused distortions of the mind, contra inadequate ideas."[19] Here is the "tremendous *intellectual faith* of Spinoza's wisdom: every affect that is a misery ceases to be one once we have a clear idea of it; for it is only a misery insofar as it is a confused, an inadequate Idea."[20]

It would be stimulating to slog through the present obscure landscape, a swamp in which the pied profusion of therapeutic flowers yet blooms, and muster them all to see just how much unconscious Spinoza has survived within it, dimmed down to the petty and complacent. Be that as it may, Spinoza himself formulated for his own time (to which Goethe, among many others, took himself to belong) precise ethical guidance for Philosophical Praxis; and, while today his works come across as imposing and inimitable, he *himself* stands as an extraordinary demonstration of its concrete actualization. Such a personal realization was attempted only once more in the far north: by Kant, whom no one would have called "the sage of Konigsberg" had his output only been an unprecedented sharpening of thought and an ingenious imperative that finally became a 'categorical mnemonic' for philosophy seminarians.

The gallery of ancestors of Philosophical Praxis is now neither complete nor closed, because since at least the so-called "saddle time"[21] in European history in 1770, with the rise of "qualitative individualism"[22] (corresponding to the opening in 1771 in Vienna of the first psychotherapeutic practice by Anton Mesmer, along with Father Hell); i.e., with the advent, according to Nietzsche, of an age of waning cheerfulness, in which problems came to the fore "with which nothing could be done once they had arisen";[23] in short, since at least the onset of the modern age, there have been numerous pioneers and predecessors of Philosophical Praxis who could be named. And they are interesting precisely because they see that their life-calculations no longer work out roundly and without remainder, so that they became embarrassed even to fashion advice.

Noteworthy in this regard is Karl Philipp Moritz, Goethe's young friend, who from 1783 to 1793 published the "Magazin zur Erfahrungsseelenkunde" under the title *Gnothi Sauton* (ΓΝΩΘΙ ΣΑΥΤΟΝ)—still today a treasure trove of observations for the philosophical practitioner. Next in line to be named, from Copenhagen, the Dane, Søren Kierkegaard, who in his book, *Either-Or,* fictionalized a long and exemplary philosophical consultation, conducted in the name of B, a court and city magistrate, in a tone entirely distinct from that of the crude righteousness of the bourgeoisie or the spiritual complacency of the clerical ground crew, yet with a hitherto unheard-of "Freedom of a Christian"[24] against all superior ordinances, under the motto "the only salutary thing, is always that a person with respect to his own life is not his uncle, but his father."[25]

Schopenhauer also clearly belongs in this pageant. Despite his efforts to once more cast an all-encompassing metaphysics *from a single mold*, he not only looked closely, but reoriented looking itself from a practical point of view (and with subtle soteriological intent), resulting in fragments of a popular philosophy of the highest order.

At the very least, to Schopenhauer we owe that philosophy was not completely forgotten outside academic circles—to him and to Nietzsche, who, despite all the misgivings raised by his broad impact, was a veritable firestorm (one that rages still, as we see yet today), and not mere learned ash.

Finally, in the twentieth century, we have Franz Rosenzweig, a most peculiar outlier, who, before the Nazi crack-down began, when he was at an advanced age, gave a remarkably practical twist to the scholarly life by establishing in Frankfurt the *Freie Jüdishe Lehrhaus*, a kind of precursor institution of Philosophical Praxis. The very idea found richer soil in the Jewish tradition, with its rabbinically personalized synthesis of inherited and intellectually advisable wisdom, than in the Christian church's soul-collectivism. In the spirit of later Philosophical Praxis, Rosenzweig wrote to the historian Friedrich Meinecke, who had him in mind for a professorship at Berlin University:

> Wisdom [*das Erkennen*] has become a service to me. A service to man. . . . Wisdom . . . does not let anyone dictate its answers, . . . only its questions. Not every question is worth being asked. . . . I ask only where I am asked. Asked by people, not by scholars, not by 'science.'[26]

Philosophical Praxis affiliates itself with these and many other figures. But it could never rely upon them, as if any one of them had already finally settled what Philosophical Praxis is or should be.

Put bluntly: there is no place in the history of philosophy that Philosophical Praxis can find its bed ready-made, into which we need only slip to make ourselves comfortable. This claim clearly subverts the cliché that avers that philosophy, unlike the sciences, cannot grow antiquated, that Aristotle is more than ancient history. But, alas, this prejudice is so far true that tradition-circumcised thinking easily and without resistance falls victim to the prevailing pressures to conform, and becomes stupid.

It must therefore be owned that *ideas too are mortal*. And if any philosophical life-plan, torn from its temporal context, should endeavor to clothe itself in the pathos of eternal validity, it would instantaneously be disgraced.

Inevitably, Adorno, Habermas and others raised the question in all seriousness as to whether philosophy was not utterly outmoded.[27] It is at the very least indisputable that the intellectual labors [*Kopfwerk*] of the guild of philosophers have for a good while now lost their unquestionable right to existence; all the more so as regards Philosophical Praxis.

The most immediate question about Philosophical Praxis—which has not only traded under the questionable label "philosophical" but also thereby—*note well!*—damaged its own business—is whether *as a practice* it is still even possible at all in a genuinely philosophical sense. And the question is urgent, since whatever Philosophical Praxis may have been in the past—be it ancient or Hellenistic or Roman or enlightened Königsbergian dietetics stylized into fixed-principle life-instruction, or even Oriental crypto-matriarchal-taoistic life-guidance—all such forms of praxis, though they were assuredly philosophical *in their day*, cannot endure as philosophical. In effect, praxis would be calling upon philosophy only to spurn it, if it were to overlook the fact that, already by the twentieth century, the most representative figures of philosophy had lost all relation to questions concerning the conduct of life, lost indeed even the competence to deliberate over crises of existential importance.

Unable any longer to underwrite individual life-risks, philosophy can no more provide deception-free advice on questions of the meaning of life than it can on the so-called ‘ultimate things’—notwithstanding fundamental *Daseinanalyse*[28] nor the existentialist revolt in its aftermath, which anyway both already belong to the past, even if they might yet strike some vestige of justice against the flat, comically ignorant collective consciousness of the lonely masses. So the time is over for philosophical teachings and exemplary [*vorbildlicher*] life-instruction; indeed, even to want in some binding way to say what is right is a presumptuous stupidity.

But if this is the case, as I maintain, if every traditional form of Philosophical Praxis transposed without further ado into the present would be an instant curiosity, the question arises once again how it is even possible for philosophy to become practical anew.

In order to make plausible in outline a fitting answer to this question, I would like to sketch out, in a dangerously brief overview, those irreversible developments that rendered philosophy “unserviceable as a technique for the subjugation of life,” “with which philosophy was once so closely entwined.”[29]

According to Habermas’ incisive reconstruction of these developments, the interrelation of philosophy and praxis is fragile, and its results have been tenuous from the very beginning; that is, since the revolt of philosophy against myth, which we know to have been already instigated long before Socrates. The price to be paid for this philosophically perpetrated “depersonalization of the interpretation of the world,”[30] with its concomitant aestheticization of myth, was the relinquishing of any “link between the mythical narrative and ritual action”;[31] thus, philosophy was unable to replace myth “in its stabilization function for the practice of life.”[32] It was still allowed to appear as a practice-guiding science, at least insofar as it was able once again to latch itself parasitically onto existing traditions and worldviews, i.e., to manage a portfolio of found cultural assets [*Beständen*], namely common knowledge and shared norms, in order theoretically to underpin them or at best to adapt them to purpose.

But this mostly precarious unity of philosophy with received tradition has shattered, says Habermas.[33] Due to the effective pluralization of high culture traditions, ushered in by the Enlightenment, along with the concomitant politicization of worldviews, philosophy was no longer able, even in appearance, to support what it itself needed as support. Ever since then, it is ideological particularism that has been calling the philosophical tune. And so, instead of crystallizing out into a totalizing worldview (which Karl Marx was the last actually to accomplish, although the associated violence[34] was contrary to his intentions) philosophy, insofar as it still sought any connection at all with people’s practical interests, luxuriated as the outstretched intellectual wing of ideological programs.

At exactly the same time, philosophy—quite remarkably—also lost its ties to the theological interpretation of the world. Habermas: "Philosophical thinking sees itself confronted not only with the fixations of a technocratic consciousness but at the same time with the collapse of religious consciousness."[35] He goes on:

> Only today is it clear that the philosophical interpretation of the world confined to a cultured elite depended precisely upon coexistence with a widely influential religion. Philosophy, even after assimilating utopian impulses form the Judeo-Christian tradition, has not been capable of mastering by means of consolation and trust the *de facto* meaninglessness of death in its contingency, that of individual suffering, or that of the private loss of happiness—in general, the meaninglessness of the negativity of the risks built into life—in a way that has been possible in the religious hope in salvation.[36]

This failure has far-reaching consequences for philosophy, at least to the extent that it does not salvage itself in the academy as compartmentalized knowledge-adjudication and retreat entirely from the cares and conflicts of everyday life. Indeed, philosophy has never seen itself as mandated, or even in a position (as Habermas puts it) to offer "to replace the certainty of salvation of religious faith. It never offered a promise of redemption, confident expectation, or consolation."[37] Whenever it even tried—for instance, with the Stoic self-preparation for death—it only revealed, contrary to intention, the very "lack of consolation that pertains to philosophical thinking *in principle*."[38]

The question arises once again, and it poses itself with all due severity, as to how, just now, under current circumstances, at apparently the worst possible time, *philosophical* praxis is supposed to be possible, let alone justifiable.

Now I assure you that I do not ask this question rhetorically, as if to demonstrate integrity by parading all possible doubts, only to slice through this gnarled knot of thought at a stroke. Such indeed is the customary philosophical dramaturgy of serious style—which nevertheless would be (at best) merely an intellectual pleasure.

For, as I see it, especially as regards the individual who arrives in Philosophical Praxis, there is no other solution than what appeared already to Adorno, and after him to Habermas, as the last and most urgent onus upon philosophy—a solution that certainly seems risky and precarious enough—*Philosophy is no longer necessary or conceivable except as critique,* and can no longer feign itself almighty in its answers, as if it were yet certain of the absolute and a broker of the unconditionally valid—a stance that inevitably discredited philosophy and justified the fun had at its expense.

As critique, however, philosophy does not merely affirm itself as the "frenzy of eradication"[39] (Hegel), nor does it, with the "School of Suspicion"[40] (Nietzsche), conquer a ghostly dominion over long-departed spirits. It must be vigilant that life, in coming to self-understanding through speaking and expressing itself—however provisionally and tenuously—not let itself be infected by benumbed silence, the arrogant disinterest of aloof intellectuals or the seemingly superior cluelessness, which plays it cool, as if everything were in the rearview mirror.

Here lie dangers to which the supposedly experienced all too easily fall prey. Philosophy, opposing this critique-posturing, does not let go of questioning, not even where answers are not forthcoming. But nor does philosophy senselessly 'search' for answers that it secretly no longer hopes are there, as a different cliché insists; rather, philosophy cleaves to the question, in order if possible to revolutionize it. It scorns to serve needs as they come, but rather strives to differentiate amongst the needs themselves—in old vocabulary—to 'cultivate' them.

There is an old, and perhaps long since worn-out trope, which ought to be used only very cautiously, according to which philosophy, however, is the radicalization of problems that, without philosophy, are only ever served up half-cooked. The *philosophical* in Philosophical Praxis would then amount to thinking further and beyond [*weiterdenken*] the suffering—the hardships, worries and apathy, the speechlessness, the inhibitions and anxiety expressed in the conversation, the rampant disinterest (which may finally turn out to be an ominous deficit of love)—to think further and beyond with an *intensity* that slowly and finally transforms them by making their philosophical contours salient. Thereby, what emerges as perhaps the essential learning [*Erfarhung*] from Philosophical Praxis so far, philosophy thinks differently, and finally comes up with new thoughts, which is what is wanting.[41]

What new thoughts?

Take, for instance, questions posed by Peter Sloterdijk—in intimate relation to the findings [*Erfarhungen*] of Philosophical Praxis—regarding "algodicy" and the "logic of pain":

> Algodicy means a metaphysical interpretation of pain that gives it meaning. In modernity it takes the place of theodicy, as its converse. In the latter, it was asked, How are evil, pain, suffering, and injustice to be reconciled with the existence of God? Now the question is, If there is no God and no higher meaning, how can we sill bear the pain?[42]

How is it possible for the practitioner to obtain an non-fleeting perception of a failing, duped, defeated or suspended life, one subject to the optics of self-sacrifice, without thereby co-generating in the visitor a thirst for revenge or a lust for retribution, and without degrading the necessary and desirable intimacy through accusatory poses and imputations of guilt, thereby setting oneself in a better light?

What program of training (concealed from awareness) have people undergone who experience their pain, grief, disillusionment as 'mental defects' or malfunctions and expect readjustment or a reset from a qualified soul-repair specialist?

When does assignment of guilt generate psychological payoffs, and when not? And how in general terms should we regard such profit-and-loss accounts? What if hating, scorning, abhorring, and murdering were more digestible to people than forgiving, forbearance, and hope?

Is there any 'argument' for life? Could it be that such an argument, if it ever existed, would always come too late, whenever it was needed? It may be that life is an altogether different question—one that arguments cannot even reach—maybe life is a 'seduction,' and some are simply incapable of being seduced.

Is it just possible that those who argue 'cleanly' are swine? Could it be in certain cases that one who argues 'factually' is in league with death? How would it be, then, if it were impossible to counter such 'factual' argumentation without oneself becoming contaminated, to touch on death without being touched by it?

And does this exist: goodwill intending to save playing the part of sacrificer and slaughterer, turning goats into lambs? (It does.)

Isn't it possible, vice versa, that the victim wants to become master of the victimizer? (Which succeeds not at all rarely.) How can it be that this, which is so intractable, 'works out,' is 'logical' in a loose sense of the word? (A question that ought to fascinate not only people with psychological interests, but above all religiously and philosophically responsive minds. . . .)

How much violence is latent in a love unalterable? And what is to be thought of a person who, having fallen in love, visits his doctor in order to have tranquilizers prescribed—because he becomes aware of the antisocial, violent dimension of love in himself?

Or, to address something quite different and very particular, which also bears a relation to philosophical texts: Could Schopenhauer's "Metaphysics of Sexual Love"[43] give a valid insight into private events, such as a young, freshly emancipated 'enlightened' woman taking the pill, who with the onset of spring becomes 'restless' and 'no longer understands herself'? Would it be "reasonable" if, against the surges of the blood, she "reasonably" remained faithful to her partner whom she chose only after going through the trouble of reasonable deliberation?

What is revealed about our normal assessments when the neurotic who struggles to pay tribute to them lies, but the psychotic who disregards them speaks the truth and frightens us, unless we insist on his 'madness'?[44] What "language" do symptoms speak? Are they context-bound, i.e., would they have to fall silent if the context were to be changed?

How far can the assumption of a 'meaning' of illness be generalized; and concerning ourselves: What are we doing when we insist on its 'meaninglessness' in an individual case, before this question has even been raised?

Could an illness also be based on an "error"? (Novalis: "Many diseases are errors, which man must exhaust."[45]) And to what extent does psychosomatic suffering involve a "pathology of truth"?[46]

Or what does it mean when a person who notices something which no one is allowed to notice,[47] becomes ill, in order by this detour to fall into the hands of those who will drive the noticing out of him again?

And what, after all, aggrieves us?

Is there a hope for the hopeless? Or is such talk in Walter Benjamin[48] and Herbert Marcuse (among others) mere fiction, a solace-addled lie? Even if the proposition (as one says ever since Kant) is neither a lie nor the truth, but a pretension beyond the competence of human reason (an embezzling of competence), the question stands out: what difference does it make to the hopeless one to be met with such a "presumption" rather than an enlightened silence? If hope were in error and had not kept silent, or if the hopeless one were in error and had not kept silent—are these at all comparable, are they one and the same? In other words: is there a yet enduring relevance of Pascal's wager here?

Stories place demands upon another sort of human reason, a narrative reason, a faculty that refuses to dissolve contingencies using reductive formulas, but constrains them to the logic of story, according them a meaningful place. The random is thus transformed into 'intelligible contingency.'

Finally, through Philosophical Praxis a new philosophical question arises: whether it might not be possible and even necessary for philosophy to revive again its age-old community of interest and action with medicine. Now, as far as this question is concerned, I have the impression that it is more often spoken to by physicians who have recognized the philosophical significance of their assessments and interventions, than by philosophers who understand how illness, or a particular illness, and ultimately the individual patient, present a challenge to philosophical-medical understanding and philosophy becoming practical. Notwithstanding that insights into a medically relevant dietetics dawned upon an aged Kant, inspired by his friend Hufeland, insights of a medically relevant dietetics;[49] that Schelling sketched a philosophy of illness; that brilliant insights into morbidity and sick decrepitude can be found in Novalis; and, as is well-known, Nietzsche was a great philosophical experimentalist with his illnesses and healthinesses.

The alliance of interests of medicine and philosophy (for which, I freely confess, I hope and aim, and which in the last century also men like Ludwig Binswanger, Medard Boss,[50] Viktor von Weizsäcker and their Hamburg colleague Arthur Jores championed) would probably have to find its common field of action where—whether philosophically or medically—a "meaning" of the disease is insinuated, the apprehension of which was already exhorted by Richard Koch, who once said—addressing himself to the colleagues providing therapy: "One often has too little respect for the meaning of being ill. Many treatments consist in explaining to the sick person the meaning of his being sick."[51]

Whoever is able to accomplish this adequately would embody once more the ideal of a doctor due to old Galen, who encapsulated his programmatic vision in the title of one of his works: "That the best doctor is also a philosopher." The converse, that 'the best philosopher would also be a doctor' still sounds like a distant prospect at best. But let it be well noted what these two sentences do *not* say: namely that the doctor is 'the best philosopher,' still less that that the philosopher is 'the best doctor.' Such a reading would rather be the worst of all possible misunderstandings, and would certainly annul any community of interests between doctor and philosopher.

NOTES

1. Theodor W. Adorno, Why still Philosophy?, in C*ritical Models: Interventions and Catchwords* (1998), 16. Translated by Henry W. Pickford. Columbia University Press, 2005. Used with permission.

2. Achenbach note: Originally a lecture at the University of Dusseldorf held in 1985. In the tone of this lecture one may hear that it was in part specifically addressed to the group of "Pathognostics" who were big in Dusseldorf at that time. Thus a strong connection to Adorno's critical theory and thought played a role here. It was also necessary to contradict the ideas of "applied philosophy" that circulated at the time. Here the lecture is slightly shortened.

3. As translated in Plutarch, *Lives of the Ten Orators* (832B–834B), in *The Older Sophists*, ed. by Rosamond Kent Sprague (Columbia, SC: University of South Carolina Press, 1972), 117. See also 120–122. Word order and punctuation have been adjusted somewhat to fit Achenbach's text, and slightly more has been quoted than Achenbach does, also for reasons of clarity. Achenbach quotes Plutarch in German from Paul Watzlawick, *Die Möglichkeit des Andersseins* (Bern-Stuttgart-Vienna: Huber, 1978), 12, which in turn cites Hermann Diels, *Fragmente der Vorsokratiker,* 2. Auflage, 2. Band, 1. Hälfte (Berlin: Weidmannshce, 1907), 590. Diels is also the source for the Kent Sprague collection.

4. A common theme in ancient philosophy, notably but not exclusively in Stoicism; see for example Seneca's *De Tranquillitate Animi*. The Latin '*tranquillitate animi*' is

Seneca's translation of *euthymia*, which can mean cheerfulness, and occurs in the title of a lost treatise by Democritus, the Laughing Philosopher. There is also an essay on *euthymia* by Plutarch (quoted by Achenbach elsewhere in this book), which appears in a translation by Robin Wakefield under the title, Contentment, in Plutarch's *Essays* (Penguin, 1992).

5. Achenbach note: Compare Hermann Lübbe, Wozu Philosophie? Aspekte einer ärgerlichen Frage, in: *Wozu Philosophie? Stellungnahmen eines Arbeitskreises*, ed. H. Lübbe (Berlin-New York: Gruyter, 1978), 137.

6. Panaitios: Die Ethik, Das Werk über die Pflichten, in Das Sittliche, as cited in *Stoa und Stoiker, Die Gründer, Panaitios, Poseidonios*, Bd. 1 (Bibliothek der Alten Welt, Griechishe Reihe). Ed. and trans. by M. Pohlenz (Zurich: Artemis, 1950), 238. I have not been able to locate this passage in English. For a related discussion on the four "roles" or *personas* in Panaetius, see Long & Sedley, *The Hellenistic Philosophers*, 424, 427–428.

7. Hegel, *Hegel's Lectures on the History of Philosophy*, 2. Trans. by E. S. Haldane and Frances H. Simson (London: Routledge and Kegan Paul, 1968), 238–239. Note that this 1894 translation of this passage has been altered in minor ways. The Achenbach citation of Hegel reads: *Theorie-Ausg*. Bd. XIX, S. 257.

8. Achenbach note: This realization we owe above all to the work of Pierre Hadot, which only became known to me when it appeared in German translation a few years later. (See references below.) Also, only a year after I delivered this lecture in Dusseldorf, Michel Foucault's important books on Hellenistic philosophies appeared [in German], which worked in their own way toward the idea of a Philosophical Praxis. Notably *Der Gebrauch der Lüste* and *Die Sorge um sich* (both Frankfurt a.M., 1986). [Editorial Addendum:] The Foucault books cited by Achenbach appeared in French as *L'usage des plaisirs* (Paris, 1984) and *Le souci de soi* (Paris, 1984), later in English as, respectively, *The Use of Pleasure* (1985) and *Care of the Self* (1986), both translated into English for Vintage by Robert Hurley. The Hadot books Achenbach cites in German are: *Philosophie als Lebensform. Geistige Übungen der Antike* (Berlin, 1991); *Die innere Burg: Anleitung zu einer Lektüre Marc Aurels* (Frankfurt a.M., 1996); und *Wege zur Weisheit—oder: Was lehrt uns die antike Philosophie?* (Berlin, 1999). They too appeared originally in French, and were also later translated into English; French sources in Bibliography. English translations of the books cited are Pierre Hadot: *Philosophy as a Way of Life* (OUP, 1995); *The Inner Citadel; the Meditations of Marcus Aurelius* (Harvard, 1998); and *What is Ancient Philosophy?* (Harvard, 2002).

9. Seneca, *Letters from a Stoic*, Letter XVI to Lucilius. Translated by Robin Campbell (London: Penguin, 1969), 63–64.

10. Epictetus, *Handbook*, 50/50.1. In *Discourses, Fragments, Handbook.* Trans. by Robin Hard (OUP, 2014), 303.

11. Augustine, *Confessions*, 4.3.5. This 1838 translation is due to E. B. Pusey.

12. Heinrich Seuse, *Henry Suso: The Exemplar, with Two German Sermons*. The Classics of Western Spirituality. Ed. Frank J. Tobin (New York: Paulist Press, 1989).

13. I have translated the phrase myself. The original appears to be Tauler's 'Sermon For New-Year's Day,' which I quote here in English translation (italics added): "A

man must in all things turn inward, wait inwardly, watch there for God, let God act, and be to God nothing but an instrument in His hands. Let him do *God's will simply, passively and not actively*, acknowledging as God's his every effort, act and word. Surrender thy will to God in all things, and live and act interiorly. *Draw thyself in to the innermost recesses of thy soul*, for it is there that God dwells. . . ." In *The Sermons and Spiritual Conferences of John Tauler, the Illuminated Doctor.* Trans. by Walter Elliot (Washington, DC: Apostolic Mission House, 1910), 84.

14. Michel de Montaigne, 'Apology for Raymond Sebond,' in *The Complete Essays of Montaigne,* II, 12. Here and below I quote the 1877 edited version of Charles Cotton's translation, with one significant amendment: for "moeurs" I put the more exact "mores" in where Cotton has "manners." The latter weakens the moral connotation of "moeurs," unlike the German translation Achenbach consults (by Lüthy), which uses "Sitten." Donald Frame's translation of Montaigne, cited elsewhere in this book, is worse; it uses "behavior," which weakens the moral significance further and even undermines the sense of agency, besides forcing the rest of the sentence into the singular.

15. Michel de Montaigne, 'Apology for Raymond Sebond,' in *The Complete Essays of Montaigne*, II, 12. Trans. by Charles Cotton. 1877. Achenbach later added the following note: "Montaigne in the same location cites Cicero's saying that 'nothing so absurd can be said that it has not been said by some philosopher,' [displaying a] cheerfulness in self-appraisal that seems to me to be no less meritorious in Montaigne, and which Philosophical Praxis today will not want to do without." (Cicero translation as in Frame.)

16. This phrase originates in Montaigne in the sentence immediately prior to the passage just quoted: "Ils soyent nez chez moy et sans patron." Achenbach quotes the German phrase, "*von ungefähr und ohne Vorbedacht*" (by chance and without forethought), which in Frame's translation runs: "born with me and without a model." (See Montaigne, *Complete Essays,* II, 12, 409.) The phrase in Charles Cotton's translation is: "spun out of myself, and without any pattern."

17. *Populärphilosophie* is associated with the Enlightenment philosopher, Christian Garve (1742–1798), translator of Cicero and Adam Smith, and interlocutor of Kant; he was a popularizer of philosophy who attempted a union of British empiricism and German rationalism. Kant derides *Populärphilosophie* in Chapter 2 of *Groundwork of the Metaphysic of Morals*, Ch. 2, saying it produces a "disgusting hotch-potch of second-hand observations and semi-rational principles on which the empty-headed regale themselves" (409/31) and which "goes no further than it can get fumbling about with the aid of examples" (412/36). H. J. Paton translation (New York: Harper Torchbooks, 1964).

18. Ernst Bloch, Philosophische Aufsätze zur objektiven Phantasie, *Gesamtausgabe,* X (Frankfurt a.M.: Suhrkamp, 1969), 374 ("Über den Begriff Weisheit"). Picard translation. As far as I know, this does not exist in English.

19. Bloch, *Philosophische Aufsätze*, 374. Picard translation.

20. Bloch, *Philosophische Aufsätze*, 374. Picard translation.

21. This concept was introduced by historian Reinhard Koselleck.

22. Achenbach Note: As per Michael Landmann. Cf. "Georg Simmel als Prügelknabe" (Georg Simmel as a whipping boy), in *Philosophische Rundschau* Vol. 14, 1967, p. 259.

23. Achenbach note: Arnold Gehlen, *Moral und Hypermoral. Eine pluralistische Ethik* (Frankfurt: Klostermann, 1969), 154. "The darkening of the atmosphere can no longer be denied; according to Nietzsche, it began precisely in the wake of the Enlightenment; around 1770, one noticed a decrease in cheerfulness. It began the age of criticism and of problems with which nothing could be done once they had arisen." Gehlen is likely referencing Nietzsche's *Nachlaß* of 1885 (36[49]), where it says: "The eclipse, the pessimistic coloring, comes necessarily in the wake of the Enlightenment. Around 1770 the decline of of cheerfulness began to be noticed. . . ." See *The Will to Power,* Bk 1 (91). Trans. by W. Kaufmann and R. J. Hollingdale (New York: Vintage Books, 1968), 55–56 (Achenbach cites Nietzsche, KSA, XI, p. 571).

24. An allusion to Martin Luther, "Freedom of a Christian," 1520. In Martin Luther, *Three Treatises* (Philadelphia: Fortress Press, 1960).

25. Søren Kierkegaard, *Either-Or*, II, 266. Hong translation. Achenbach refers to the German edition, *Entweder-Oder*, edited by H. Diem and W. Rest (Cologne, 1960), mistakenly to page 843 (it is page 834).

26. Franz Rosenzweig, Letter to Friedrich Meinecke. In *Das Buchlein vom gesunden und kranken Menschenverstand* (Düsseldorf: Melzer Verlag, 1964), quoted by Achenbach from the 1992 Frankfurt edition, p. 11. Picard translation. The *Buchlein,* written in 1921 was published in 1964; it appears in English as Franz Rosenzweig, *Understanding the Sick and the Healthy: A View of World, Man, and God.* Translated by Nahum Norbert Galtzer (Boston, MA: Harvard University Press, 1999). However, this English edition does not appear to contain the letter Achenbach cites.

27. Theodor W. Adorno, "Why Still Philosophy?," in *Critical Models: Interventions and Catchwords* (1998), 5–17. Translated by Henry W. Pickford (New York: Columbia University Press, 2005). Jürgen Habermas, "Does Philosophy Still Have a Purpose? (1971)" in *Philosophical-Political Profiles*, trans. by Frederick G. Lawrence (Cambridge, MA: MIT Press, 1985), 1–19.

28. A reference to the work of Ludwig Binswanger. See *Being-in-the-World: Selected Papers of Ludwig Binswanger.* Trans. by Jacob Needleman (New York: Basic Books, 1963).

29. Adorno, "Why Still Philosophy?" 5–6. Pickford translation. However, the prior phrase "unserviceable . . . for the subjugation of life" has been freshly translated, since Pickford overlooks the difference between *Lebensmeisterung* (life-mastery) and *Lebensbemeisterung.*

30. Habermas writes: "Philosophy, like mythology, was a system of interpretation that comprehended nature and the human world at once. It apprehended the cosmos—being as a whole. In this respect, philosophy could replace myth. Of course, it did not tell naive stories but inquired methodically after reasons." Habermas, "Does Philosophy Still Have a Purpose?" 9.

31. Habermas writes: "Then, too, philosophy had to give up the link of mythical narrative with ritual action. A certain form of cultic practice survived in highly sublimated forms (even in the operations of university departments), but it was not to be

permitted in a thematic way. Consequently philosophy could not replace myth in its stabilizing function for the practice of life." Habermas, "Does Philosophy Still Have a Purpose?" 9.

32. Habermas, "Does Philosophy Still Have a Purpose?" 9.

33. Habermas, "Does Philosophy Still Have a Purpose?" 12.

34. Achenbach note: In addition here mention should be made at least Rudolf Steiner and Mao.

35. Habermas, "Does Philosophy Still Have a Purpose?" 17.

36. Habermas, "Does Philosophy Still Have a Purpose?" 17–18. This quotation is more complete in English than the German.

37. Habermas, "Does Philosophy Still Have a Purpose?" 11.

38. Habermas, "Does Philosophy Still Have a Purpose?" 11.

39. G. W. F. Hegel, *The Phenomenology of Spirit*, para. 253. Trans. by Peter Fuss and John Dobbins (Notre Dame, IN: University of Notre Dame Press, 2019), 295.

40. Friedrich Nietzsche, *Human, All Too Human*, Preface. §1: "My writings have been called a School of Suspicion, even more for Contempt, fortunately also for Courage and, in fact, for Daring." Trans. by Marion Faber, with Stephen Lehman (Lincoln and London: University of Nebraska Press, 1984), 4.

41. Achenbach note: With the enumeration of problems that follows, I begin to translate experience from practice into the lecture wording. The problems mentioned are not 'imaginary abstractions' but were all of them encountered by me at that time in consultations, and my concern here lies in naming these difficulties.

42. Peter Sloterdijk, *Critique of Cynical Reason.* Trans. by Michael Eldred (Minneapolis: University of Minnesota Press, 1987), 460.

43. Arthur Schopenhauer, Chapter 44 of *The World as Will and Representation*, 2. CUP, 2018.

44. Achenbach note: This question, among the group of 'pathognostics' active in the 1980s in Düsseldorf under the aegis of Rudolf Heinz, was regarded almost as a mark of understanding.

45. Novalis, *Werke, Tagebücher und Briefe*, II. Ed. by Joachim Mähl und Richard Samuel (Darmstadt: Carl Hanser, 1978), 797. Fragmente und Studien 1799/1800, Physicalishes und Medizinisches, Nr. 268. Picard translation.

46. Achenbach note: This question already occupied Viktor von Weizsäcker.

47. To notice—*bemerken*.

48. Walter Benjamin, Goethe's Elective Affinities, in *Selected Writings, 1913–1926*, Vol. 1, Harvard/Belknap Press, 1996, 297–360. Achenbach cites "Goethes Wahlverwandtschaften" in Benjamin's *Illuminationen* (Frankfurt a.M., 1980), 135.

49. Achenbach note: On this, see the Third Part of Kant's *Conflict of the Faculties,* titled "The conflict of the philosophy faculty with the faculty of medicine." See "A Letter in reply to Privy Councillor and Professor Hufeland," in Immanuel Kant, *Conflict of the Faculties*, 313–327.

50. See on this the events initiated by Medard Boss with Martin Heidegger, published as *Zollikon Seminars* (Frankfurt a.M.: Klostermann, 1987).

51. Richard Koch, *Ärztliches Denken. Abhandlungen über die philosophischen Grundlagen der Medizin* (München: J.F. Bergmann-Verlag, 1923), 94; here quoted

from D. v. Engelhardt, H. Schipperges, *Die inneren Verbindungen zwischen Philosophie und Medizin im 20. Jahrhundert* (Darmstadt: Wissenschaftliche Buchgesellschaft, 1980), 22. [Achenbach note]

Chapter 3

Philosophical Praxis Bears the Insignia of *Lebenskönnerschaft*

> One of the worst temptations in our dangerous and endangered world is the status of patient offered us everywhere. Our difficulties are too great for us, we feel overwhelmed, and we look for someone, not to strengthen us, but to treat us. We surrender our shortcomings to someone else, who usually confirms that our weakness is due to this or that experience. Objective problems are turned into relationship problems. We acquiesce in our moral absolution. Modern therapism promises healing at a price: one must declare oneself ill. This procedure increases . . . the incapacitation of the individual.
>
> —Hartmut von Hentig[1]

The novel German compound word *Lebenskönnerschaft* is not likely known to my readers, even to German readers, and that is just as well. But I have my reasons for introducing this neologism or word-creation. Decades ago, when I first decided to bring Philosophical Praxis into the conversation, I needed an 'unoccupied' term, as broad as possible but not yet determinate, with which to unite in a path-breaking way the requisite reflections, needed prospects, and emerging experiences. All the same, I welcomed the ease with which this virgin terminology could join company with ancient and venerable traditions. Indeed: just as 'Philosophical Praxis,' when first introduced, evoked the ancient tradition of a philosophy that demonstrates itself in practical terms, and strives for a form of life worthy of recognition; so too today, I can readily relate *Lebenskönnerschaft* to the notion of 'virtue' so long elevated by philosophers. For what else are the virtues but praiseworthy 'mastery' [*Könnerschaften*]—skillful, cultivated, honed, consummate—the 'right resources and fine wherewithal'? The new terms, then, allow us to rehabilitate traditions that are spent or fallen into decline, or that have been deprived of their former prestige by a spirit that has since strayed elsewhere; also to call these traditions back into the conversation and to help them to gain fresh respectability; whereby I presuppose that such attempts at reanimation are meaningful and desirable, possibly even necessary.

The justification of this presupposition in sufficiently persuasive terms is, therefore, the task of the proper introduction and promotion of any new idea. With regard to Philosophical Praxis, much work has been carried out since 1981. The present chapter takes up that task in regard to the concept of *Lebenskönnerschaft*.[2]

So much, then, by way of introduction. And now, as announced, some considerations that are intended to offer an initial outline of the idea of *Lebenskönnerschaft*.

I call to mind Nietzsche's "last man," who "invented happiness."[3] What does he do when he notices that, contrary to his vaunted destiny, he is unhappy? He goes to therapy. "I've forgotten how to blink," he tells his therapist, wondering how it could have come about. He is dejected and despondent. Something must be to blame, he tells himself, something must have happened to me, something has steered me off course in life. But what? "I have lost my laughter," says the last man. Neither can he mourn. Let the therapy begin.

Nietzsche's "last man" would most likely never show up at a Philosophical Praxis. One who visits there wants neither to be treated nor cured. He seeks to enlighten himself. "I have tried hard, but I have failed. Surely I am doing something wrong. I just ask: what?" He does not complain of being someone held back from life, yet admits, maybe implicitly, to not yet having understood how to live well. He is eager to learn. He is a welcome guest at Philosophical Praxis.

What is the difference?

Whereas the client of therapy assumes that life is something that "normally" succeeds, as long as it has not been thwarted or subject to bad influences, the visitor to Philosophical Praxis suspects that life is to be led, surmounted, mastered, if it is to come out well. Slogging through the day in the usual way, run down and washed out by the prosaic routines of everyday life, thoughtlessly strung between here and there—life at last becomes pale and insipid, distracted, fleeting, and flat, ultimately a deadline that meaninglessly runs out. Days spent in this way lack the ballast that would keep us walking upright. We are like a boat without a keel. We are not set right on our hinges, have lost the tension in which far-off aims would hold us.

Without worldly counter-weight, without demands placed upon oneself, life falls under the dictates of small, petty desires, stumbles about aimlessly, dreaming of better days as if they should fall into one's lap. That decision that must be made is put off; that beginning, which ought to be made, must wait again; and imperceptibly the moments pass, one after another.

Meanwhile the essential question remains shut out, the very one which beckons us into wholesome philosophical dis-ease. This is the question: what firstly and finally life comes down to, what life taken in utter seriousness would be. Only those whose life takes shape as an answer to this question find the cheerfulness that arises from composure, the suppleness that springs from judicious understanding. To these people Philosophical Praxis is devoted. It takes them in under the sign of *Lebenskönnerschaft*.

And now you may ask: Not the art of living [*Lebenskunst*]? No.

What is the difference?

In order to quickly eliminate the most obvious misunderstandings and to forestall confusion, I shall briefly sketch an initial profile of *Lebenskönnerschaft* by contrasting it with the currently popular "art of living." This precaution has become all the more necessary, since some decades ago[4] I myself sought to revive the term "art of living" (dormant for centuries) which unfortunately afterwards due to popularization fell into bad company and lost its philosophically demanding content. Here then is the characteristic distinction:

> The aim of the art of life is *happiness*; Lebenskönnerschaft aims at being *worthy of happiness*.
> Life-artists *shape* their lives; the Lebenskönner *prove* themselves in life.
> Artists of life *win over*; the Lebenskönner *stands upon* what is right.
> Artists of life are *flexible*; the Lebenskönner is *upright*.
> Artists of life *attach* a meaning to their life; the Lebenskönner *lives* up to one.
> The art of living *seeks joy* in life; Lebenskönnerschaft *seeks to survive* a vain, pale and wrongful life.
> The one knows to makes *virtue out of necessity*; the other proves *virtue in need*.
> The art of life flees *shadow* and seeks *light*; Lebenskönnerschaft flees *twilight*, seeks both *light and shadow*.
> Artists of life give an *answer* to life's questions; the Lebenskönner seeks the *question* to which life is the answer.[5]

Perhaps, however, even given all this, the decisive point has not yet been made. And that is: the *Lebenskönnerschaft* goes beyond know-how [*klug*], or even care for self; and it is far rather a praxis-orientated world-understanding [*Weltkenntnis*]. No one is a *Lebenskönner* who does not know how to gauge the relations in which he must take his stand and wage his life. This does not mean going with the flow in the aim of installing oneself in the greatest convenience. That would be the task of know-how [*Lebensklugheit*], which selects effective means in the service of arbitrary life ends:[6] to turn a profit, it rolls unhesitatingly with whatever opportunities arise. Knowing-how [*Klugheit*] adapts itself to the world, says Joubert, whereas "wisdom seeks accord with heaven."[7] *Wisdom*, however, is the north star of the *Lebenskönner*, and it is not possible to articulate their mission more ambitiously.

What—for the third time—is the difference?

Lebenskönnerschaft does not in the main seek success, still less does it regard as justified any old means that would serve success. Rather, it is mindful of ends. In so doing, it defies the prevailing cynicism that transacts with a compromised reality. It runs with the wolves as little as Socrates danced to the tune of his judges. In a word, it seeks accord with the heavens: the *Lebenskönner* strives to live as if ever standing before the final authority, be that ever so distant. Of that we know nothing anymore (or so it would seem, at least in *our* case). Yet the *Lebenskönner* is able anticipate its hint, which they accomplish through *remembrance*. For, what is right, *we* may no longer know; the best, however, once knew, and they stood up for it. *Lebenskönners* take their measure against the best, the exemplary and the straight arrows, those whose disobedience was their submission, whose doubts about the system arose from their belief in what is right. Thus they were devoted to virtue, which is only another word for excellence, and to liberating themselves from the half-and-half mediocrity of the socialized human animal. They take the high road and the narrow door. Here lies escape from the immaturity in which we now are firmly held, no longer by a word lorded over us from above, but rather in the broad, friendly, shallow babble that lulls us to sleep in the lap of public opinion. In contrast to this wallowing of mind, philosophy is the courage to think differently—which does not mean arbitrarily. Our thoughts are justified neither by the charm of being different, nor the allure of the merely interesting, but by being sewn in to the long 'red thread' running throughout the development of thought, which is present as the history of thinking to those who remember.[8]

So much for now by way of a first perspicuous overview. In all this, it should not be overlooked that *Lebenskönnerschaft* is first and foremost a requirement placed on the individual philosophical practitioner: only the *Lebenskönner* will be able to meet the demands made on the philosopher in practice.

But now the question arises: what problems does Philosophical Praxis make for itself when it is not satisfied to aim with its guests at health, or mere absence of disorder, or to eliminate the causes of complaint, but instead follows the scent of *Lebenskönnerschaft*?

This raises once more—in quite practical terms—the very old problem that already occupied Socrates, namely, the question whether virtue is 'teachable.' The question now runs: Can one impart *Lebenskönnerschaft* in counseling?

Necessary first, I think, is the courage to realize the extent to which we are dilettantes, in what respect we are bunglers, in what respect apprentices; for which, it is necessary that in our self-image we remain learners. It is just the same in respect to the virtues: it is hard to make them palatable when their counterparts, the vices, have been withdrawn from linguistic circulation, in the process becoming incomprehensible. Yet just this is what has happened.

And this absence initially complicates any attempt to promote *Lebenskönnerschaft*. How can we even conceive of it if we are forbidden to cast a critical glance at whether there are in fact defective lives, even total losers [*Nichtkönner*], as if the whole phalanx of vices cannot be called by name? Such as—settle in for a long list!—incorrigibility, obstinacy, hardheadedness, envy, malice, spite, rancor, cynicism, sloth, indolence, heedlessness, closed-mindedness, thickheadedness, dullness, bigotry, idleness, crudity, silliness, ridiculousness, small-mindedness, narrow-mindedness, pettiness, short-sightedness, arrogance, unreliability, duplicity, mendacity, impetuosity, irascibility, capriciousness, being bitchy, petulance, incontinence, deviousness, intransigence, egotism, iniquity, self-centeredness, egomania, cantankerousness, vilification, callousness, ruthlessness, depravity, laxity (where it does not belong), dilatoriness (where resolution and action are needed), inability to forgive, to forebear or to extend benevolence, deviance, aloofness, ineptitude, timidity, reticence, mistrust, suspicion, pusillanimity and self-importance, stodginess, grouchiness, philistinism, dogmatism, fanaticism, miserliness, greediness, pretension, smugness, stupidity and lack of imagination, or (to become dignified again in tone . . .) indiscretion, despondency, imprudence, folly (a word that has gone entirely extinct, though it is only the word that is rare) and foolishness (same applies).

With this long list I had in mind the following: to make it plain that in Philosophical Praxis the practitioner needs the facility to bring to the attention of the guest what is wrong, muddled, misguided, without thereby discouraging him or forcing him to 'defend himself' or to 'salvage his honor.' How such facility is to be acquired, however, is a question that would require all too lengthy considerations, and cannot be answered in detail within the confines of this chapter. Maybe just a hint instead, introduced by way of a remark by Goethe: "When we take people merely as they are, we make them worse. When we treat them as if they were what they should be, we improve them as far as they can be improved."[9]

Meaning? Only the philosophical practitioner who does not conflate his guest with the overt reality they present may dare to venture an elucidation that inevitably risks being understood as mere critique and objection. Or: to say the same more poetically: only one who is able to see the other with a serene unshakability—"as God intended him."[10] Or again: if we are compelled to speak in the terms of today's worldview: as his 'destiny' demands. And toward this end we have this one great aid: all that is thus false, errant and less-than true, loses its gravity in such elucidation; it becomes the stuff of comedy, and therefore falls under the jurisdiction of humor. Insofar as it reveals the guest's shortcomings as comic reality, humor is already colluding with the potential *Könnerschaft* of the guest.

But as I said: This question is a sensitive one and would require a far longer chapter for a thorough treatment. Yet this much is certain: Philosophical Praxis is obliged to answer the question of how wholesome critique is possible, i.e., a naming of the wrong that does not paralyze, but strengthens confidence, that does not discourage, but lends courage.

Here now is another point. If it were indeed possible to help a person in this way to the insight into what is wrong, would we have finally settled the age-old question of whether virtue can be taught? Alas, we cannot even *make* anyone a *Lebenskönner*. We can only help him or her to become a *Lebenskönner*. The question therefore becomes: what can we do on our part to achieve this?

Let me choose an example. How does one become a master of chess? Certainly, acquiring knowledge of the rules that can be taught will not suffice. Knowledge of correct moves, of good moves, ideally of best moves, far outstrips knowledge of 'permissible' or 'allowed' moves. (This is worth mentioning in passing if only to prevent confusion of our endeavors concerning *Lebenskönnerschaft* with the so-called academic 'ethics' industry, currently booming, which primarily concerns decisions as to what is 'permissible' and 'impermissible.') All chess moves are technically correct that do not violate any chess rules. But—correct moves are not thereby good moves. And a chess master will say: 'The move you played there is indeed allowed, but it is wrong.' Why? Because a better move was possible. He may even say, 'Look, in your situation, this move is the only right one.'

So, as far as it goes, the game of chess appears to offer a charming analogy for questions concerning *Lebenskönnerschaft*. One is not a *Lebenskönner* who does only what is allowed. To do that is merely to be bourgeois, a pedant, or a bore.

Even less could we say of anyone who does only what is expected of everyone, that he is a *Lebenskönner*. We may praise him for it, but such correctness we simply expect as a matter of course, the way we expect our opponent in chess not to cheat. So far, it is still a question of rules and moral codes, duties or precepts that decency dictates, customs to be observed, and suchlike. Something more is needed for *Lebenskönnerschaft*—namely, understanding how to *live well*.

So now we ask: isn't that the same as saying that the chess master knows how to *play well*?

Yes and no. One difference is that, in the case of chess, it has already been decided what the game is—and even which are the rules to be played by. Besides, the stakes are clear, namely to win in the end. Not so in the case of life. But a further point of difference is far more important. The game of chess, though at first sight it offers itself as an analogy, is governed and defined by only one faculty: let us call it the intellect. Pure rationality and calculating are the only factors that matter in selecting amongst possible moves. Thus chess programs can be written for computers that leave no chance even to above-average players.

Lebenskönnerschaft, on the other hand, is not simply a question of strict logical rigor or rational calculation. Either that or we call someone a *Lebenskönner* who knows that he has every reason to be cheerful—but is not. In this context our question now becomes: How are we to "teach" him to feel joy?

Someone else says he does not love life. Does anyone know an argument that will "persuade" him to change his mind and make him love life from now on?

Is it clear where this is leading? What is lacking in these real-life scenarios is not know-how [*Wissen*] that can be transmitted in the propositional form, nor teachable information [*Kenntnisse*]. What then is missing? Whatever it is, wouldn't it be precisely what the philosopher in Philosophical Praxis is responsible for, in other words, for something other than and more than propositional and disciplinary knowledge?[11]

Allow me at this juncture to interject. With this quest for *Lebenskönnerschaft* we wind our way back to a (largely forgotten) duty of philosophy, one that demanded of it more than insights and theories that might be true or false, namely what might better be clothed in the question: How is philosophy to get through to a particular person? As Aristotle, with only mild didactic overstatement, reminded us: "What we wish is to be courageous, not to know what courage is; to be just, not to know what justice is; in the same way as we wish to be healthy rather than know what it is to be healthy."[12] Philosophy devoted to such a quest, perhaps the most daunting there is, reveals itself, for example, in questions of the following type. Quoting Paul Feyerabend: "What is the use of an argument that leaves people unmoved?"[13] A corresponding aphorism by Hans Kudszus reads: "Where we have failed to convince a brain, we have failed to convert a heart."[14]

Do you hear how this tone resonates with the problem that is our theme? Thus speaks one who wonders how one becomes good—how to pave the way to *Lebenskönnerschaft*. And at the moment I am exploring what sort of knowledge or philosophy or philosopher is helpful in view of this. What is

Philosophical Praxis capable of achieving in this regard—and how? We know the answer of Socrates, handed down by Xenophon. When Hippias asked him what justice is, the master said it was a question he answered daily, "not by words but by my deeds."[15] This was his only convincing teaching. The disciples of Socrates beheld from a front-row seat an astonishing living exemplar of *Lebenskönnerschaft*; they witnessed it first hand, and the consequences were lasting. The effect Socrates had was to "convert hearts"—to re-use Kudszus' phrase—which then prepared the brains to suitably appropriate the "arguments." His words take carried greater weight by not "leaving people unmoved." In short: the person lends credence to the claim.

And this holds true not only for Socrates, but for all "paradigmatic individuals" (as Jaspers[16] called them): Confucius, Buddha, the Nazarene, Francis of Assisi, and others, to whom we are all indebted for their idea of human possibility; for they were what they said, and—no need to shy away from the allusion—their *words became flesh*.

To venture a conclusion: what reaches people are images and stories. In them wisdom becomes understandable—and in a way that does not "leave unmoved."

So, if our question is how Philosophical Praxis can help people to become *Lebenskönner*, then I answer—admittedly still very generally—first of all: with examples and with stories. Walter Benjamin has called them the very medium of advice. I quote:

> All this points to the nature of every real story. It contains, openly or covertly, something useful. The usefulness may, in one case, consist in a moral; in another, in some practical advice; in a third, in a proverb or maxim. In every case the story-teller is a man who has counsel for his readers. But if today "having counsel" is beginning to have an old-fashioned ring, this is because the communicability of experience is decreasing. In consequence we have no counsel either for ourselves or for others. After all, counsel is less an answer to a question than a proposal concerning the continuation of a story which is just unfolding. To seek this counsel one would first have to be able to tell the story. (Quite apart from the fact that a man is receptive to counsel only to the extent that he allows his situation to speak.) Counsel woven into the fabric of real life is wisdom.[17]

Let us count this passage among the signposts to Philosophical Praxis. Correspondingly, in my book, *Lebenskönnerschaft*, I accord stories a central role. For the *Lebenskönner* apprentices for wisdom, and what is heard along the way are stories. Why stories? Because they develop in us a sense for the individual, for what is incomparably right. The more we develop this sense, the more well-versed we are in the forms of life, and ultimately able to master life in an exemplary way. Here lies the path to *Lebenskönnerschaft*.

Once more I will resort to an example. How does one 'learn' to compose? Listen to the symphonies of Beethoven! None of them fails to stand for itself, each has its own unique character. The great work of art, it is said, is *sui generis*, not 'an instance' of a general type or rule, but 'one of a kind.' Scholarship may strive for a 'theory of the symphony'—the eminent composer in each case writes *just this one*.

But the question before us interests us in its relation to the *Lebenskönnerschaft*, and to our yet outstanding question, how to become *Lebenskönners*. So we ask: what has equipped the composer? How has he become a *Könner* in music? He is unlikely to have written this *unique* symphony according to a 'theory of the symphony' or according to a set of rules on 'how to compose symphonies.' Thus, he does not orient himself via a schema. For nothing would come of that but mass-produced goods.

No, he got there in a different way (apart from talent, genius, giftedness—as one used to say). He has heard and studied many masterpieces, he knows all the important works, and he knows them each as individuals. In other words, he knows models without using them as templates, and he will not 'copy' what he admires. Beethoven looked very closely at how Bach and Mozart and Haydn composed. But what did he make out of Bach and Mozart and Haydn? He made Beethoven!

This is how we learn to live from those who lived excellently. Since ancient times they were called the wise, and they were revered as wise. Philosophical Praxis takes its cue from them, and bears their insignia on its shield. With them it follows the scent which leads to the *Lebenskönnerschaft*.

NOTES

1. Hartmut von Hentig, Fragmente einer zukünftigen Pädagogik. *Frankfurter Hefte* (1984), 128. Picard translation.

2. Gerd B. Achenbach, *Lebenskönnerschaft* (Freiburg-Wien-Basel: Herder, 2001); 2nd ed. (Cologne: Dinter, 2010).

3. Friedrich Nietzsche, *Thus Spoke Zarathustra* (1969), Prologue, 5, alluded to multiple times in this paragraph.

4. "Lebenskunst." Opening Lecture of the 4th GPP Colloquium, Oct., 1986 in Klagenfurt. Appeared in *Weisheit: Archäologie der literarishen Kommunickation*, III (München: Wilhelm Fink Verlag, 1991), 231–238. Reprinted in Achenbach, *Zur Einführung der Philosophischen Praxis*, 329–339.

5. Achenbach, *Lebenskönnerschaft*, 9.

6. Know-how—*Klugheit/Lebensklugheit*. Achenbach is here alluding to Immanuel Kant, and indeed intends the term in Kant's sense: "Nun kann man die Geschicklichkeit in der Wahl der Mittel zu seinem eigenen größten Wohlsein Klugheit im engsten Verstande nennen. Also ist der Imperativ, der sich auf die Wahl der Mittel zur eigenen

Glückseligkeit bezieht, d.i. die Vorschrift der Klugheit, noch immer hypothetisch; die Handlung wird nciht schlechthin, sondern nur als Mittel zu einer andern Absicht geboten." Immannuel Kant, *Grundlegung zur Metaphysik der Sitten*, 416. Both James W. Ellington and H. J. Paton, in their respective translations of the *Grundlegung*, render *Klugheit* as 'prudence' (associated with the Greek, *phronesis*, practical wisdom). After considerable discussion, however, we decided to go with the plainer expression, 'know-how.' I now quote Ellington's version of the above passage, but with our translation of *Klugheit*: "Now skill in the choice of means to one's own greatest well-being can be called 'know-how' in the narrow sense. And thus the imperative that refers to the choice of means to one's own happiness, i.e., the precept of know-how, still remains hypothetical; the action is commanded not absolutely but only as a means to a further purpose." Kant, *Ethical Philosophy* (Indianapolis, IN: Hackett, 1983), 26 (416 in marginal pagination).

7. Joseph Joubert, "Le bon sens s'accommode au monde; la sagesse tâche d'être conforme au ciel." *Pensées, essais, maximes et correspondance de J. Joubert* (Paris: Le Normant), 262. "Common sense suits itself to the ways of the world. Wisdom tries to conform to the ways of Heaven." *Joubert: A Selection from His Thoughts*. Translated by Katharine Lyttelton (New York: Dodd, Mead, and Co., 1899), 86. Achenbach cites a German translation, which includes the phrase "Weisheit sucht Einklang im Himmel," and the term, "Einklang," which surfaces again later, I have rendered in both places as "accord," to keeping close to both the German and the French, "conformer."

8. Here "history of thinking" renders "*Geschichte des Geistes*," whereas "development of thought" stands for "*entwicklenden Denkens*." The "red thread" is metaphorical allusion to a distinctively red thread allegedly woven into the British Royal Navy's ropes, which allowed even the shortest segments of them to be identified.

9. Goethe, *Meister Wilhelm's Apprenticeship and Travels*, Carlyle's 1858 translation. Volume 2, Book VIII, Ch. 4, page 88. The words are being attributed to Natalia.

10. Achenbach attributes the quoted German phrase to Paul Stöcklein, *Wege zum späten Goethe* (Darmstadt: Wissenschaftliche Buchgesellschaft, 1973), 28, whose concern was, not philosopher-practitioners, but love: "Liebe sieht einen Menschen, wie Gott ihn gemeint hat." ("Love sees a person as God meant him to be.") The colloquial English does little justice to the "zauberhafte Wendung" in the German.

11. Propositional and disciplinary knowledge—*Sach- und Satzwissen*.

12. Aristotle, *Eudemian Ethics,* Book I, 5, 22–25. Translated by Michael Woods (Oxford: Clarendon, 1982). Editorial markings removed.

13. Paul Feyerabend, *Against Method* (London: Verso, 1978), 25.

14. Hans Kudszus, *Jaworte, Neinworte. Aphorismen* (Frankfurt a.M.: Suhrkamp, 1970), 42.

15. For simplicity, and to fit the context, I opt here to translate the German directly: "nicht durch Worte, sondern durch die Tat lege ich es an den Tag." The line is a reference to Xenophon's "Memoirs of Socrates," 4.4, which in the Tredinnick-Waterfield translation appears in context as follows: "I never stop revealing what I think is right. . . . If I don't reveal my views in a formal account, I do so by my conduct." Xenophon, *Conversations of Socrates*, revised edition. Translated by Hugh Tredinnick and Robin H. Waterfield (editor) (London: Penguin Classics, 1990), 197.

16. Karl Jaspers, *Socrates, Buddha, Confucius, Jesus: The Paradigmatic Individuals.* Translated by Ralph Manheim (New York: Harcourt, Brace & World, 1962). From Jasper's, *The Great Philosophers*, Vol. 1.

17. Walter Benjamin, "The Story-teller," in *Illuminations: Essays and Reflections.* Trans. by Harry Zohn (New York: Schocken, 1969), 86–87. Achenbach cites "Der Erzähler," in *Gesammelte Schriften*, Bd. II/2, 442.

Chapter 4

Conversational Mastery

What one does not bespeak with another, one does not rightly bethink.

—Goethe[1]

To speak of conversational mastery [*Gesprächskönnerschaft*] is first of all to bring the very idea of it into conversation. Indeed, I intend here to introduce this term—modeled on *Lebenskönnerschaft*, to which it bears an obvious family resemblance—as an entry in the conversation about conversation. Such is the purpose of the following endeavor.

First of all, however: why 'conversational mastery'? Why not the 'professional conversation' or even a 'conversation profession'? For is it not generally understood that 'professional' and 'masterful' are one and the same in being proficient? Don't we sometimes say such things as, 'leave it to the pros—they do it best'?

But with these alternate phrases we are caught in the very snare I am trying to evade with the title 'conversational mastery.' Do we really want to say—that is, in every case—that someone can do something *because* it is their profession, their occupation? If so, then in order to establish what someone can or cannot do, it would suffice simply to point out the person's occupation. But of course we know that in every occupation, as amongst all professionals, there are the competent and the incompetent, the masters and misfits. There are those who are 'good' in their profession, others who are 'better,' some indeed are 'exceptionally good'; yet others, on the contrary, are merely mediocre, while not a few are 'inferior,' and many simply 'lousy.' Here we find the experienced expert, there a novice in the discipline, and so on and so forth. Yet, in all these cases, the relative 'mastery' serves as the yardstick by which we assess the professionalism—not the opposite, which would indeed be impossible. For whether anyone is 'good at' or 'a master of' something is not to be determined by whether they qualify as a professional or ply their trade professionally.

Accordingly, a 'professionally' conducted conversation is not automatically a good conversation, let alone a masterful conversation. It is indeed quite conceivable that some conversations are *lousy* precisely *because* they are the conversations of professionals.

At any rate, the possibility is one we shall not be able entirely to exclude. Isn't it, after all, exactly our experience today when, for instance, we watch or listen to (*endure*) so-called 'talk shows,' which are populated so extensively by professional talking heads? Or perhaps there is an even more grave problem: could it be that conversations are ruined precisely by *routine*, which is only one of the many attainments of the professional?

Let that suffice as my opening question, and as allusion to the justification of my title, unusual enough to demand some elucidation.

And now let me indicate in brief overview what will here be brought to the conversation, not merely talked about, but *maieutically* brought into the world.

I intend to speak up for *listening as the soul of conversation*. To that end I would like to launch a new idea, a neologism, that is not even in German dictionaries, namely that of *Eingelassenheit*, which will step by step be elucidated below in its many senses. After that, I shall speak about *agreement and contradiction*, both of which also belong to a good conversation and thus at the center of Philosophical Praxis.

LISTENING IS THE SOUL OF CONVERSATION

A German proverb says, "One learns to gab earlier than to listen." And, for that matter, to *hear* sooner than to *listen*. Mere hearing is a gift of nature; to be able to listen, by contrast, is a resource that few have at their disposal. For it is not naturally given to anyone, but must be cultivated into proficiency. Put differently: listening must be *mastered*, being adept at listening [*zuhören zu können*] is the very essence of conversational mastery.

In his *Elective Affinities*, Goethe very impressively had Ottilie note as much in her diary: "To share of oneself is nature, to take what is shared as it was given is honorable [*Bildung*]."[2] But listening is much more than even this. *To take what is shared as it was given is the actual basis of every conversation.* Say two are present, and one speaks, but the other does not listen: it has not yet become a conversation. Indeed, one could provisionally say: the conversation begins with the *readiness* and *wherewithal* to listen. The latter are what make the beginning, *not* the speaking.[3] Why is that?

If speaking could start the conversation, then a beginning would be possible without any Other whatsoever. Though I can speak by myself, I can only listen to another. One may speak, but one only *converses* once one finds a listener. And I should prefer, in the context of praxis, to speak of a hearkener rather than a listener.[4] For to hearken is to pay close and respectful attention. What matters is to understand listening not as pure passivity or mere reception, but as activity.

"Listen patiently to the one who speaks to you," says the wise Heykar in *One Thousand and One Nights*, "and do not hurry to interrupt him. You don't start a conversation with answers."[5]

The French moralist, La Rochefoucauld, opined:

> One reason we find in conversation so few persons reasonable and agreeable is that nearly everyone thinks more about what he wants to say than about responding precisely to what is said to him. The cleverest and most obliging are content to display the mien of attention, while one can see in their eyes, and in their mind, that they are disengaged from what is being said to them, and preoccupied with returning to what it is they want to say; . . . to listen well and to respond well are among the greatest charms we can have in conversation.[6]

Just now I said that being adept at listening is of the essence in conversational mastery. Let me now add that, in the extreme case, this hearkening can take the form of a very long silence, even, as one says, a 'deep' silence.

Thus it happens that a guest in my Philosophical Praxis, after he has been speaking for some time, recounting his problems, says to me: 'You haven't said a thing.' In response one might venture a disclosure such as: 'Yes, quite so—I am still considering it.' This at least makes it clear that listening to the other person demands more than hearing what is said—it aspires to understand. It further implies that the Other, by sharing with me, really gives me something to think about. What he *has been thinking*, I, as hearkener, *re*think, as it were, or think through myself. And that is something different again from the easy understanding that rushes to say, 'I hear you' and 'I know what you mean,' or that shifts direction entirely by saying 'what that brings up for me is . . . ' (as when the other merely provokes my thoughts, but then falls out of them), or any other way in which to keep the conversation going at the expense of dialogue. To *rethink-through together*, it is essential to get beyond empathetic understanding, and never to lose sight of the obstacle course concealed within the ordinary run of events, the many points of doubt glossed over in the plain retelling. Trying to make the Other understandable is dangerous to understanding the Other. As in Socrates, agreement prevents philosophy.[7]

Put differently: what my guest has said is not the occasion for me now to say something in return, but first and foremost—as long as I am a listener—to try to understand how he is trying to make himself understood to me, how he would desire to be understood; that is, to understand *how he understands himself*. This is hard to do, rarely done, and only a beginning.[8] For it must not be supposed that *his* way of making himself understood conforms to *my* way of making myself understood, as if some kind of 'intuitive understanding' were possible.

This relation, that I in hearkening am striving to understand how the other understands himself, is brought to light in my Philosophical Praxis by a symbol. Two armchairs face each other at an angle across a small low table. I sit in one, my guest sits a little to my left in the other; while, a little to my right, between us across the table, there hangs on the wall a mirror. In it too I see my visitor, who has taken his seat obliquely before me; but I see him reversed left-to-right, the same way he is accustomed to seeing himself in the mirror. Just this is expressed by the symbol: it is this aspect of the others, as I have them immediately face-to-face before me, that the conversation ought to "reflect"—as in a mirror. The conversation thus affords me, within a bounded framework—just as a mirror is framed and presents only a slice—at least a delimited glimpse of the "self-image" of my visitor.

Now in this context it is of the utmost importance to me expressly and emphatically to underscore the limitations operative here (*nota bene*: 'within a bounded framework,' 'delimited glimpse'); for, to speak exactly, one can not *know* how the other understands himself; even in the best case, that is rather a matter of *conjecture*.

Why such caution? Aren't there plenty of theories standing at the ready to *decode* the human being? Oh, to be sure, I should say; but let us not fail to see that at best it is 'THE human being' that our theories decode, not and never *this very one* with whom we are conversing. In each and every case it is only with *this one* that conversation is possible at all. You can't have a conversation with humanity, only with a human.

Moreover, in conversation, I understand the other not by knowing, or having discerned, how others have understood human being, nor by having transposed their understanding into theory, but only by my hearkening[9] to how this other is presenting him or her self to me to be understood (though, in most cases, it is only to how the other person *struggles* to present themselves to me to be understood).

And here another problem of every conversation surfaces: not only is it difficult for an auditor to understand the other (and possible at best only within limits), but the same applies to the one who wants to commune with us: he himself usually finds it difficult to make himself understood to us, and he achieves it at best within limits. If therefore a meddlesome auditor, well-meaning but recklessly assertive, should declare: 'Ah, yes! I have well understood. I know exactly what you mean,' etc., he would be making light of what falls hard upon the other. And so he would *not* have understood the other in the distress[10] they experience in trying to express themselves adequately.

Yet such difficulties accord with the insight of Schleiermacher,[11] who thought that, more than anything else, what properly belongs to the 'true' conversation is a consciousness that the apprehension and understanding[12] of the Other erects an enormous demand, one that overburdens all and sundry, even the most masterful. Or, to put it differently: it is mastery that is most cognizant of this excessive demand. By this we recognize the masters. Yet this insight itself marks only a beginning: as listeners we understand at best 'something,' perhaps 'some,' sometimes 'a little,' much 'to some extent,' but never 'everything' and certainly not 'completely.' In other words, conversational mastery begins once I have understood how difficult, extraordinarily rare, and hence quite improbable, genuine understanding is. Whoever has understood this, shifts his business to listening intensely, to hearkening well. In this he evinces respect for the other. Goethe understood this and, with a subtle allusion to the traditional theologumenon, expressed it in his letter to Lavater with the words: "Individuum est ineffabile."[13]

Let me now lean in a little more to this beginning of conversation, to listening, which—according to Byung-Chul Han—is "not a passive act," but "a bestowal, a giving, a gift. It helps the Other to speak in the first place." Again: "I listen so that the Other will speak." Thus, the listening that hearkens is "a hospitable silence" that invites the visitor to "speak themselves free."[14]

Eingelassenheit

Listening, I said, is not passivity, but rather utter activity, and of such a manner, I would add, that a new word is needed specifically for it, which I now wish to propose. Such mastery of listening is a conversational virtue that I would call *Eingelassenheit*.

Of course, I know that a proposal does not ensure a career. Introducing new concepts is no trifle. Nevertheless, I will allow myself to make this suggestion and explain why I would take some delight in this word, if only it existed.

At first sight, *Eingelassenheit* brings to mind *Gelassenheit*, a word meaning serenity, spiritual repose, or composure of mind. That is, it conjures that lofty virtue of the wise Greeks and astute Romans, without which no one is really a listener. Not only does repose urge one as listener to 'let it be'—that is, to afford the other person the time, to provide a space of calm, to talk out, through to the last word, whatever it is they have to say—it is also the wherewithal to step back for the duration from one's own desires, opinions and expectations, to distance oneself from oneself—at least while one persists as hearkener. To hearken requires being 'with the other' but also at the same time being 'with the matter at hand,' that is, with the matter at the hand of the other. If, on the contrary, that which is one's own all too intrusively interposes, listening becomes a torment, as speaking does to the speaker. Peter Sloterdijk came up with a mischievously amusing formulation of this: "Those who will not hear are left to feel."[15] And who is it who does not want to hear? Those to whom the clutter in their own head is incomparably more important than anything that might be discovered in the other.

But let me return to *Eingelassenheit*, my proposed new term of art. The word also suggests the verb *einlassen*, meaning 'to let in' or to let enter.' And this in a double sense: first, transitively, e.g., 'to let someone in' (we let the other in to us in a figurative sense when we hearken unto them); and second, reflexively, e.g., 'to let oneself in' [*sich einlassen*] (in hearkening unto the other, we let ourselves in to them, as it were).

It goes on. It seems as if every association and evocation of meaning that the word '*Eingelassenheit*' harbors is welcome. We not only *admit* ourselves, give ourselves entry to another, in hearkening unto them, but we also *attend* them, we are there with them. We all know the fundamental importance of this latter aspect in peace diplomacy: whoever sits down at the negotiating table and even just hears out the opponent is already 'there with them'; even if it remains merely giving them a hearing and is not yet tantamount to listening.

But it seems to me that what really deserves the name listening is most aptly depicted in the common figure of speech according to which the listener 'lends an ear' to the one listened to. Anyone pondering this metaphor as if for the first time will find it a strange image indeed! To 'lend one's voice' to another who does not know how to speak for himself—this is easy to understand. Thus one person uses his mouth to speak for another, whose spokesperson he becomes.

But 'to lend an ear'? Could it be that the one to whom I listen has no ears of their own, and now needs mine as a surrogate? Certainly not. And yet the figure is to be taken precisely: If I lend my ear to the other, they have my ear; if only on loan, it 'belongs' [*gehört*] with him,[16] and is *for their use*. But note well: the other is merely in 'possession' of it, and that only for a limited time, without it actually being their property, to deal with as they see fit. The ear is *borrowed*, and precisely *not* their own. From the point of view of one lucky enough to have found such a listener, this means: There is an ear listening *as if* it belonged to me, and yet it is not my own. By listening to me, it belongs with me,[17] and yet it is not my own, otherwise I would be as if talking to myself. Put differently: one who listens to me is close to me, is 'at my place' and yet, at the same time, is another, has only lent me this hearing.

It can hardly be expressed better than with this image of the borrowed ear: only he listens who hears—not what he wants, but—what the other of himself lets be heard.

ABOUT WHAT IS HEARD, AGREEMENT AND CONTRADICTION

But, to go one step further, such hearkening is the very precondition of any reply, any contradiction, any rebuttal, and, if this should prove necessary, any effort to move the other. Blaise Pascal saw this clearly. I quote:

> When we wish to correct with advantage, and to show another that he errs, we must notice from what side he views the matter, for on that side it is usually true, and admit that truth to him, but reveal to him the side on which it is false. He is satisfied with that, for he sees that he was not mistaken, and that he only failed to see all sides.[18]

This would appear to be an essential and invariable rule of good conversation, applied here to the special case of advice-seeking conversation. Walter Benjamin was to make the same point a few centuries later, so pithily and persuasively, in fact, that I cannot pass up any occasion that comes my way to quote it unabridged. Thus I do so again now. Benjamin's advice on the advising conversations, published as a piece of his *Ibizan Sequence*, reads as follows:

> *Do Not Seek to Dissuade*. Anyone who is asked for his advice would do well to begin by finding out the asker's own opinion and then endorsing it. No one is easily persuaded of another's greater cleverness, and few people ask for advice with the intention of following someone else's. The fact is that they have already [come to their decision in the privacy of their own mind] and now wish to hear it from the outside, to accept it as the "advice" of another. This confirmation is what they seek, and they are right to do so. For it is very risky to set out to implement one's own decisions without passing them through the give-and-take of conversation, as if through a filter. This is why the person who seeks advice is already halfway to a decision; and if what he is planning to do is a mistake, it is better to lend it skeptical support than to contradict it with conviction.[19]

The well-advised person consults himself, the well-*advising* person only assists him in doing so. That is the whole point of the advice-seeking conversation. Yet I find it appealing and appropriate here, through a slight amplification of Benjamin's text, to sketch some features of conversational mastery as they relate to conversations concerning advice.

Thus: "Anyone who is asked for his advice"—Benjamin correctly opens with what belongs at the beginning of all advice: *it must be asked for.* Advice, given without being asked, is annoying, if not ridiculous. "I always pass on good advice," says Lord Goring in Oscar Wilde's play, *An Ideal Husband.* "It is the only thing to do with it."[20]

Benjamin's second recommendation is just as correct: It involves first "finding out the asker's own opinion." Again, whoever's advice is sought must first of all prove himself a hearkener, a point already made above with sufficient force. So the question now is: what is it to "find out" the advice-seeker's "own opinion," as Benjamin says? Or, for that matter, what does it mean to have "come to their decision in the privacy of their own mind"?[21] Experience in philosophical praxis teaches me that few seek advice unless they already know their opinion—only, they do not trust it. Or, a decision has in reality already been half-made, and all that is wanted is that it be reinforced. One who lacks even self-advice is usually totally confused, unclear as to what to think, does not know his way around, or even where to turn. Here the adviser is forced to be an improviser: like a hieroglyph-reader, he must decipher fragments of a biographical narrative, discern its character and inner logic. After all, what those without direction are seeking by way of advice is meaningful fulfillment, or at least how to follow on from what has happened so far in their own story. What is hoped for is not so much that the adviser knows all the answers, only that he see how one might move on. And even if the adviser does not possess the 'solution,' much would already be gained if he discerns which knot needs untying. To the ill-advised, life in which they are entrapped has tied itself in knots in him.

A "give-and-take conversation"[22] might then begin, the well-advised person lets his thoughts pass through it "as through a filter." The image is splendid. He who seeks the advice of another consults *himself* through another,[23] and yet this other, who "lends him his ear," as we said, is not simply a silent extra, and certainly not merely the forbearing listener. Rather, everything hinges on whether the narrator, speaking to that other ear that the adviser 'lent' him, now hears his own story differently. And if it is a fine, sensitive ear that is listening to him, as closely as if he were listening to himself, he will now hear intermediate tones, undertones, and overtones that have so far escaped him in his own 'version' of his misfortune or misadventure.

But most importantly, as Benjamin says, the conversation with the adviser becomes a "filter" for him, through which neither the first nor any random idea will pass, but only the purified thought, the examined decision. For this it is necessary that the adviser *not* be someone who has advice on hand ready to hand out, but someone who is seeking it, just like the person seeking advice. Just as only he is called to be a writer who finds writing arduous, so too a good adviser is one who knows that good advice is not only rare and 'costly,' but only in the most exceptional instances truly on the mark. By contrast, advice tossed out ready-made is quite rightly disregarded. Generic advice misses the misfortune, which is grasped only if it is understood in its uniqueness. "One does not treat in a universal way what God wanted to set asunder" Gustav Thibon says.[24]

Finally, what about Benjamin's concluding dictum that it would be better, when the advice-seeker has a misguided plan, to confirm him skeptically in this rather than contradict him with firm conviction? Will I go so far as to agree with this thought? Indeed. For, it affirms that the one seeking advice is the agent [*Täter*] of his life, and also remains such while being advised. That the adviser confirms him *skeptically* is objection enough, and it may give pause for thought. Anything more is meddling.

"The one seeks a helper for the birth of his thoughts," says Nietzsche in *Beyond Good and Evil*, "the other someone who he can help; thus arises a good conversation."[25] Perhaps this is the key to well-crafted conversation, at least as regards a conversation wherein advice is being sought together.

OBSTETRICS: A BRIEF LOOK BACK AT SOCRATES

With the catchword "obstetrics" borrowed from Nietzsche, I have opened up the possibility finally of casting a glance back to the very beginnings of conversational mastery. And this beginning we commonly associate with the name of Socrates and his midwifery or maieutics.

To begin let us remind ourselves that the interchanges of this first master of conversation were not consensus-building exercises or the forging of unanimity, but the high-risk scrutiny of prevailing opinions, ingrained attitudes, hand-me-down judgments, tradition-honored validities, sacred norms and standard practices, and all conventional maxims. In short: the Socratic conversation enters the world as a shake-up, an unsettling that cunningly contests the opinion-holder's ownership of truth. With ironic assurance, Socrates sought to bring his interlocutors to safety on solid ground, that they may secure a foothold beneath their feet. But in fact he leads them onto thin ice with his 'what-is-it?' questions and with his insistence on knowing what a thing actually is, what it is essentially and in reality.

This dream, dreamt first perhaps by Socrates, and then after him by countless other philosophical master-thinkers, was that we might arrive, by way of conversation, at binding deliverances of reason that were valid and that, once firmly established as entrenched foundations and rock-bottom truths, were thereafter to be withdrawn from further conversation. It was assumed that henceforth they would instead play the role of incontrovertible cornerstones, or serve to help settle later disputes as unassailable points of appeal.

In reality, however, even the most rigorous philosophical discussions have never led to such resounding results, and consequently, we have to get used to the fact that *the conversation will go on and not end*, unlike the results, the 'fixed outcomes' that so many expect, but which emerge only now and then. Thus centuries—indeed, millennia—after Socrates, the philosopher, Robert Spaemann, can declare that it is not the business of philosophy to make the solutions simpler, but to make the problems harder.[26] This indeed is the fundamental precept for the mastery of philosophical conversation, to wit: to sound out the actual depths of problems—*if they have any*—perchance even to discover that some are bottomless, such as no plumb-bob may fathom; to comprehend their intractability due, for instance, to their being understandable only as entwined with other problems; or as descendants of preexistent troubles; or simply as questions that are always raised but ever beyond answer.

Does the point made by Spaemann not ring out like some late echo of the novel tone of conversation first struck by Socrates? For certainly it is with him that a whole culture of conversation and speech first came into the world. Hans Blumenberg puts the point in similar terms: "Every type of philosophy can be defined by the fact that it finds easy questions difficult, or renders them difficult."[27] In all correctness, we must allow one amendment: Philosophy takes the *supposedly* easy questions as hard, thereby taking them seriously.

I maintain: conversational mastery is not a practice of facilitation, not the provision of relief, but a burdening of those who are wide-awake and to which they have always deliberately exposed themselves, which destined them to stand for others—including especially for the best amongst us—as exemplary.

But there is something else that can also be identified as a peculiarity and innovation of Socratic conversation, that in my view is even more decidedly the basis of all conversational mastery.

Socrates was probably the first to protractedly *fasten upon a thought*, however it may have entered the conversation, long enough till, through the unraveling of its own contradictions, it begins to move; and this is called *thinking*. Hegel put this innovation into a commonsensical, even folksy formula: "the main thing is to keep to the point."[28] And then he incisively explained what distinguishes such a culture of conversation from others and from everyday banter.

> The spirit of dogmatism, self-assertion, stopping short when we seem to get into difficulties, and escaping them by a jest, or by setting them aside—all these attitudes and methods are here excluded: they do not constitute good manners, nor do they have a place in Socrates' dialogues.[29]

What Hegel here calls "good manners" in a Socratic dialogue, I call conversational mastery, as inaugurated by Socrates: the perseverance to stay on point; or: sustained concentration.

But this, in order to persevere on my own part, can also be understood as an exercise in *re-thoughtfulness*,[30] itself the keyword that I put forward to which all the present considerations are to lead. For surely it can be said that conversational mastery is in essence an exercise in re-thoughtfulness, for which there is also the good, traditional word: judiciousness.[31]

According to Herbert Schnädelbach, philosophical conversation, especially with Socrates, was tantamount to:

> a culture of re-thoughtfulness. It is the conversation of the thoughtful, *i.e.*, of those who not only think, but think through, think over and under their thoughts in order to clarify them, to improve them, and to put them to the test. As a rule, the occasions for this reflection do not come from thinking itself, but from the domain of pre-philosophical experiences with problem-situations that compel us to think things through. Our progenitor Socrates has laid down the example of this for us; we trace back to him the critical re-thinking of our thoughts through conversation, which we call elucidation. Philosophy as elucidation is a spiritual [*gedankliche*] reaction to the loss of the self-evident certainties of the life-world, to the unsettling and upheaval of the familiar, which the thoughtful descendants of Socrates do not, like many contemporaries, merely feel but try to analyze and master.[32]

And so it is. It remains only to complete the point, or at least to supplement it: we have had, in the meantime, to learn to live with conversations that generate a minimum of resolution, harmony and agreement, and even to welcome within them a multiplicity of clear-cut stances and well-founded insights. Truly, the authentic conversation,[33] and so conversation in Philosophical Praxis, does not serve—and never has—to transform polyphony into a boring unison without tension or suspense, but rather to arrange a counterpoint of voices in a polyphonic composition—to exploit metaphors of music. And indeed, I should like to promote the idea that, besides philosophy, which very much presents as conversation, it was music above all else that made a most crucial contribution to conversational mastery—music and, of course, drama and epic.

But let us stick with music as an example. What would a symphony by Haydn be for us, in which there was no tension between musical phrases, no movement from the first theme to the second, whereby the two themes, having made themselves known to each other in their utterly distinct characters, nevertheless come into relation with each other, which, to adopt the tone of official music theory, is called *Durchführung* (literally, 'working out or through; development').[34] In the end, however, at least in the classical sonata, the two themes, having undergone many alterations and modifications, are, one might almost say, "persevered," precisely by having taking up the other theme or bound themselves together; and they emerge once again in the recapitulation, so to speak, purified and strengthened. Is this not the image of a successful conversation?

The Romantics thought so: for example, Adam Müller, whose great 1816 essay "On Conversation" I recommend reading once again. As the image of a good conversation, he took the "relationship of the sexes to each other, where nature has arranged the highest diversity of inclinations, opinions, and social and moral characteristics, where it seems most to argue with itself and to contradict itself." For it is here that "the liveliest and most irresistible feeling of being determined for each other" shows itself.[35]

This speaks volumes for the dialectic—which, of course, if it is to be represented by 'gender differences,' might seem to be moribund today. In Philosophical Praxis, we don't fail to notice it.

NOTES

1. Johann Wolfgang von Goethe, *Wilhelm Meisters Lehrjahre*, Vol. 7, 12th ed. (Munich: C. H. Beck, 1989), 451. Translation by Laura V. Adrian. Used with permission.

2. Goethe, *Elective Affinities.* From Ottilie's Journal, Part 2, Ch. 4. Laura V. Adrian translation. Note that "honorable" here translates *Bildung*. Though by no means literal, Adrian's translation is a marked improvement upon R. J. Hollingdale's not incorrect version, which runs as follows: "It is natural to communicate yourself to others, but to receive the communication of others without falsifying it requires culture" (Penguin Classics, 1978), 180–181.

3. Achenbach's note: Recently, Byung-Chul Han in *The Expulsion of the Other* has thankfully pointed out that listening is precisely what is lacking today, concluding from this that "in the future, there may be a profession known as a '*listener*.'" He has thus passed off as "possible" what actually exists as the Philosophical Praxis. Quote: "For a fee, the listener gives and ear to the Other. People go to the listener because there is hardly anyone else left who will listen to the Other. Today, we are increasingly losing the ability to listen. It is hampered most of all by the intensifying focus on the ego, by the narcissization of society." Han, *The Expulsion of the Other: Society, Perception and Communication Today*. Trans. by Wieland Hoban. (Cambridge, UK: Polity, 2018), 70.

4. The German phrase is: "statt vom Zuhörer vom Zuhörenden zu sprechen," which one might quite literally render as, "instead of the listener, speak of the listening-er," to emphasize the active character of listening.

5. Though attributed to *One Thousand and One Nights*, the story is cited indirectly by Achenbach via Marie-Claude Tarnero-Pansart. Der Patient als Dulder, in *Geduld: Die Kunst des Wartens.* Ed. by Ruthard Stäblein (Darmstadt: Bühl-Moos/Elster, 1994), 179.

6. La Rochefoucauld, *Maximes et Reflections Diverses* (Librairie Larousse: Paris, 1971), #139. Picard translation, taking small advantage of the old translation by J. W. Willis Bund and J. Hain Friswell (Simpson Low, Son, and Marston: London, 1871). Note that Achenbach cites a German translation, and his quotation is not continuous, though it does closely follow the original French. I have restored the final phrase of Rochefoucauld's "maxim," which seems entirely *apropos*, but is not quoted by Achenbach.

7. The final four sentences of this paragraph do not exist in the German. They capture an interpretation of a conversation with Achenbach intended to clarify this passage. The final two sentences approach direct quotations of Achenbach from that conversation.

8. In these three strokes I have tried to capture the meaning of the multivalent German expression, 'es versteht sich nicht von selbst.'

9. Hearkening—*aufmerksam sein.*

10. Elsewhere in this book, in regard to the difficulty of guests expressing themselves, Achenbach refers to Goethe's play, *Torquato Tasso*. See chapter 6, note 5.

11. Friedrich Daniel Schleiermacher Ernst, Das eigentliche Gespräch. From *Einleitung in die Dialektik.* In *Friedrich Schleiermachers Dialektik.* Ed. by Rudolf Odebrecht (Leipzig: J. C. Hinrichs, 1942; Darmstadt: Wissenschaftliche Buchgesellschaft, 1976), 7–10. For an English translation, see *Dialectic or The Art of Doing Philosophy*. Ed. by Terrence N. Tice (Atlanta, GA: Scholars Press, 1996).

12. Apprehension and understanding—*Verständnis und Verstehen.*

13. Letter to Lavatar from September 20, 1780. Cited from *Goethes Werke, Weimarer Ausgabe*, IV. *Abteilung*, *Briefe*, 4 (Munich: Deutscher Taschenbuch Verlag, 1987), 300.

14. All quotations in this paragraph are taken from Byung-Chul Han, *The Expulsion of the Other*, 70–71. Achenbach note: The art of listening conjured by Carl Zuckmayer in a striking example: On long walks in Austria, he had fantasized together the sequence of scenes of the later 'Hauptmann von Köpenik,' but then, when Max Rheinhardt met him in a hotel and asked him what he was working on—at that time there was still "not a single written word"—he suddenly began "to recite the play, or rather: I played it, for hours, with all the scenes and characters, often blindly surprised by my own ideas. There arose unplanned scenarios, dialogue, the endings of acts—the play was there. It had taken shape through Reinhardt's magical listening, with which he could raise people into a trance of productivity." Carl Zuckmayer, *Als wär's ein Stück von mir: Horen der Freundschaft.* Volume 2 of *Werkausgabe in 10 Bänden* (Frankfurt a.M.: Fischer, 1966), 455.

15. Peter Sloterdijk. Personal communication. The quote in German runs: "Wer nicht hören will, läßt fühlen." Sloterdijk here plays on the parental threat "Wer nicht hören will, muß fühlen," which means those who do not obey must be (made to) feel the consequences. But in Sloterdijk's amended version, the point would seem to be that 'those who are incapable of listening are abandoned to, or left imprisoned within, mere feeling'; i.e., isolated from others and without understanding of the matter or situation at hand ('*die Sache*').

16. The force of the pun is lost in translation: *gehört* means both 'heard' and 'belongs to or with.' If the borrowed ear *belongs* with a person, they are heard.

17. "Es ist mir, indem es mir zuhört, zugehörig."

18. Blaise Pascal, *Pensées.* Transl. by W.F. Trotter (New York: E. P. Dutton, 1958), #9.

19. Adapted slightly from Walter Benjamin, *Selected Writings*, vol. 2, part 2, 1931–1934. Ed. by Michael W. Jennings, Howard Eiland and Gary Smith (Cambridge, MA: Belknap, 1999), 588. See the Ibizan Sequence, April–May, 1932. I have had to add the words "come to their decision in the privacy of their own mind" to highlight the intent of "im Stillen schon gefaßt," a phrase Achenbach specifically references later, but which is not rendered literally in the existing translation. Achenbach quotes the *Gesammelte Schriften*, vol. IV/1, 403.

20. Oscar Wilde, *An Ideal Husband*, 1895. Achenbach quotes a German translation as an instance of the ridiculous. The immediate context of the quotation revels the comic intent of the passage, and is itself worth quoting. Lord Goring, without prompting, has just said, "You should go to bed, Miss Mabel," to a Mabel Chiltern, who is shocked. In response, Lord Goring says, "My father told me to go to bed an hour ago. I don't see why I shouldn't give you the same advice. I always pass on good advice. It is the only thing to do with it. It is never of any use to oneself." See *The Plays of Oscar Wilde*, Wordsworth Editions, 2000.

21. Come to their decision in the privacy of their mind—*eigener Entschluß, im Stillen schon gefaßt.*

22. In the Benjamin quote, the phrase 'give-and-take conversation' renders "Rede und Gegenrede," and concerns the "Agreement and Contradiction" ("Zustimmung und Widerspruch") in the title of this section. The issue being raised concerns in part contradicting and otherwise arguing with visitors to Philosophical Praxis.

23. The usual but peculiar German expression here is: 'sich beraten mit jemandem'; literally: to consult yourself with someone. Achenbach is suggesting there is some wisdom in the common expression. In this connection, one might recall an opposite saying, that a person who acts as their own lawyer has a fool for a client. But perhaps the real fool is one who never acts as their own philosopher.

24. "Man behandelt nicht auf universelle Art, was Gott grundverschieden haben wollte." Gustave Thibon, *Nietzsche und Johannes vom Kreuz* (Paderborn: Ferdinand Schöningh, 1957), 44.

25. Friedrich Nietzsche, *Beyond Good and Evil*, #136. Picard translation. I have translated "Geburtshelfer" literally as "helper for the birth," in order to bring to the surface the shared root "helf-." But "Geburtshelferschaft" I have rendered as "obstetrics," since "midwifery" and "maieutics" are used later.

26. Robert Spaemann, "Die zwei Grundbegriffe der Moral," in *Grenzen. Zur ethischen Dimension des Handelns* (Stuttgart: De Gruyter, 2001), 78. Picard translation.

27. Hans Blumenberg, Die Frage, an der Plato starb, in *Frankfurter Allgemeine Zeitung*, 81 (4.4.1996), 33.

28. Hegel, Georg. *Hegel's Lectures on the History of Philosophy*, I. Trans. by E.S. Haldane and Frances H. Simson (London: Routledge and Kegan Paul, 1892; 1968), 403.

29. Hegel, *Lectures on the History of Philosophy*, I, 403.

30. Re-thoughfulness—*Nachdenklicheit.*

31. The German word is *Besonnenheit*, but the reference is to the central notion of Greek practical philosophy, *sophrosyne*, variously translated by soundness of mind, moderation, temperance, restraint, self-control. See, for example, Plato *Cratylus*, 411e. It is perhaps noteworthy that Aquila, in his translation of Schopenhauer, is well pleased with his rendition of this important term as *thoughtful awareness*.

32. Herbert Schnädelbach, *Das Gespräch der Philosophie*. Farewell Lecture at the Humboldt University, June 18, 2002. Picard translation.

33. Authentic conversation—*eigentliche Gespräch*, an allusion again to Schlieremacher.

34. *Durchführung* in English musical terminology is 'development,' sometimes more interestingly called 'free fantasia.'

35. Adam Müller, Vom Gespräch, in *Zwölf Reden über die Beredsamkeit und deren Verfall in Deutschland* (Leipzig: Georg Joachim Göschen, 1816), 27f.

Chapter 5

The Ground-Rule of Philosophical Praxis

> Philosophy always comes up against non-philosophy, because it has no object of its own. It thinks over experience, over all experience, over the totality of experience . . .
>
> —Paul Ricœur[1]

Philosophical Praxis is confronted with a requirement that has been alien to academic philosophy: instead of showcasing for people the stock problems that preoccupy the academic philosopher, Philosophical Praxis must calibrate itself to the themes, problems and question-formulations that burden others, those who in their need have turned to philosophy for help. So the opening move is not made by philosophy; the opening is made by the questions brought to the philosopher.

I would like to try to explain the far-reaching implications of acceding [*Anerkennen*] to this ground-rule.

> 1) *Philosophy that begins where others begin with it stands in stark contrast to the sciences in having an unlimited purview. It is neither a specialty nor a discipline in the academic sense of the word. And the philosopher is no expert. What practical philosophy is, therefore, cannot be delimited by the declaration of a 'specific responsibility,' cannot be departmentalized.*[2]

Let's imagine a man living in a bad marriage, and despairing therein, who seeks a way out of his situation. The man consults a lawyer and begins to recount all his sorrows. If the lawyer should then listen to all that the client has to say, that would certainly be nice, a humane gesture—but people's sorrows are not his responsibility *as a lawyer*. That is very likely why, after a decent span of patience, he will at last interrupt his client and ask: 'What is it then: do you want a divorce or don't you? If so, I would be happy to help you.' In fact, he is responsible [*zuständig*] for *this* way out, and *only* this way out, though our man may not yet know if divorce is indeed the way out he seeks. Whether he should or should not get divorced is not a question of law.

'You need to figure out what you want,' the lawyer tells him, 'if I am to help you any further.' The dilemma, however, that has led our man to the wrong address, is that *he does not know* what he wants.

Thus hanging, he cannot live well where or how he now lives. All manner of scruples keep him from 'breaking free' of the situation. No surprise if our man should fall ill over it. He suffers from a pain in his throat that makes it difficult for him to swallow—a phenomenon that often accompanies separation anxieties and is tied to fears stemming from an impending loss. Thus he repairs to the physician.

And we let him find a doctor who—up with all the latest—is well aware already that many ailments of which patients lament are in some way related to their life situations, their fears and sorrows.

And so this doctor, like the lawyer before him, will for some time forebear to hear his patient's lamentation; he may go so far as to weigh up for himself the extent to which the man's illness could be the effect and expression of unresolved conflict—in medical terms, a 'symptom.' As a *physician*, however, he is responsible [*zuständig*] only for eliminating or alleviating those effects. For the sorrows that originally brought the man to the doctor's office, medicine is not responsible. It does not fall within its competence even to begin to understand this sorrow, let alone to understand it helpfully, that is, in such a way that the potential solutions enfolded within it become practically accessible.

For how could one possibly say *medically* how to conduct a marriage, whether it is possible to save a marriage gone astray, or better not even to want to save it but to dissolve it? Now this doctor—assuming he is any good—may well be able to advise the man what he should do if he wants to get healthy again, and not merely have the illness outwardly cured, just as a good lawyer could have advised him what he should do to carry out the divorce. But the question remains: *Is* health the way the man seeks out of his misery, which, after all, health will not solve or dissolve? Were this self-evident—and it does seem self-evident to many today—we should have to conclude that a healthy life cannot at the same time be a false life. Health would undoubtedly be—in an old philosophical turn of phrase—the 'highest good,' a reliable manifestation of the good life. But such an equation, as popular as it may be, is only the expression of fashionable naivety.

In consultation with the doctor, our patient's indecision may have become evident—his hesitation, his unhappy perseverance in unhappiness, his powerlessness to pull himself out of paralysis. So the doctor (for he is a modern, 'enlightened' physician and practitioner) recommends to him (as supplement to his own pharmacological prescription—a light sedative) that he enter psychotherapy. 'It will do you good,' he tells him. 'Talk through everything thoroughly for once, and you will see that things will soon be looking up.'

So the doctor releases our man, and he takes himself to psychotherapy. What awaits him there, however, thanks to the extraordinary variety of psychotherapeutic procedures, schools, and methods, can hardly be adequately imagined. One could say: for him there now, almost anything could sprout up. . . .

However, a *crucial problem* can be stated—and precisely in our fictitious case—a constitutive problem and deficiency that no therapy—whatever form it takes—can ever get clear of. I would like to make this problem understandable by interposing a quotation, a diary note by Eugène Ionesco:

> H. tells me that a psychotherapist friend of his has been taken up with two difficult cases, two people who don't know each other and who have been coming to see him every day for the past two or three months: a man and a woman. The man would like to be divorced, but inwardly he cannot face divorce, so he never achieves it. The psychotherapist tries to explain to him the reasons for his behaviour, he does his best to help the poor man to separate from his wife. The other patient, the woman, is suffering from nervous depression because her husband wants to leave her. The psychotherapist tries to explain to her that to keep her husband she must behave in a different way. He tries to make her admit that it is largely her own fault if her husband wants to leave her.[3]

To my knowledge, the most trenchant commentary that can be attached to this diary note is again a quotation, namely a fragment from Max Horkheimer's *Notizen*, titled 'Psychoanalysis as the Cause of its Necessity': "The clueless certainty with which the therapist feels called upon to remove the obstacle," Horkheimer writes, is the result of a powerful misjudgment:

> By placing the rupture of painful [. . .] spousal love at the discretion of the subject in analysis, the analyst negates the taboo already gnawed upon by the progressive decay of the bourgeoisie; in dangerous carelessness, like a mini-Nietzsche, he continues to push what is falling, and thrusts the dagger into the partner's heart. What he calls healing is the empowerment of a fashionable lack of scruples by that party to the family conflict to whom he can present a bill.[4]

Now I do not want to tell the little fictitious story of our misery-laden man any further—which, after all, could easily be done and would be quite tempting; especially if we were now also to have him seek an audience with a priest or pastor, and we would have the opportunity to observe what parades itself as the special competence of the theologian.

But I must resist this temptation, which in the end would amount to a never-ending story, and I can do so all the more readily because the interpolated narrative was only intended to demonstrate the significance of my first thesis.

And now I will try to summarize what has been circuitously presented: By their necessary specialization on a particular responsibility [*Zuständigkeit*], the various helping professions force the complex problem of our man under the rule of a *single* point of view, by adopting which they become utterly unable to judge whether this particular way to intervene in the problem at hand is even appropriate. 'I am competent to prosecute your divorce,' says the lawyer. 'I am here for you to get well again,' says the doctor. 'If you want to understand and work through your inhibitions, I'll take you into therapy'; so says the psychotherapist in the tone of professional empathy.

And the philosopher? For what is the philosopher 'responsible'? The answer is: there is not 'something' that the philosopher is responsible for and—before being called for in an individual case—nothing exceptional, particular, or special that already falls within his wheelhouse, and to which the individual case is now to be submitted. Rather, a philosopher's responsibility in a particular case is first to be determined by the very problem presented. In short, one becomes responsible for *this particular case*. And the first question to ask oneself is: What does it mean to be responsible *in this particular case*?

Whether he is responsible for divorces, convalescence, psycho-hygienic mood stabilization or human technically driven behavioral adjustments to normal behavioral expectations, the expert perceives in the case presented *those* questions for which he, as an expert, has ready solutions. For the philosopher, by contrast, the problem becomes the problem, and that also means that, to the philosopher, the answers which are to be sought must first become liable to question.

After this summary, I repeat the first thesis: philosophy that begins where others begin with it stands in stark contrast to the sciences in having an unlimited purview. It is neither a specialty nor a discipline in the academic sense of the word. And the philosopher is no expert. What Philosophical Praxis is, therefore, cannot be departmentalized by the declaration of a particular 'responsibility.'

The ground-rule mentioned at the beginning (according to which it is not philosophy that makes the opening move, but rather the matter laid before philosophy that must come first) has a further significance that now emerges as the following second thesis:

2) *Philosophy that begins where others begin with it can only live up to this rule to the extent that it is already open to taking up every problem as a philosophical problem and thereby dignifying every question philosophically, that is, admitting it as a question for philosophy.*

Such philosophy joins the call of the Romantic, Novalis: "philosophy is actually homesickness—the *urge to be everywhere at home*."[5] To do so, however, it is necessary to break with the predilection prevailing among certain philosophers to distinguish sharply between 'philosophical' and 'non-philosophical' questions, to draw an insurmountable gulf separating a supposedly 'philosophical' terrain from the domains of other sciences, and to fend off all 'encroachments.'

Karl Popper declared that all his "philosophical work [was] interrelated with non-philosophical problems," and added: "Genuine philosophical problems are always rooted in urgent problems outside philosophy, [and die if these roots decay]."[6] As examples of such "areas not belonging to philosophy" he lists "politics, social coexistence, religion, cosmology, mathematics, natural science, history."[7] Popper himself came quite close to fulfilling his requirement, in that he essentially abolished the difference, which at the same time, however, he held onto (undialectically—he could not do otherwise): namely, the distinction between "philosophical" and "non-philosophical" domains. Yet the mission to overcome that opposition (which in any case must first of all be recognized as having become *de facto* an alienation) had been embraced already by Ludwig Feuerbach who—a good student of Hegel—foresaw it as a basic principle of a philosophy of the future. I quote Feuerbach directly, because with particular decisiveness he insists on what is also a requirement of my second thesis:

> The philosopher must include in the text of philosophy *that* in man which does *not* philosophize, that which is rather opposed to philosophy, which opposes [. . .] thinking. Only in this way does philosophy become a universal, ungainsayable, irrefutable, irresistible power. Philosophy, therefore, has to begin not with itself but with its antithesis, with non-philosophy.[8]

To put it in a phrase: Philosophy is unfettered interest and endless hearkening. Thus the conventional, small-minded admonition to 'stay in your lane!'[9] can indeed still be addressed—albeit figuratively—to representatives of the sciences, at least to the extent that they have not long found their security in the division of labor that is the basis of the scientific order, anointing themselves thereby. But as a protest against philosophy, the saying would be completely meaningless, since philosophy has no lane to force its thoughts into. Philosophy, where it deserves its name, does not produce thoughts according to a pre-cast mold, but rather seeks lead-ins by which anything at all can reach us as thought. And—to say it once more—*anything and everything* may become the occasion of such thoughtfulness.

To illustrate in an amusing way this intent to dissolve boundaries, Kierkegaard contemplated a possible philosophy of the kiss, finding it "curious that there is no book on this topic,"[10] and asked: "can the reason for this deficiency in the literature be that philosophers do not think about such things or that they do not understand them?"[11] He followed up this question with some initial "hints" such as that "a perfect kiss requires that the agents be a girl and a man."[12] The man-to-man kiss he found to be in "bad taste, or, worse yet, it tastes bad."[13] The same applies to any sort of kiss, if routinized. "This is the case with the conjugal domestic kiss, by which husband and wife, for want of a napkin, wipe each other's mouth while saying, 'May it do us good.'"[14]

So much for this little diversion and digression. Now back to the more serious and fundamental questions raised—for example—by Rüdiger Bubner, who is quoted as agreeing that "the thoughts formulated by philosophers take their cue from the pre-established knowledge that they . . . find extant, in the rational shortcomings of which they discover their discipline's core problems."[15]

Incidentally, and without further ado, one may with perfect consistency extend Bubner's line of thinking by noting that the philosophical endeavor takes off not only from pre-established knowledge, but just as much from pre-established forms of action and decision-making, and indeed from the very modes and models of life as lived.[16] Let us listen longer to Bubner: "The awareness of problems arising where none are seen by either the sciences or normal everyday knowledge-bearing practice demands that philosophical concepts be set to work." Thus, for Bubner, "philosophy grasps at problems that, outside of philosophy, are not recognized as problems at all."[17]

But how do these considerations fit into the attempt to amplify my second thesis, that is, the hope and expectation it expresses in the openness and the capacity of philosophy *to take up every problem as a philosophical problem and thereby to dignify any question philosophically, that is, to admit it as a question for philosophy*—which contains within it the requirement to dignify [*würdigen*] questions brought *to* philosophy as questions *of* philosophy, as philosophical questions?

To clear up this issue, I will rush to my own aid, as it were, with a further and yet far-reaching question: How is the principled open-endedness and boundlessness of philosophical interest possible at all, and how are we to conceive [*denken*] the actuation of this interest?

What is not meant is that every problem and every question—or all pre-established knowledge that philosophy finds extant—are in themselves already philosophical problems, philosophical questions, or philosophical knowledge. Rather, they can without exception *become* philosophical.

However, before I—with my third thesis—attempt to answer this question about the prerequisite (understood as the potency of philosophy to bring whatever it encounters into metamorphosis, to transform it into a question that now invites philosophical thought to participate in its own way in its thorough-going exploration), I want first to demonstrate with another example how the self-declarative look and feel[18] of philosophy gets a makeover as soon as it fosters respect for the requirement not to limit its interest to certain 'objects.' The fulfillment of this requirement, however, I identified as the very precondition that must be realized if philosophy is to engage in praxis by going along with the 'ground-rule,' which demands from it to not begin with itself, but to leave the opening of philosophical reflection to what it encounters and is brought before it.

As an example for this I take a small, very successful book by the equally successful philosopher Bertrand Russell, which he wrote in 1912 and to which he attached the title, *The Problems of Philosophy*. The title already signals an understanding of philosophy, consistent in the nicest or worst way with the widespread prejudice, according to which, philosophy—apart from all the sciences—administers a special stock of esoteric profundities and fundamental problems, at least when it has not risen aloft into the rarefied air of the highest and most ultimate questions, and asked (to quote a famous example): 'why is there something rather than nothing?'[19]

And Russell, wanting to introduce us to the "problems of philosophy," begins his text in Cartesian style with one of Kant's four major questions, in this case, "What can I know?" He considers such a question to be through and through a philosophical problem. And that is very true.

Now let us present this question the Russellian way. The sentence opening his book reads as follows: "Is there any knowledge in the world which is so certain that no reasonable man could doubt it?" He goes on to say that "philosophy is *merely* the attempt to answer such ultimate questions."[20]

Now: If *that* were true, the libraries of philosophy would consist in large measure of scrap paper, and the bulk of what has been handed down to us in philosophy could be safely shredded and recycled as waste paper. Nevertheless: Russell would only have to put up with a minor correction and his view, at a stroke, would lose its narrowness and one-sidedness.

It would suffice to perceive in his grandiose formulation of the question *the Socratic impulse*, which is by no means totally suppressed in Russell's inquiry, but remains rather well preserved within it. Yet this primordial Socratic impulse, the inaugural question of philosophy, concerns not whether we can with incontrovertible certainty ever know anything, but whether what we think we know, whether what seems to us incontrovertibly certain and has already become our conviction (acquired by science or in everyday life), can indeed withstand all doubt. Better put: it is whether such a re-thinking might not cause the loss of our rigid and dogmatic fixedness, perhaps even the veil of ideological delusion.[21] And this brings us to the interests of Philosophical Praxis.

In that regard, I would like to propose a necessary re-appraisal of philosophy: namely that, contrary to Russell's conception, the business of the philosopher is not to initiate thinking without any presuppositions from some fictitious zero-point, but to *urge thinking onward*[22] when its vigor has been sapped, or when it has taken shelter in deceptive certainties and now languishes in the sloth-bed of cozy thought-routines. In short: its office is to reinvigorate the power of conscience when "salt has lost its savour" (Matthew 5:13), and where the bite of thinking has been enfeebled. Philosophy may concern itself with the greatest, noblest and most sublime questions; if it does so only within the confines of its own circles, which it will not allow to be disturbed, it nevertheless becomes provincial.

Here I would like to conclude this brief—outwardly wayward—excursion. A book written in the spirit contrived here, to be juxtaposed to Russell's work, would be titled, not *The Problems of Philosophy*, but *The Problems brought to Philosophy, and what becomes of them when Philosophy takes them on board?* This indeed brings me back to my second thesis, which I must now further explicate with a third thesis. What remains in need of explanation is the assertion that only a philosophy that can engage philosophically with every question and any problem is capable of adhering to the 'ground-rule' of Philosophical Praxis, which requires it to start—not with philosophy itself but—with what it encounters in what is brought before it.

The question that arises now is: How is this even possible? Under what conditions can philosophy enter into a conversation with anything?

In reply, my third thesis:

> 3) *Philosophical thinking is able to relate to all forms of knowledge, assertion, opinion, sensations and sensitivities, attitudes and actions, and last but not least—in principle—to every scientifically established theorem, since, being one and all manifestations of thought, they belong, in Hegel's words, to the "Phenomenology of Spirit."*[23]

Take the sciences as an example: *thinking* has gone into all of them, but then become coagulated in them, methodologically fettered. And now that it has proved itself useful, it functions as a routine, which, incidentally, constitutes the success of the sciences, but at the same time increases their ominous aspect, as is presently more and more obvious. Now what happens when philosophy meets such scientific knowledge? Figuratively speaking: it awakens the sleeping reason in knowledge. Thus it brings theories back to the living movement of thought, to which they owe themselves, like the ladder up which they climbed, but which they have kicked away.

At bottom, nothing other than this happens when philosophy in praxis encounters the most everyday questions, problems written in the prose of life, difficulties tangled up in the most diverse ways with custom, habit, drilled-in valuations, decrees of thought that (precisely because they have become general) pass unnoticed. Into this disarray, philosophical thought shows up like a rookie, looking around as if it were the first day; sorting out everything together, each with its ilk; retracing every step; raising questions that concretely test every theory and explanation; going back into what has come and gone to become way-wise; exploring hitherto ignored byways, as if out of sheer curiosity; bringing unlived possibilities halfway to reality through thoughtful amplification, scrutiny and pondering; shedding a sidelight on our 'correctnesses' so that the moment of error within them is revealed, finely tuning them, making them more diverse, more cautious. What is self-evidently understood, or indeed supposed to be understood, turns out unwittingly not yet to be understood at all; which in turn may grant other matters that had hitherto passed for incomprehensible the chance at least to be taken into account.

As this impressionistic overview perhaps shows, philosophical thought everywhere ranges in its own element, and is everywhere at home; or, as Novalis puts it, seeks its home. "Philosophy," he says in another of his fragments, is "*everywhere* or nowhere."[24] That philosophy is able at all to opt for this "everywhere" is grounded in the fact that the stupidest opinion, the most stale and trivial insight, the most annoying prejudice, is wood from the same tree that burgeons philosophical thought.

So once again: philosophy is by its very nature unlimited interest. And this does not mean, as should now be clear, that it has appropriated all knowledge to itself, that everything that is thought, researched or otherwise known belongs to it, as if philosophy claimed the whole world of knowledge as its province. Yet philosophy *is* called to find access everywhere; for, into all knowing and surmising, even hoping, believing, judging, and cherishing, etc., its own element has already entered beforehand, the thinking element, which—in a justified extension—Hegel dubbed "spirit." Once this is acknowledged—and only then—philosophy will be able to pluck up the courage needed to accommodate itself, in the sense required by the basic rule of philosophical praxis, to what is dragged before it.

If, however, it does summon this courage and actually succeeds in discovering itself in its other (i.e., thought as the moving, driving moment in everything, which must be tapped into, and thought further through, that it may ferment and attain its efficacy), then it has become a philosophy worthy of the appellation 'Philosophical Praxis.'

ADDENDUM: ON "THE VALUE OF PHILOSOPHY"

With this I arrive at the end of the preliminary considerations I wanted to present here—more as hints than actually thought through thoroughly. But I would rather not close like this. So as an addendum I would like briefly to draw attention to a chapter in Russell's book, *The Problems of Philosophy*, to which so far I have only referred in order to present a conception of philosophy opposed to his own, without which it is not possible at all to practice philosophy. Entitled "The Value of Philosophy," this chapter (in commendable contradistinction to the tones struck initially, in which we recognize the pathos of foundationalist philosophy) lays out a philosophy so unpretentious, skeptically wise, vividly life-oriented, that it is hard to imagine one that would better support the aspirations of Philosophical Praxis.

Without pretending to review the chapter in its entirety, I will at least underscore some especially memorable passages in it, passages which I joyfully admit to finding inspirational. His very first point delineating the unique and characteristic *usefulness* of philosophy already assumes it to be utterly distinct from the profit we draw above all from scientific-technical research. Philosophy, he argues, has its effectiveness, unlike the other sciences, "through its effects on the lives of those who study it."[25]

Excellent! Those who philosophize live differently. The only question is: How? And *what* changes for them? In what way does philosophy influence our lives, insofar as we philosophize? This question, which seems to ask itself, Russell answers not immediately, but a couple pages later, which I again quote: "the value of philosophy," he says, "must not depend upon any supposed body of definite ascertainable knowledge to be acquired by those who study it"; rather, "the value of philosophy is . . . to be sought largely in its very uncertainty."[26] And further:

> The man who has no tincture of philosophy goes through life imprisoned in the prejudices derived from common sense, from the habitual beliefs of his age or his nation, and from convictions which have grown up in his mind without the cooperation or consent of his deliberate reason. To such a man the world tends to become definite, finite, obvious; common objects rouse no questions, and unfamiliar possibilities are contemptuously rejected. As soon as we begin to philosophize, on the contrary, we find . . . that even the most everyday things lead to problems to which only very incomplete answers can be given. Philosophy, though unable with certainty to tell us what is the true answer to the doubts

> which it raises, is able to suggest many possibilities which enlarge our thoughts and free them from the tyranny of custom. Thus, while diminishing our feeling of certainty as to what things are, it greatly increases our knowledge as to what they may be; it removes the somewhat arrogant dogmatism of those who have never travelled into the region of liberating doubt, and it keeps alive our sense of wonder by showing familiar things in an unfamiliar aspect.[27]

To vary this quotation in its very words, philosophy is the ability—or perhaps the incitement—to liberate us from the fetters of a narrow-minded life; a *vade mecum* against the stupidity of settled knowledge, a thorn in the rotten flesh of comfortable certainties. Philosophy is the wherewithal to better living with uncertainty, rather than with certainty; for truly there are no certainties—with the exception of deception, which falls in league with the inertia of the heart. So it becomes clear: such adumbrations, as they flow freely from Russell's conception of philosophy, bear witness to the late arrival of Socrates.

Indeed, it could be that only now we really understand the meaning of his confession [*Geständnis*] of knowing that he knows nothing. Perhaps only now we see that we are confronted in that confession [*Bekenntnis*] not with some characteristic peculiarity of *Socrates*, but with the situation we are all in.

So once again: those who philosophize live differently. But how? And what changes? Philosophy is the urge to want to know what there is to know, to see, to understand, to take note and to grasp it—and not thereby be deceived, neither by others, nor by the ensemble of the real (which presents itself as if it could not be otherwise), nor—most gratifyingly—by ourselves, by our desires, interests and emotional dictates.

Insofar as this interest prevails in philosophy, it liberates us—at least partially—from the interplay of forces that bring about delusion, the foremost being the reign by our egotisms, our all-too-human, all-about-me, one-sided subjective wanting. Those who even once have experienced for themselves the liberating effect of philosophy will also know the emotional stew of disgust and pity that now boils over whenever others are seen to be groping about like obsessives for so-called 'arguments' with which to engage in swordplay over their opinions.

So: philosophy transforms life by first by disuniting us with our own head.[28] And the most beautiful astonishment starts when someone has been led to throw into question [*wundern*] what he or she just so happens to think and mean and judge and feel. How does that even come about, since 'my thought'—of all things—is precisely what I take to be right? In sum, the value of philosophy—its effect on our lives—can be captured in a single word: that word is *freedom*. Once more Russell on this:

> The free intellect will see as God might see, without a *here* and *now*, without hopes and fears, without the trammels of customary beliefs and traditional prejudices, calmly, dispassionately, in the sole and exclusive desire of knowledge—knowledge as impersonal, as purely contemplative, as it is possible for man to attain. . . . The mind which has become accustomed to the freedom and impartiality of philosophical contemplation will preserve something of the same freedom and impartiality in the world of action and emotion. It will view its purposes and desires as parts of the whole, with the absence of insistence that results from seeing them as infinitesimal fragments in a world of which all the rest is unaffected by any one man's deeds.[29]

This same freedom that Russell here (in line with fine tradition) conflates with contemplation, "the unalloyed desire for truth,"[30] amounts to the hard-won capacity [*Begabung*] to affirm the world, to bestow from one depths a Yes upon it. This freedom expresses itself, so Russell tells us,

> in action, [as] justice, and in emotion [as] that universal love which can be given to all, and not only to those who are judged useful or admirable. Thus contemplation enlarges not only the objects of our thoughts, but also the objects of our actions and our affections: it makes us citizens of the universe, not only of one walled city at war with all the rest.[31]

This is what Russell promises us in what is perhaps his strongest claim regarding the efficacy and value of philosophy: "liberation from the thraldom of narrow hopes and fears."[32]

At most, the succinct résumé with which he follows this up surpasses the sharpness of this dictum. Philosophy, he assures us, diminishes our "dogmatic assurance" in thinking, while enriching our "intellectual imagination." That's a magnificent pair of words: "intellectual imagination." They name the philosophical aptitude most required for philosophy to prove itself as Philosophical Praxis.

Only a philosophy unafraid to call its own gift[33] "intellectual imagination" has, among other things, the capacity to perceive what is reasonable in the individual and in the concrete as the propelling moment in everything, and the well-honed consciousness that scouts out ways for what is reasonable and right, so that goodwill—still the name for active reason, despite the current scorn!—so that goodwill does not stop halfway and become resigned and sad or cynical—only the philosophy which brings itself to such a self-understanding is called upon and duly endowed to find its realization in Philosophical Praxis.

NOTES

1. Paul Ricœur, "Philosophie après Kierkegaard," *Revue de Théologie et de Philosophie*, 13 (1963): 303–316. Achenbach quotes "Philosophieren nach Kierkegaard" from *Materialien zur Philosophie Søren Kierkegaards*, Michael Theunissen und Wilfried Greve, eds. (Frankfurt am Main: Suhrkamp, 1979), 584.

2. The notion here of 'specific responsibility' or *Zuständigkeit* is derived from Niklas Luhmann. See his *Gesellschaft der Gesellschaft*, which appeared in English as Niklas Luhmann, *Theory of Society*, 2 vols. Translated by Rhodes Barrett (Stanford, CA: Stanford University Press, 2012/2013).

3. Eugène Ionesco, *Fragments of a Journal*. Trans. by Jean Stewart (New York: Paragon House, 1990), 94. Achenbach cites a German translation (*Tagebuch*, 2nd ed. Neuwied and Berlin, 1969, 153). The French original appeared in 1967.

4. Max Horkheimer, *Gesammelte Schriften*, Band 6: "Zur Kritik der instrumentellen Vernunft" und "Notizen 1949–1969" (Frankfurt am M: Fischer, 1991), 202. Picard translation.

5. Novalis, General Draft, #45, Ch. 8 in *Philosophical Writings*. Trans. and ed. by Margaret Mahony Stoljar (State University of New York Press, 1997), 135. Achenbach cites Novalis, *Tagebücher und Briefe*, vol. II. Edited by H.-J. Mähl and R. Samuel (Darmstadt: Wissenschaftliche Buchgesellschaft, 1978), 675.

6. Karl R. Popper, *Conjectures and Refutations: The Growth of Scientific Knowledge* (London: Routledge, 1963), 72.

7. Popper, *Conjectures and Refutations*, 72. Achenbach cites Popper via Klaus Grossner, *Verfall der Philosophie. Politik der deutschen Philosophen* (Hamburg: Reinbek, 1971), 279. I have not seen the latter, but the list of examples of non-philosophical areas Achenbach quotes is longer than the list in the English original, which refers to problems arising originally "in mathematics, for example, or in cosmology, or in politics, or in religion, or in social life." I retain the list as it appears in Achenbach's text, which make perfect sense in the context of the point Popper is making.

8. Ludwig Feuerbach, *Sämtliche Werke*, II (Leipzig: Otto Wigand, 1846), 257. Picard translation. Allusion is also made to Feuerbach's *Grundsätze der Philosophie der Zukunft*, in *Gesammelte Werke*, IX (Stuttgart: De Gruyter Akademie, 1990), 264–341, and translated by M. Vogel as *Principles of the Philosophy of the Future*, with an intro by T. E. Wartenberg (Indianapolis, IN: Hackett, 1986).

9. "Der Schuster möge bei seinem Leisten bleiben." This matches the proverbial advice in English to 'stick to your lasts,' a reference to the cobbler's lasts: molds (often made of wood) around which shoes are built. "Stick to your knitting!," as my mother would say.

10. Søren Kierkegaard. *Either-Or*, I. Trans. by Howard and Edna Hong (Princeton, NJ: Princeton University Press, 1987), 415 (marginal pagination: 383).

11. Kierkegaard, *Either-Or*, I, 383 (marginal pagination).

12. Kierkegaard, *Either-Or*, I, 383 (marginal pagination).

13. Kierkegaard, *Either-Or*, I, 383 (marginal pagination).

14. Kierkegaard, *Either-Or*, I, 383 (marginal pagination).

15. Rüdiger Bubner, "Was kann, soll und darf die Philosophie?" *Neue Rundschau* 1976, 228. Picard translation. This is a serious but funny point, though not funny in my translation.

16. The German reads "Formen und Gestalten des gelebten Lebens." I use 'modes' for the "forms of life as lived," and 'molds' for "Gestalten des gelebten Lebens." *Gestalten* is taken here in the sense of *Vorbild*, a model (e.g., role model) or paragon of a "good" life.

17. Rüdiger Bubner, "Was kann, soll und darf die Philosophie?" *Neue Rundschau* 1976, 229. Picard translation.

18. Self-declarative look and feel—*selbstankündigende Erscheinungsbild*. And, for later in this sentence: foster respect—*zur Anerkennung gelangen*.

19. Achenbach's note: To prevent possible misunderstanding: I am by no means of the opinion that such fundamental and big questions are not philosophy's business; I am only concerned to reject the assertion that philosophy has solely to deal with such stock questions.

20. Bertrand Russell, *The Problems of Philosophy* (OUP, 1912), 1. I have added the emphasis on "merely," since that is Achenbach's target here.

21. See Max Horkheimer and Theodor W. Adorno, *Dialectic of Enlightenment*. Trans. by John Cumming (New York: Continuum/Seabury, 1972), 41: "Guilt is a social delusion."

22. Urge thinking onward—*weiterdenken*. And, in the next sentence, 'conscience' stands in for *Besinnung*. The word 'thoughtfulness' might have done just as well.

23. G. W. F. Hegel, *The Phenomenology of Spirit*. Trans. by Peter Fuss and John Dobbins (Notre Dame, IN: University of Notre Dame Press, 2019).

24. Novalis, *Tagebücher und Briefe*, II. Ed. by Mühl and Samuel (Darmstadt: Wissenschaftliche Buchgesellschaft, 1978), 333.

25. Russell, *Problems*, 89. Russell concludes: "utility does not belong to philosophy," though as we shall see he later speaks of "its utility in showing unsuspecting possibilities" (91).

26. Russell, *Problems*, 91.

27. Russell, *Problems*, 91.

28. Disuniting us with our own head—*mit unserem eigenen Kopf entzweit*. Allusion to *Selbstentzweing* (self-estrangement or self-alienation), a central concept in German philosophy since Idealism.

29. Russell, *Problems*, 93.

30. Russell, *Problems*, 93. Not quoted in Achenbach.

31. Russell, *Problems*, 93.

32. Russell, *Problems*, 93.

33. *Begabung*—here rendered as 'gift'—was translated a few paragraphs back as 'capacity'; it is cognate with *begabt*, which occurs in the final line and is here given as 'duly endowed.'

Chapter 6

On Beginnings

> What the philosophers say about Reality is often as disappointing as on a sign you see in a shop window: Pressing Done Here. If you brought your clothes to be pressed, you would be fooled; for the sign is only for sale.
>
> —Søren Kierkegaard[1]

> Nothing must be so applicable to reality, or so justified, as that which comes from philosophy, nor anything so individual, alive and permanent.
>
> —G. W. F. Hegel[2]

In Philosophical Praxis, it is not philosophy that makes the beginning. In Philosophical Praxis, the guest makes the beginning. To illustrate the relation with an image from the game of chess, I might say: the visitor chooses the white pieces. That is, the one who comes to us begins.

But if we were to think of this as a rule, the first and opening thing would be precisely *not* the visitor, but at the beginning there would be the *rule*, this direction, or—to put it formally—the *setting*. Isn't that a contradiction? Obviously. But it can be remedied.

I modify the introductory sentence and say: I, the philosophical practitioner, must make the beginning so that the visitor can begin. Or: I start by making the beginning easier for him by making the beginning possible for him. I do not open the conversation, but I open the space that must be opened for the guest, so that he or she, in turn, can begin the conversation.

But how's this now? Isn't this again—or still—a contradiction? Isn't the situation exactly the same as it was before, since that implied that the rule according to which the guest begins just puts the rule at the beginning and not the guest? Nevertheless this contradiction can also be remedied.

It is up to us to open the *conversation-enabling* conversation. To take an image, it is up to us to open the door so the guest can go through it, and we follow. We have to begin the conversation that is *not yet* the conversation, at least not yet the 'actual' or definitive conversation, not yet the conversation that qualifies as Philosophical Praxis. And yet, this is not entirely correct either. For what I would like to show through these reflections on the beginning is this: that the beginning or opening prelude to Philosophical Praxis also belongs to Philosophical Praxis itself. A pretty paradox? One I hope will be allowed me.

So back to this: I said that the philosophical practitioner has the task of beginning the conversation, which in the 'actual' and strict sense is not yet 'the conversation,' but which has the task of making the conversation and its beginning possible in the first place. What kind of pre-conversation is this?

Appropriately, this conversation before the conversation is determined by courtesy, by conventions of hospitality and stock phrases.

> 'You managed to find the place?'
>
> 'Your trip here was pleasant enough, I hope?'
>
> 'Tea? Coffee?'

One should not think that such expressions say nothing, or that they are nothing but say-nothing expressions. On the one hand, it may well be true that they say nothing; but they *ought to say* nothing, since they are not yet the conversation. What says much [*vielsagend*] should come first from the guest.

On the other hand, however, I would add that the ethos of philosophy overall—and, in Philosophical Praxis, the leading ethos—lies in careful attentiveness, in hearkening [*Aufmerksamkeit*]. It is by no means easy actually to say something in such a seemingly 'nothing-saying way,' nor to hear what is said in that way. One needs the ears to hear it. To demonstrate this, it suffices to vary slightly the mentioned 'meaningless' opening phrases:

> 'My first cup of coffee today . . . '

This makes clear that there is no routine running. Or make the phrase an explicit welcome:

> 'I waited with the coffee until you got here. Now I look forward to . . . '

Or take another variation, of which there are, of course, countless:

> 'These coffee machines are a real temptation. But then, what doesn't tempt us?'

Here already an appropriate (perhaps also inappropriate) common ground is anticipated, and this move can, of course, be built upon and lead to modest reflections that, in the first instance, may seem unrelated, but at least herald the atmosphere of thought:

> 'These machines are a temptation. But then what doesn't tempt us? Maybe it's just a matter of knowing when to resist and when to be joyfully tempted.'

Such small incidental remarks have their rightful place only under the condition that—to choose again a chess metaphor—they take place 'on the board,' i.e., they are not pre-prepared moves.

In this spirit, a few ambiguities may be worked in, which, if set in a chatty tone, may worked into the later conversation naturally and without force. That this occurs so often with explicit ambiguities is perhaps no wonder, for they work like 'insights in a state of limbo,' which everyone then in their own way reduces to their own level. An example:

> 'Let us give in to temptation as long as we still can. One becomes reasonable soon enough.'

Such a formulation can open up many things. On the one hand, I may be welcoming a guest who has his own problems with aging. But also, in the most inconspicuous way, such a remark calls into question a prejudice that some people bring to the consultation, namely that philosophy, in an exceptionless and uncompromising way, is about the 'reasonable.' (Interposed question: How 'reasonable' is the 'nothing-but-reasonable'?) During the preparation of coffee, a similar yet different role can fall to a small story or anecdote. Example:

> 'A historian of antiquity and connoisseur of the Orient once told me that the ancient Bedouins had a compulsory tradition that the one with whom one eats or drinks together as a guest enjoys all the privileges of a friend. But that only applied as long as you sat together. After that . . . Well, let us be glad that we are Central Europeans and not desert people.'

A vacuous yarn like this can prove astute if, for example, a conflict-laden consultation is in the offing, as will usually be evident at once. For then, in the most elegant way in the world, one would have already communicated a precaution: Be on your guard! You may enjoy hospitality here, but don't settle your accounts without the host.

It would have its own legitimate attractions to illustrate the eloquence of such supposedly say-nothing introductory phrases with further variations, and by reflecting on their consequences. But I leave all that aside now, since otherwise certain considerations that I should like to present would be neglected.

So let's go one step further, relocating now from the coffee machine to the conversation corner, where the real conversation is supposed actually to begin.

We have to begin, I had said, so that the guest can begin. To meet this challenge, it might seem natural to open with a question, laboring under the assumption that it is not yet the question that starts the conversation, but only the answer. But that underlying assumption is not only dubious, it is quite possibly fundamentally wrong.

I demonstrate this in an ordinary case. Imagine one starts with the inquiry as we know some doctors do:

> 'What brings you to me?'

Viktor von Weizsäcker has suggested opening with the question of what the patient was 'missing,' which at least points in a different direction than asking what he 'has.' Or imagine, as an alternative, the opening question:

> 'What is your problem?'

The crudity of the inquiry is buried in the formality of politeness, as is usual. With these opening questions much would be prejudged at the outset, and the guest of the philosophical practitioner would possibly have been lured along a wrong path. Are we as advisers urgently interested in the 'problems' of the guest? Not more importantly in him or her?

In any case, the visitor's answer to such an inquiry would quite probably be:

> 'Yes, if only I knew . . . '

Even so: such an opening would be a precarious start. For now the very fact that the visitor *does not know* what her problem is would be set up as her 'problem.' But is it really?

All right. Perhaps we avoid such insidious questions, and open instead with the more innocuous simple remark:

> 'Now we have time!'

In principle the guest is now free for *his* part to use the time to open. Then however it is not unlikely that we first hear:

> 'Yes, how do I begin . . . ?'

We may surmise that there really are difficulties here for the guest to open up the conversation appropriately. Now consider how two further interventions might play out. The first runs:

> 'Nothing dumber than the assertion that all beginnings are easy. Or simple.'

The second says just about the same thing:

> 'Indeed, all beginnings are difficult.'

Examined logically and semantically, the two expressions show no important distinction in meaning. If we take a closer look, however, we notice first that the negating sentence ('Nothing dumber than . . . ') expresses solidarity with the visitor—and with good reason, incidentally, since further reflections on the beginning are bound to make clear to what extent all beginning is difficult. But what's more, this first twist affords the guest a fine opportunity to reply, since quite probably he or she prefers the more common proverbial phrase, 'All beginnings are difficult.' So now the visitor says (and this has happened):

> 'Don't they say, all beginnings are difficult?'

And already the beginning would have been made, a lifeline laid out, to which we as philosophical practitioner must only connect.

But let us take a different, frequently recurring variant of the opening. The visitor begins, for example:

> 'I don't really know where I should start.'

Or, with significant difference:

> 'I don't really know how I should start.'

With this opening, our guest would have given us an excellent template that can be made use of in a variety of ways. And depending on how we react to it, we can inconspicuously steer the further conversation along certain tracks, which demands prudence and sensitivity. Let me take an example:

> 'Oh, you know, that is not a problem. Because basically it's always like that. Beginnings always come afterwards.'

This sounds unusual, possibly contradictory, at least interesting, and to some it may even appear paradoxical, which might be welcome since that typically arouses curiosity and invites questions. The guest, for example, reacts:

> 'What do you mean by that?'

(I assume the guest is grateful that the entire burden of the beginning was not immediately passed over to him . . .)

> "Well, you see, we start to relate, but what we relate is already late—it occurred to us long since. Or: we want to recount, but we have not yet understood what counts in what has come to pass. Or: we begin to think. But what about? About what has long been our unthought case. Or: we are in the middle of a story before we ask ourselves, 'What kind of story will we find ourselves in?' and so on."

We might add here a little of what we've garnered from Sloterdijk's lovely reflections on beginnings, such as:

> 'It's like that with our whole lives: When we first emerge, our beginnings are far back. Nobody is able to begin at the real beginning. We always just set in, or set forth what has already started with us or has been started with us.'[3]

These are very general reflections, and can of course be varied in many ways. With a bit of luck, or a lucky hand, such *general* reflections may be brought to bear on what already weighs on the heart of the visitor *in particular*. Indeed, that would be the very function of *general reflections* in this context. It is not unlikely therefore that the guest will reply something like:

> 'That's saying something. . . .'

Indeed I say: just like that, we already are in the middle of a conversation. And we can count on it, now our visitor will begin to relate.

I present another variant that is by no means uncommon. The visitor, after drinking a sip of coffee, begins:

> 'I have a problem.'

Here the presentation is completely different. And not a little tricky. Because here too, we could with various reactions already make an extraordinary number of preliminary decisions. I would like to illustrate this with an example. Once a guest actually began in exactly this way. I replied:

> 'Lucky you!'
>
> 'How?'
>
> 'You are lucky! I do not have one. I have many problems.'

Undoubtedly dangerous! A walk on a high ridge! But if you can pull it off—if without scorn or envy you are able to intervene in this small way, and to actually mean it in all earnestness—then it is *possible* to loosen and relax the tension. Disarming people by surprise, we may pave the way for a sort of 'problem depotentiation.' Soon probably some qualification will be necessary, and with that the actual conversation may be opened.

> 'Of course this is only half true. It is just as true that those who have many problems actually have none. It's like with many gods and the one God. Under the swarm of the many gods, one lives comparatively commodiously, under the regiment of the One, things get serious.'

With this, the conversation moves to safer ground and—after only a small detour—back to the guest's opening sentence, and he may move on.

There are naturally many ways that this sort of opening, working by means of surprise, can be intensified or in effect weakened. Let me go into this a bit further in order to convey a feeling for the richness of variations already within sight of the first 'moves.'

> He: 'I have a problem.'
>
> I, smiling ambiguously: 'I don't believe that.'

If asked, one can prove very correctly that you never have *only one* problem, but usually as a rule you have the additional problem of not knowing how to deal with the one. That already makes two problems out of one. Or: one problem has arisen, and because of it now you have another problem with yourself for having a problem. Which again makes two problems out of one. Or: you have problems with others because (allegedly) you have this one problem, etc. All this readily explains itself and, in this way, guests come to know they have time and space that would not be necessary at all, if it were only a matter of presenting 'the one problem.'

In this context a general consideration may be added. Much has already been achieved if visitors get the impression that the difficulties that led them to the consultation do not have to be related in condensed manner, as we are used to during lawyer and doctor visits. The root resource of Philosophical Praxis is the time at the disposal of the guest.

The variations I have so far described have this in common: they all contain a surprise or something somehow unexpected. It can be a benefit to signal in this way to visitors that in Philosophical Praxis a conversation awaits like nothing in which they are likely to engage with their friends, and even more rarely with intimate partners. Consider a further variation:

> He: 'I have a problem.'
>
> I: 'OK, good. You tell me about it, and I will return the favor by renouncing all explanation.'

Here with casual move, I throw in a bit of the theory behind Philosophical Praxis.

But—to wrap all this up with a question: What exactly am I doing here? I am drawing attention to incidental matters that have their own, not insignificant role to play. This could obviously be continued *ad ultimo*, as I must repeat. But I refrain from doing so in order to take the opportunity to point to a further, equally fascinating subject, which belongs to thinking about the beginning. Specifically, I would like to distinguish, not different types of persons exactly, but various types of openings that guests characteristically make.

Trigger Happy. The first type of opening comes from one I would like to name *Trigger Happy*, understood as one who thinks that, for safety's sake, he must preemptively self-defend. First he lurks a little, demonstratively hesitates, next perhaps explains that he has already been here and there and tried this and that, which of course have all brought him 'exactly nothing.' Then he adds to this introductory report his declaration of war:

> He: 'It's rather curious, isn't it? What you're offering here? I mean, "Philosophical Praxis"—doesn't it sound a bit extravagant?'

Should one of that clientèle (known in therapy circles as the 'therapist eater') find their way to your praxis, it might be advisable to take immediate, decisive—though *friendly*—counter-measures. I remember how once I responded to such an opening:

> I: 'You've come at the wrong time of day.'
>
> He: '?'
>
> I: 'The duel takes place at dawn.'

I don't want, by citing this instance, to rule out the possibility of a more conciliatory response to such petty entry-way impudences. Like this:

I: 'Curious? You are quite right. But consider this: only a curious institution can deal with curious guests.'

It should be noted that the Trigger Happy visitors portrayed here do not reveal themselves only when they first speak. On the contrary, we can and should expect belligerent interventions long after we first meet them.

Another Quick Shot. I don't know what to call this next guest, who certainly belongs to the larger group of Trigger Happy visitors. He is one who first must assure himself that he is meeting you eye-to-eye, must test the hardiness of the philosopher he is visiting, and discover whether you are able to withstand anything he might throw at you. So with even greater vigor, our imaginary guest expresses his aggression (be it from whatever source) and begins something like this:

'Can you handle the Truth?'

Now this might be place to reflect a moment on so-called 'quick-wittedness,' which some people are thought to 'possess' and others to lack. That thought, by the way, is probably wrong. It can indeed be acquired, at least to some extent. At least one can put oneself in a frame of mind that allows ideas to 'come.'

In the right spirit, with real presence of mind, a brilliant parry might look like this:

'You want to know whether I can handle the Truth? What a question! Much more difficult and interesting is whether the Truth can handle me!'

Perhaps so stark a response is not for everyone. Still, let's go on. The guest says in a pronounced, matter-of-fact tone:

He: 'To be honest, I don't pin much hope on my visit to you.'

I: 'Hmmm. Nor do I.'

Then you can explain that. Here too, of course, a more moderate, relaxed variation would be possible:

'It is always darkest before the dawn.'

Or, put another way:

'If you say so. But my principle is never to curse the evening before the dawn.'

The Examiner. Let's take another type of visitor as an example: call him the *Examiner*. He has already spent several hours visiting you. The one day, finally, he starts out with the following remark:

> He: 'You hardly asked me anything . . .'
>
> I: 'You would prefer to sit there and answer for yourself?'

It is foundational to Philosophical Praxis to keep your distance from any loaded questions. This must now somehow be made clear.

The Questioner. Another common opener is a question like: 'What is Philosophical Praxis?' etc., etc. While it is possible to respond by introducing some tentative definitions, they ought to be presented in such a way that they can be broken off at any time. For in all likelihood, the guest has not come to be educated about our profession.

The Referred Guest. Those who do not come immediately on their own initiative, but are sent to us by others, present a special challenge for opening. Typically the guest is a youth, but sometimes it is the spouse. In these cases, I take care to begin *myself*, perhaps somewhat as follows:

> I: 'Suppose I first tell you what I already know about you. Or rather: what I have heard about you, that is, of you. Because what one has heard about, or of, someone, has obviously not yet been heard from them.'

Here one nicely highlights the possible or even the likely distinction between the one who was sent to us and the one who did the sending.

The Friendly Fan. Another opening comes from a guest I would like to call the *Friendly Fan*. I sketch a typical case:

> 'I saw you on a TV show the other day.'

Here it is best to let the visitor know right away that they don't have to choose their words as a service to the consultant.

> I: 'And despite that you came!?'

In this way, by irritating the other person's assessment of me (which was probably based too much on that broadcast), I also give myself room to maneuver.

The Couple. Another special challenge with opening: *he and she* have come together.

> She: 'Do you want to start?'
>
> He: 'You go ahead.'

After a while, I do:

> I: 'White moves and wins.'

Or:

> I: 'Scenes of a marriage. Only one of them is the problem.'

She goes into it—then:

> I: 'My good woman, you misunderstand me. The one who thinks the other is the problem is the problem, you understand? But the really potent problem is the one who has succeeded in making the one who is allegedly the problem begin to believe it. But to clear up such stimulating things, that's what you're here for.'

Easily Intimidated. This second-to-last type of opening allows me to draw attention to the *basic problem*, regardless of type, which can be formulated roughly as follows: above all it is essential to enable the other person *to continue on* from the *conversation opener.* Take this example:

> Guest: (pointing to the walls of books lining the office): 'Have you read them all?'
>
> I: 'Already read. For the most part anyway.'

Much is inevitably left out of any such statement. Should the guest inquire, I can go on to clarify:

> I: 'Thank God I forgot most of it again. Some people think that the secret of the brain is how it stores. But probably its real secret is how this organ manages to forget, above all else, that which can be forgotten with a clear conscience. And that is not a little.'

Let this be my cue for an interjection—not unimportant, to my mind: what is really worthwhile about chess-playing computer programs is their reduced level of play. This is also an ideal for leading philosophical conversations.

But let me return once more to my selective list of *types* of guest openings. A broad generalization is perhaps also in order, which I preface with a longish quotation from Adorno:

> I must explain to you a little more closely the idea that philosophy does not have its object, but seeks it. First, it brings the Subject into play quite differently than is the case in the individual objectified and objectifying sciences. This is connected with the *moment of expression*: philosophy wants to express the nonconceptual in a concept. If Wittgenstein's famous sentence states that one should only say what one can clearly say, and keep silent about the rest, then I would directly oppose that conception of philosophy and claim instead that philosophy is the permanent and ever-frustrated effort to say what cannot actually be said. . . . In Tasso one reads that, when man falls silent in his agony, he has a God-given power to say what he is suffering.
>
> Precisely this is what inspires philosophy, which, one might almost say, would translate pain into the medium of the concept. Philosophy, then, is not a mirror turned out to the external world depicting whatever reality is there, but rather an attempt to make [subjective] experience an object [of thought], and to realize this will-to-articulate.
>
> Thinking in this *expressive* sense (that is, where it is not already structured according to the requirements of whatever discipline or purpose) certainly always has something to gain from philosophy [of this sort].
>
> And the most grave matters, where truth is really at stake, are always the most fragile. The truth is not something firm that one can hold in one's hand and carry confidently home. . . . It is always and without exception something extraordinarily fragile, and so is the concept of philosophy.[4]

We do well to point out that Adorno misconstrues Tasso here.[5] The whole point is that Tasso knows to say, not just 'that' or 'what' he suffers, but 'how' he suffers. It is precisely *as poet* that he is able to say what "man" is *not* given to say. But after this correction one can now say: the aim of Philosophical Praxis to help guests to become "poets," at least as far as is necessary to express *how* they are suffering.

This, however, *is* the problem most visitors to Philosophical Praxis have—*they are no poets*. Let the ambition of Philosophical Praxis be proclaimed: a new maieutic is needed. We have to provide obstetric services. Everything depends upon giving guests the opportunity to say *how* they suffer.

Speechless. *This* being the difficulty, we see clearly the reason why so many guests falter at first, if not despair, and why it is that they doubt whether what they feel driven to say can be said at all. Many visitors cry.

> I: 'Indeed, sometimes words fail us.'

A variant of doubt-laden beginning of despondent visitors occurs when they downplay their problems from the start:

> 'It is silly, but. . . .'

In this regard, the high purpose of Philosophical Praxis is to be a refuge for the feelings, which are *not* to be forced into speech, interpreted, and worked over with words (as is common in therapies). Instead of talking *about* feelings, sensations, moods, they are directly given a say, a say in their *own* diction, which needs to be understood in its 'speechlessness.'

In view of everything presented, it has hopefully become clear that to indicate rules according to which one should proceed to begin a session of Philosophical Praxis is strictly impossible. And if rules were possible, if they didn't simply spoil everything from the outset, they would be an outright hindrance.

So how then can we learn?

Study the beginnings of novels! Study *many* beginnings of novels. Often there is much to be learned about the problem of beginning, of opening space for narrative. A superb case in point: the beginning of Thomas Mann's most outstanding novel, *Joseph and his Brothers*: "Deep is the well of the past. Should we not call it bottomless?"[6]

Here a large space for thorough narration is created. As it happens, this lead-in reads like an allusion to Thomas Mann's favorite philosopher, Arthur Schopenhauer, who opened the second volume of his *Parerga und Paralipomena* with the following image:

> The very ground upon which all our knowledge and science rest is the inexplicable. Therefore every explanation leads back to this, by means of middle terms more or less, as on the sea the sounding lead now finds the bottom in greater, now in lesser depths, yet ultimates must reach it everywhere.[7]

Undoubtedly a great beginning! The mysterious, the unfathomable—*that* is the ground of all narration. And we have a few more words for whoever still needs it: *productive imagination*. Plus: *presence of mind.*[8] Ideally, the opening of *every consultation should be as unique and in-exchangeable as the opening of a novel.*

The dictum of Novalis points our direction: philosophers in Philosophical Praxis have to "romanticize" [*romantisieren*]. We help to develop a germ of a story into an infinite novel [*Roman*].

CONCLUDING REMARKS

The beginning is not made by understanding a problem. Rather, what is shown at the beginning is whether we have understood the problem of the beginning, whether from the beginning we understand ourselves. (This we call knowing our way around. [*Umgangswissen*].)

Nor is the beginning to be made from the problem the other person supposedly has. We begin with our guest, and only then, second in line, with his or her problems.

NOTES

1. Søren Kierkegaard, *Either/Or*. Vol. 1, Translated by David F. Swenson and Lillian Marvin Swenson (Princeton, NJ: Princeton University Press), 31. Used with permission.

2. G. W. F. Hegel, "Über die wissenschaftliche Behandlungsart des Naturrechts, seine Stelle in der praktischen Philosophie und sein Verhältnis zu den positiven Rechtswissenschaften" IV, Absatz 3, *Werkausgabe*, II (Frankfurt a.M.: Suhrkamp, 1986), 510. Picard translation. The sentence also occurs in translation in Hegel, *Natural Law*, trans. by T. M. Knox (Philadelphia: University of Pennsylvania Press, 1975), 117.

3. Peter Sloterdijk, *Zur Welt kommen—Zur Sprache kommen* (Frankfurt a.M.: Suhrkamp, 1988); in particular the second lecture, "Poetik des Anfangens."

4. Theodor W. Adorno, *Philosophische Terminologie*, I (Frankfurt a.M.: Suhrkamp, 1973), 82–83. Picard translation.

5. The reference is Goethe's play *Torquato Tasso*, in particular to Tasso's last words, rendered on page 150 of the J. Cartwright translation (London: D. Nutt, 1861) as follows:

> Nature vouchsafes to us the gift of tears,—
> The cry of agony, when man, at last,
> Can bear no more.—And I, besides all this,
> Have, in my woe, the gift of speech and song,
> To find fit accents for each deepest pang.
> And whilst some men endure silently
> I am permitted to make known how I hurt.

However, Cartwright's translation, like Adorno, misses the point Achenbach wishes to stress, so I have replaced the last two words ("my loss") with "how I hurt," which indeed reflects the original German, reproduced here:

> Die Trän hat uns die Natur verliehen,
> Den Schrei des Schmerzes, wenn der Mann zuletzt

Es nicht mehr trägt—Und mir noch über alles—
Sie ließ im Schmerz mir Melodie und Rede,
Die tiefste Fülle meiner Not zu klagen:
Und wenn der Mensch in seiner Qual verstummt,
Gab mir ein Gott, zu sagen wie ich leide.

6. Thomas Mann, *Joseph and his Brothers*. Trans. by John E. Woods (New York: Knopf Doubleday, 2005), 3.

7. Arthur Schopenhauer, *Parerga and Paralipomena: Short Philosophical Essays*, II. Trans. by Adrian Del Caro and Christopher Janaway (CUP: 2015), 3. (Marginal pagination.)

8. Presence of mind—*Geistesgegenwart.*

Chapter 7

Philosophy as a Profession

> Common parlance has always designated as philosophers those who on every occasion choose the best and most tonic discourse: it aims at the center.
>
> —Alain[1]

> Just as bees extract honey from thyme, the most pungent and the driest of plants, sensible people often in like manner draw from the most unfavourable circumstances something which suits them and is useful.
>
> —Plutarch[2]

Philosophical Praxis is not only no 'new therapy': it is most decidedly no therapy at all.[3] This much has already been established. So what is it instead?

Answer: Philosophy is to become praxis, communicative action, a dialogical reconnaissance and problem-framing, which amounts—in a phrase—to a *critique of the distorted communication* at work in any therapeutic 'treatment.' The question as to what underlies this conception of Philosophical Praxis I will here try to answer, initially only in outline.

I would like to open with a simple fact: human being is a complicated being. Unable merely to live or simply to be there, we must—whether we like it or not—take a stand on our own life. So we make thoughts about it to ourselves. But that's not all. We are also able to think back over our thoughts, and, in some situations, we do well to make use of this possibility. That we are given overall to reflect upon our own thoughts makes each of us *constitutionally* a philosophizing being.

In other words, we don't just *have* thoughts (the way we have hands to work with); we must also struggle and grapple with them. What I have in mind is the category (introduced into anthropology by Helmuth Plessner) of the "eccentricity" of human being, the fact that man is able "to distance himself from himself, to open a rift between himself and his experiences."[4]

This rift we rarely open without reason, since these 'second thoughts,' as I would like to call them, are sharply uncomfortable. Just how much discomfort these second thoughts can cause becomes painfully clear in those situations—and there are enough of them—when automated thought-processes divide us in two. Such occasions and reasons may include, for example, the experience: of going round in circles of your own thoughts and views; of moving in place, as it were; of our familiar and accustomed ways of thinking no longer making headway; of being stuck in problems you can neither solve nor rid yourself of.

Today it is more often the case, however, that the self-evident, habitual way of thinking is experienced not so much as pain, but by and large as inanimate and schematic, for the most part boring. One feels, given such thought-habits, that new, genuine experiences are no longer possible, which makes life implacable, routinized and, in some terrible way, finished, shut down, finally impassive. We are tried and tested, but lack the knack to enrich our lives.

The overpowering groundswell of feeling that happens to people in these circumstances is apathy, loss of interest, the inner sense of being burnt out, the desire to live having somehow died away, and the drive to start anything new fizzled out.

I would like now to dare a hypothesis that might explain this condition. Sublime and elevated needs, suspended and unresolved due to long-enduring frustration, have sunk to ever deeper and more inaccessible levels of sensitivity and quasi-pathological feeling, ultimately down to the body itself, where they exert further, obscure and diffuse effects as ambitions unknown even to ourselves. In the end, these sunken needs drain all color from life, which runs gray. Inevitably, one begins to suffer. But: from what? Not from pain actually (or not necessarily). The feeling isn't so much painful as dull, depressed, as if somehow we've been deceived or robbed of something. Worse: our condition seems permanent, and there is no way out. A bitter mindset settles in: we are bored by the known, while what stimulates our interest, sympathy and liveliness is unknown.

We ought to call this what it is, namely a deficit in education [*Bildung*], though I hesitate to do so because that term [*Bildung*] has over time become unspeakably perverted. Yet this deficit is what precipitates the disenchantment with life just described.

This lack of education, however, might just as well be defined as a reduced capacity to love:

> Education is precisely that for which there are no real customs; it can only be acquired through spontaneous effort and interest, not guaranteed by courses

> alone, still less by the typical curriculum. Yes, in truth it does not even fall to effort but to open-mindedness, to the ability to let something spiritual come to mind in the first place, and to take it productively into one's own consciousness instead of, as an unbearable cliché reads, merely learning to struggle with it [*sich auseinandersetzen*]. If I were not afraid of the misunderstanding of sentimentality, I would say that education requires love; its deficiency is in the capacity to love.[5]

If the impression I have just given is correct, what is lacking is not a fixed set of beliefs to adhere to, a 'philosophy' to ascribe to, or a place to stand. What is lacking is the *spirit* expressed in this Adorno quote—this deficit in education and reduced capacity to love—which spirit we may also characterize as:

- the opening up of other and new perspectives and of previously blocked vistas;
- a liberation of life from the rut of a boring monotony impoverished of experience;
- the arousal of a long-exhausted curiosity;
- a readying of surprises; a being woken up, alerted, tensed;
- a movement of the rigid and the weary;
- a shaking of the established from its fixed position.

This is what education means. And it has a far greater chance of occurring in a philosophical conversation than it does in any form of instruction.[6]

In any case, my own experience to date *contradicts* the assumption—still current among academic philosophers—that the spiritual and metaphysical needs people have are for certainty and foundational truths, that we hunger anxiously for certain 'ultimate principles,' fixed in stone, which cannot be further challenged. (A sort of militaristic philosophy, where you make your points like bullets and are done.) On the contrary, I am convinced that what we lack instead is experience in thinking, of eye-opening flashes of insight that awaken our inner excitability, leaving us open and responsive to repressed possibilities, to unforeseen or unthought opportunities for existence and growth.

The task of Philosophical Praxis arises from this (presumed) lack. To put it as briefly as possible, I can say it with an aphorism of Novalis: "To philosophize is to de-phlegmatize—to vivify."[7] Elsewhere[8] I have proposed to translate this aphorism as follows: to philosophize means 'help to get a jump on things, to enliven.'

But this inevitably raises the question: to what extent are philosophers—of all people—the ones destined to accomplish all this?

The first answer should probably be that many philosophers, if not most, are quite certainly incapable of doing so. To have studied philosophy is certainly not enough, because study makes no one a philosopher.

As a second answer, however, one may surely maintain that the study of philosophy, more than an education in any individual science, has the advantage of fostering a free spirit, not narrow or fixated, but suddenly open, wide-awake, alive to its problems. This consciousness, rather than seeking to eliminate contradictions and conflicts, lets itself be moved by them, and is, in other words, a *concrete living thinking*. But this is exactly what Philosophical Praxis requires first and foremost.

To put it briefly in a sentence that, amplified philosophically, would spool out the entire philosophy of Philosophical Praxis: Philosophical Praxis is a free conversation.

But what does that mean? Or at least: What does that mean, if a comprehensive amplification of this claim cannot be achieved at the moment? It means that praxis does not bother with philosophical systems, constructs no philosophy, administers no philosophical insights, prescribes no philosopheme. It just sets thinking in motion: it *philosophizes*.

And now, in order not to bore readers with known stipulations as to what is to be regarded as philosophizing, I will provide several associations in free style, which perhaps also serve to give an initial impression of what actually happens in Philosophical Praxis.

Philosophizing, I would say in this free, associative style, is . . .

- an understanding that lays open but does not reveal
- a perception that looks within with no intention of seeing through
- making plain rather than explaining
- non-judgmental openness that names what is false, yet "neither approves nor censures"[9]
- skepticism towards conventional methods, even a desire for insight that evades theory
- unstressed concentration, calm concern, speaking without malice, convincing without ulterior motives
- a sensitivity to contradictions, not immediately to clear them out or reconcile them, but to check whether or not they can be made fruitful
- taking the trouble to relate opposites and to draw disordered voices into harmony
- the seduction of monologue to dialogue

The result is often the silencing of an old lyre, the putting to rest of a worn-out theme, and the spinning of a new, common thread that may become a motif beyond the lived moment, give direction to life, to accompany it always and inwardly pervade it, thus giving shape to the path of life.

Philosophical thinking . . .

- doesn't know, but sometimes keeps going
- checks in, not out
- argues discursively and not strategically (is anti-strategy par excellence)
- turns what is most simple into an adventure (hermeneutics of everyday life) and also the most difficult into a simple problem (as far as possible)
- entails amplifying (expanding, concretizing, making accurate) against the seduction to reduction
- is the risk-ridden management of contingency through the application of provisionally presupposed plausible, synthesizing insights

And philosophical thinking has these three enemies (among others): premature conviction, cold correctness, and soulless truth. Its reasonableness is that of the "thinking heart"[10] (Hegel). I translate: The utopia of Philosophical Praxis would be a reasoning soul or a feeling reason.

So much then for the conception of Philosophical Praxis—and not the *concept* of Philosophical Praxis, because it is not based on a concept.

What does this mean for the visitor? It means (ideally) that with each guest a thoroughly individual philosophical story begins (revealing what in a more esoteric context was known as a "way of thought" [*Denkweg*]), along with a process of *self-appropriation* through elaborating and organizing memory into a narratable biography. Only such a "mini-tradition"[11] of the individual can achieve the sort of surveyability that is the indispensable condition not only of justified approval but also of any ground-up questioning. No philosophical consultation [*Kur*] will be like any other, unless it be a very poor one.

> No, I answer, just such a [philosophy, as it is "doubly necessary in this altogether unclear time,"] could not be prescribed. For who can say: true philosophy is here, or it is there? Philosophy should never—and by its nature cannot—exert any influence except through free conviction; it must start all over again with each one, must prove itself anew to each, for no one can believe for someone else, or be convinced for another.[12]

Philosophical Praxis therefore does not fly out to find others to nest in with. It sets itself up in such a way that others can turn to it. It does not claim others, but lets others claim it. Briefly, in an image: Socrates opens a practice.

This has major consequences. No longer is *the philosopher* the gadfly, the insect that God set at the neck of the sleepy Athenians. Now the problems and suffering of those who come to a philosopher stick it to the *corpus philosophicum*, and we cannot rule out that it will be awakened from its long night of speculative dreams by this sting, or be pricked yet further until its gaze, accommodating to daylight, discovers its proper object—the prose of everyday presence, the actuality of the individual life-world.

Since Socrates we are accustomed to examine others—in philosophical counseling this relationship is reversed: it is not the philosopher who presses their questions upon others; rather, the questions of others press upon the philosopher. Whereas others once went through the purgatory of critical inquisition, which the philosopher thought justified in stoking, now philosophy is in the hot seat, and it will be seen on the contrary whether philosophical thought goes up in flames and consumes itself, or whether it proves itself and withstands the blaze.

This trial by fire is the test that philosophy risks by becoming praxis. Perhaps it is the most difficult and tricky acid test ever to embroil philosophers—and not just their thinking, but their very selves. For we can no longer keep to hand-me-down questions filtered through a long tradition (and therefore usually preconceived), but must face quite unforeseen problems that the person who seeks out practice does not know how to solve on their own.

While philosophers have hitherto been mere trustees for the difficulties that the discipline has placed before us, we must now accept responsibility for questions that seem to come from outside: we must engage the questions of the other.

The philosopher, who dares to take the step into practice, stands before such aspirations 'at the beginning.' But having always to begin anew ought to be familiar. It is the practical variant of the oldest theoretical pathos of all philosophy, from which nothing could be farther than routine. A quote from Walter Schulz may prove this and at the same time conclude my own considerations:

> Philosophy in the sense of a special profession: that can and may . . . mean nothing other than the readiness to transform the questions that come from life itself into forms of expression and in that way to radicalize them; that is, to return these questions to their roots and to think back over them from the roots. Schopenhauer once declared: 'The first two requirements for philosophizing are these: firstly, that one has the courage to hold a question in one's heart; and secondly, that everything that goes without saying is brought to clear consciousness in order to grasp it as a problem.' These two requirements—not to suppress any question and to render everything self-evident into a problem—are indispensable basic conditions for anyone who decides to philosophize.[13]

NOTES

1. Alain (Émile Chartier), *Propose sur le bonheur*, in Cahiers du Capricorne, no. 1 (Paris: 1925). The quote also appears in Éditions Gallimard in 1928: "Le commun langage a toujours nommé philosophes ceux qui choisissent en toute occasion le meilleur discours et le plus tonique c'est viser au centre." This entry is dated November 4, 1907. Achenbach quotes Alain in rather free German translation: "Der Sprachgebrauch hat immer den als Philosophen bezeichnet, der jedem Vorkommnis die beste Seite abzugewinnen weiß; denn einzig das hilft." Alain, *Die Pflicht, glücklich zu sein* (Frankfurt a.M: Suhrkamp, 1979), 156.

2. Plutarch, *Moralia. On the Tranquility of Mind.* Trans. by W. C. Helmbold. Loeb Classical Library, Vol. VI, 1939, 183. Accessed on June 22, 2023, at https://penelope.uchicago.edu/Thayer/E/Roman/Texts/Plutarch/Moralia/De_tranquillitate_animi*.html#ref40. The quotation has been altered in minor ways. The same essay appears as Contentment, in Plutarch, *Essays,* trans. by Robin Wakefield (Hammondsworth: Penguin, 1992), 467C (marginal pagination).

3. Achenbach note: Here I offer only a short excerpt from an early lecture on Philosophical Praxis that I gave at the University of Osnabrück in 1982. For the full version, see Gerd B. Achenbach, *Zur Einführung der Philosophischen Praxis* (Köln: Dinter, 2010), 147–159.

4. Helmuth Plessner, *Die Stufen des Organischen und der Mensch* (Berlin/New York: de Gruyter, 1975), 291.

5. Theodor W. Adorno, Philosophie und Lehrer, in *Gesammelte Schriften*, X/2 (Frankfurt a.M.: Suhrkamp, 2003), 485. Picard translation.

6. The sense of education [*Bildung*] intended here was developed by Robert Spaemann in a speech celebrating a graduation, which was published under the title "Wer ist ein gebildeter Mensch?" in *Grenzen. Zur ethischen Dimension des Handelns* (Stuttgart: Klett-Cotta, 2001), 513–516.

7. Novalis, *Werke, Tagebücher und Briefe*, II. Ed. by H. J. Mähl and R. Samuel (Darmstadt: Wissenschaftliche Buchgesellschaft, 1978), 317. Achenbach note: Since Novalis' idiosyncratic style of writing and expression has provoked misunderstandings, it is worthwhile to quote the cited fragment a few lines further. He goes on to say: "So far in philosophical investigation, philosophy has only been struck dead, then dismembered and dissolved. The constituent parts of *caput mortuum* were believed to be the constituent parts of philosophy. But always every attempt at. . . . recomposition failed."

8. Achenbach, Der Philosoph als Praktiker, in *Zur Einführung der Philosophischen Praxis* (Köln: Dinter, 2010), 132.

9. Johann Wolfgang von Goethe, *From My Life: Poetry and Truth*, Part 3. Vol. 4 of *Goethe: Collected Works* (Princeton, NJ: Princeton University Press, 1994), 433.

10. "The heart and feeling that directly sense the truth of religion are not the heart and feeling of an animal but of a thinking human being; they are a thinking heart and a thinking feeling, and whatever [measure] of religion is in this heart and feeling is a thought of this heart and feeling." *Hegel's Lectures on the Philosophy of Religion: The Lectures of 1827*. Trans. by R. F. Brown, P. C. Hodgson, and J. M. Stewart,

with H. S. Harris (Berkeley, LA: University of California Press, 1988), 399 (184 in the marginal pagination). Achenbach cites G. W. F. Hegel, *Vorlesungen über die Philosophie der Religion*, II (Frankfurt a.M.: Suhrkamp, 1969), 199.

11. Achenbach attributes the notion of a "mini-tradition" to Paul Feyerabend, for whom the related distinction between "historical tradition" and "abstract tradition" plays an important role; see Paul Feyerabend, *Philosophical Papers*, II: *Problems of Empiricism* (CUP, 1981), 5–8. Note that individualized "mini-traditions" are historical, in Feyerabend's sense (indeed, a key point is that abstract traditions are also historical traditions). Achenbach cites Feyerabend in the German: *Erkenntnis für freie Menschen* (Frankfurt a.M.: Suhrkamp, 1980), 116, fn 4; indeed, the 11th edition from 2016 is cited, specifically the "Drei Fragen" of the "Zweiter Teil," which bears the title, "Wissenschaft für freie Menschen." Now the English version of this work, which in fact appeared earlier, is *Science in a Free Society* (London: New Left Books, 1978). However, "Part Two" of that work (which shares an *identical* title with the book itself) only discusses "Two Questions," and omits mention of historical "mini-traditions." "Traditions" are introduced and discussed on pages 27–31.

12. Friedrich Wilhelm Joseph Schelling, Erste Vorlesung in München vom 26. November 1827, *Ausgewählte Werke, Schriften von 1813–1830* (Darmstadt: Wissenschaftliche Buchgesellschaft, 1976), 276. In the original Achenbach cites a standard reference: Schelling, *Werke*, I/9 (Stuttgart/Augsburg: Verlag Cotta, 1861), 360.

13. Walter Schulz, Philosophie als Beruf, in *Philosophie als Beruf.* Ed. by J. Schickel (Frankfurt a.M.: Fischer-Taschenbuch, 1982), 60. Picard translation.

Chapter 8

Education and Philosophical Praxis

Søren Kierkegaard and the Question of Who Is a Philosophical Practitioner

> When it comes to the *philosopher*, one cannot regard him as a *worker on the edifice of science*, i.e., not as a scholar, but rather as a *seeker of wisdom*.
>
> —Immanuel Kant[1]

> The only possible criticism of any philosophy, and the only one that proves anything, is trying to see if one can live by this philosophy, and this has never been taught at any university. The only think taught there is the critique of words about words.
>
> —Friedrich Nietzsche[2]

"Philosophical Praxis—A Question of *Bildung*?"[3] The question before us[4] is whether—and, if so, in what way—Philosophical Praxis is a practice of education [*Bildung*].

Since this query is raised in Copenhagen, however, we might just as well ask about the relation of Philosophical Praxis to Søren Kierkegaard himself. In this setting, we could even justify the title, 'Philosophical Praxis in the Footsteps of Søren Kierkegaard,' since the Dane is surely bound to become one of the main sources of guidance for our practical philosophy, if he is not already. I add: For me, he is indeed among the most important contributors and inciters of ideas.

Who like him could have presented, even before Philosophical Praxis existed as an institution, an exemplary model course of a philosophical consultation at the highest level as poetry—with his ingenious *Either-Or*? The dialectical refinement with which the ethicist, husband and family father catches up the existential man of spontaneity, the responsibility-fugitive and virtuoso of seduction, in his own contradictions, in order thereby to usher him into insights that remain necessarily closed off to artists of life—are these not all object lessons of Philosophical Praxis?

So why should we not take up 'the idea of education' in its meaning for Philosophical Praxis 'with continual reference to Kierkegaard'?[5]

I am well aware that the philosophy of the Dane is not normally associated with 'education.' But why ever not? Isn't his charmingly tossed-off juvenalia exactly an instance of an education wisely staged with practical deliberation?

What, then, does our philosopher bring to the table to open the eyes of his contemporaries upon themselves? An interpretation of Antigone; thoughts on the tragic; reflections on Goethe's *Elective Affinities*; the expansive amplification of Mozart's Don Giovanni; a casual theory of opera; an ironic demonstration of the so-called "art of living"; and the wily mockery of the ubiquitous entertainment and distraction economies of his day, which he subsumed under the rubric of the "exchange economy." Besides all this, let us not forget his unequaled masterpiece, "The Diary of the Seducer": the presentation of a seemingly gracelessly graceless[6] consciousness; the caricature of happiness that is objectively despair; the presumption of power that is in truth in flight; the figure of the victorious conqueror, who in reality ends up empty-handed, etc. . . .

Any philosopher able to make use of these registers, and to make his thoughts spring to life with such a wealth of images and traditions, we may, in my opinion, call an *educated* [*gebildeten*] philosopher. Here we find, not the narrowness of the parlor, nor merely the specialized knowledge of the book-scholar and library-denizen, but the very breadth and multifariousness of the world opening up, especially the depths of history. To be more precise: we may call the philosopher who has this knowledge *educated in a first sense of the term*, which presumably must be considered a sense of 'education,' since it is so widely recognized. The proof of education in this sense is an expansive knowledge of tradition, the acquired ability to know beyond all limits of specialization in literature, music, art and theater. And 'to know'[7] here means: 'to know one's way around,' to live and move in it as in a second home.

I am all-too-aware that education in this first sense is not seldom despised. There is a widespread prejudice that mocks the cultured 'citizen.'[8] But what of citizen? Isn't the educated person in this first understanding just an 'intellectual' and perhaps 'intellectual' in the grandest sense? In Denmark, this ideal was exemplified by Morris Cohen, the Dane from Copenhagen and prototype of the modern, pan-European intellectual and masterly educated person with the broadest overview, who called himself Georg Brandes, and who obtained Nietzsche's promise to read Kierkegaard (—albeit too late, since Nietzsche collapsed shortly afterwards).

Despite all the despising, I should like still to put in a good word for this first conception of education and, moreover, to show in what way it is indispensable to Philosophical Praxis. What needs saying, firstly, is that the educated person lives in *more than one world*, and is by no means enslaved to the present age. This is what counts for him. A saying of Nietzsche could serve him as a motto: "We philosophers need a rest from *one thing* above all: anything to do with 'today.'"[9] And how does the educated person procure rest from the tyranny of 'today'? By being equally at home in other ages, and in that way making the greats of earlier epochs into his virtual contemporaries. One thing only provides this advantage: namely our first and quite general sense of education.

But to what extent does Philosophical Praxis also demand this sort of education? Why are vast horizons and earned home-rights in the many and varied epochs of the spirit a prerequisite for the philosophical practitioner? Why do we require him or her to have left behind and overcome the bigotry of the thoroughly modern? It is because—perhaps without knowing it—those who seek out practitioners suffer under the dictates of 'today'! It is because in praxis one meets people aptly characterized as cripples of the present, victims of contemporary thinking and feeling. Or to employ the dramatic image that Kierkegaard found for it: it is because people come who have signed themselves up to fall in with the "demands of the times" as if to "military service," but who yet strive to disavow such drudge-work, maybe due to some indistinct idea they have that, rather than yielding to 'the press of the present,' they ought instead to stay true to themselves. Lots more pertaining to this image is to be found in Kierkegaard's "Literary Review." I quote:

> I myself . . . , thank God, have never had anything to do with the demands of the times by being obligated to its active service. My experience with the demands of the times has been like my experience with military service. I got my discharge immediately, and both times it was what I wanted. But when one begins with being discharged, one always has the advantage of not getting into it too deeply.[10]

Indeed, it is my impression that, for the majority of people, when it comes to legitimating demands upon our selves, there presently exists no authority more extensive than this dubious 'today.' Also principles (insofar as there is still talk of them) derive their pseudo-self-evidence simply from being in circulation currently. Indeed, modernity may without injustice be described as the tyranny of the now, a despotism of the present, the dictatorship of the day, the pitiless prepotence of fashion, which overtakes everything, including not least thinking, judging, wishing, valuing, hoping, fearing. But what is true of many dictatorships is also true of this one: many feel comfortable in its custody, whereas some are crushed under it. Most ride the wave, but some few sink below it. And I add from experience: it is these few and rare ones who seek out Philosophical Praxis. And what could they expect there, if they had *no chance o*f encountering someone *educated* (in this first comprehensive sense), someone, like Kierkegaard, whose discharge from "military service" to the "demands of the times" he cordially accepted? What would await them there is a mere 'contemporary,' a 'denizen of the present,' that is, an exemplar of the very species from which they seek refuge with us!

To the connoisseurs of Kierkegaard, the question may now be put: are we not compelled to say that he, like few of his philosophical companions from Plato to Habermas, was precisely a representative of education? Indeed, who—besides perhaps Nietzsche—was more than he a critic of modernity and a dissident of the present? Thus is Kierkegaard the natural ally of all those who suffer from the absolutism of 'today.' Moreover, the education of Kierkegaard may be discerned in the fact that he was closer to Socrates than to many of his buttoned-down and obdurate contemporaries. Accordingly, with whom did he converse? With Hegel! And he chose well! For in whom could he have found a brainier, more capacious interlocutor? Should one possibly raise the objection that Hegel was no longer alive—but how laughable this objection! For Kierkegaard, Hegel lived; for Kierkegaard, he was present and alive like no one else! Yet this is the very relation which I take as constitutive of any kind of education. But more about that a little later and as necessary.

Before then (more as a side note and hint): the educated Kierkegaard is further to be recognized in his virtually instinctive detestation of the press. He laments: "Woe, woe to the daily press! If Christ were to come into the world today, as I live, he would take aim, not at the high priests but at the journalists."[11] His lamentation is on a par with Nietzsche's invective: "Another century of newspapers—and all words will stink."[12] Neither Nietzsche nor Kierkegaard could unhear 'le jour' in 'journalism,' 'today' in *The Daily*, or the times in the *Times*.[13] Education, however, has always aspired beyond day and hour; days and years were ever as one to it. Education never only has its nose to the wind, but always also breathes the spirit of the centuries, of the ages, if not of eons.

Just now I said that it has always been constitutive for education that its knowledge and its wisdom be nothing distant or worn out, but living and present. With this I arrive by an indirect route at *a second sense of education*; for education not only moves the all-too-near to a salutary distance: it is also the re-enchantment of the present. For one who is educated, the past is precisely not over. If we linger awhile at this viewpoint, it will become crystal clear that, of all the formations of philosophy, none is more intimately related to this second sense of education [*Bildung*] than Philosophical Praxis. To see this, all that is required is to step back for a bit of explanation.

Truly great philosophy has always been advanced also as a *critique* of education, as *Bildungskritik*. Hegel, Schelling, Schopenhauer, Kierkegaard and Nietzsche (to select them as representatives of great philosophy from relatively recent times) all offered critiques of education so that no one confuse a false idea of education with what is called for philosophically.

Now, for my part, I should like, first, *to characterize the education that is the result of such education-critique* and, second, to demonstrate its importance for Philosophical Praxis.

Hegel presents an exemplary radical critique of education in his *Phenomenology of Spirit*, in the chapter "Self-Estranged Spirit—Culture [*Bildung*]."[14] The alienated (and equally alienating) spirit of education, as Hegel presents it there, is a "judging and speaking" whose sole concern is to "overwhelm everything" in a "language full of spirited wit."[15] This educated spirit is really just the "vanity" that "knows, not only how to judge and comment on everything, but also how to articulate with consummate wit the 'solid facts' of reality as well as the 'fixed norms' established by judgment in all their contradictoriness."[16]

Allow me now to point out what havoc such a spirit would wreak in Philosophical Praxis. Its power is to annihilate every problem in the acid bath of analytical acuity, to vaporize intellectually everything burdensome, until finally nothing remains but hazy talk. In *Rameau's Nephew* by Diderot (translated into German by no less than Goethe), Hegel found a literary embodiment of this sort of education, with its universally corrosive and all-atomizing power, whose history Hegel saw as the rise and uncautioned refinement of sophistry. The ultimate triumph of this sort of intellectual education is cynicism, which is beyond all nuance, free floating in the void, exalted above the wastelands where the wretched and downtrodden eke out their pathetic lives. Surely we need not expend many words to comprehend the extent to which the spirit of philosophical counseling can only be grasped as the exact opposite of such fecklessness.

Still, Hegel criticized not just the flamboyant figure of the "educated" salon-intellectual, but also an opposite image, that of the mere amassing, hoarding and preservation of heritage, which is the office of those 'bookkeepers of the spirit,' who like a "counting house clerk or cashier,"[17] is "engaged not with [their] own cognition but with cognition of other people's representations,"[18] and "all the active bustle is concerned with the alien truths of others."[19] Philosophical truth, in their hands, becomes a storehouse of opinions and thought-tokens, which they treat like stones or charms, as if they were gems to be displayed in neat showcases. Those with this sort of philosophical education—to continue Hegel's picture—hoard treasures which since long ago have been no longer in circulation as means of payment, with which nothing at all may be purchased.

Yet I urge caution for anyone tempted to adopt as their own Hegel's critique of either of these forms of education. For what objection does he raise against them both? That they are impervious to truth, to what is substantial, and so have no idea what is objectively required or of the content of valid norms incumbent upon them. Framed in terms of his philosophy of history, education, in Hegel's estimation, steps onto the stage the moment the subject no longer knows anything about what is bindingly true. Education is the veil thrown over spiritual nihilism. The moribund adorns himself with education as one who ties his bow-tie over a cancer of the larynx.

Thus, as I said, I advise caution! With all due sympathy for the philosophy of Hegel, I provisionally distrust anyone who, especially as a philosophical practitioner, generates in me the appearance of having ever been all buddy-buddy with the Truth. For the practical philosopher in counseling, few things are as potentially fatal as arousing the appearance of having at one's disposal blessings which we do not possess and which we would not know where to obtain.

It is well worth our while, in my view, to cast a glance also at the critique of education that Nietzsche brought into play. It appears to be every bit as scathing as Hegel's critique. Yet I suspect that the demands it places upon the practical philosopher are more likely to be met.

What does he excoriate? All mere knowledge which has not been really appropriated and made one's own. The modern, educated man, he says for instance in the second *Unfashionable Observations*, "drags around with him a huge number of indigestible stones of knowledge, which then on occasion, as in the fairy tale, make quite a racket inside his stomach."[20] It is just this racket that betrays "education." "We are dealing with a race of eunuchs; and for a eunuch, one woman is just like any other, just a woman." But he adds: "they themselves are neither man nor woman, nor even hermaphrodite, but instead always only neuters—or, in more cultivated terms, simply the Eternally Objective."[21] Such are "those hollowed-out by cultivation,"[22] "reduced to eternal subjectlessness—or, as they say, to 'objectivity.'"[23]

Finally, the heightening and exaggeration of this type of educated person are the scholars that Zarathustra mocks:

> Like those who stand in the street and stare at the people passing by, so they too wait and stare at thoughts that others have thought.

> If one takes hold of them, they involuntarily raise a dust like sacks of flour; but who could guess that their dust derived from corn and from the golden joy of summer fields. . . .
>
> They work like mills and rammers: just throw seed-corn into them!—they know how to grind corn small and make white dust of it.[24]

But I am careful not to quote further, for in the end I too have presented nothing but a pile of "scraps of paper glued together"[25] such as Zarathustra finds everywhere in the "Land of Culture" [*Bildung*].

I break off here to ask, after all this, what Philosophical Praxis has to do with such critiques of education? More than any other form of philosophy, Philosophical Praxis makes this critique of education its very business. How can that be?

Another 'scrap,' as a first reply, simply because I love it, also because what needs explanation and clarification here is to be found nowhere else more fittingly or strikingly expressed. The scrap is from the hand of Schopenhauer: "One cannot nourish others with undigested waste, but only with the milk that has secreted itself from one's own blood."[26] Ergo: with only what is merely read, rehearsed and regurgitated, the philosophical practitioner will necessarily fail in practice, and worse still: will become a laughingstock. No one who in their need turns to us will be served by being thrown leavings and crumbs from other people's tables; and no one comes to us in order to have us disgorge what others have chewed up. Rather, our guest comes to converse *with us.* This conversation, however, has its beginning or its basis not in lecture or being able to recite what we have learned, but *in that we listen and understand.* Thus is the core of the philosophical critique of education expressed: whether the philosophy we have been able to appropriate has really become our own is proved not by our repeating it, nor even by our having understood it, but only by our understanding through it!

If something has grown philosophical in us, or something in us has attained to the dignity of a philosophical education, it is not shown in what we are able to share with our visitor, but in how we ourselves are able to understand what it is that our visitor shares with us. *Philosophical education* in this second clarified sense is thus not *schooling of the mouth,* but *refinement of the ear.* I recognize the *philosophically educated* in this second sense *not by what he says, but by how he listens*. And this I expect from him: that he has learned to listen to very many philosophers, and thus to the most diverse thinking imaginable, as well as to vastly different mentalities and characters; that he has fostered a fine ear for nuances, for overtones, undertones and in-between tones, for idiosyncrasies, moods and dispositions—finally that he does not handle thoughts like glass arguments, to be held up as if with pincers, flipped back and forth, and fiddled with; but has nurtured a sensibility for the shades and colors in which a thought shrouds itself, decks itself out, perhaps hides itself, maybe disguises itself, so that one gets the thought only by guessing at it.

Is it even necessary still to point out that such demands presuppose the critique of superficial education, that Philosophical Praxis is not about mere knowing or knowledge-gathering; that therefore the philosophical practitioner does not need to spoon-feed anything to his visitors? For the question is whether he himself is for his own part philosophically well-nourished and strengthened, that is, whether he is able to digest what the guest has to feed him.

And *that* is a question of education, as it arises in view of Philosophical Praxis, education in a second, formidable sense. It stands the test by establishing itself as the aptitude to meaningfully listen, just as the ethicist in *Either-Or* knows how to listen to and observe that ungrounded virtuoso of life until that aesthete is understood better and more thoroughly than he was ever able to understand himself.

But put aside *Either-Or* for a moment. I relish the opportunity to refer here to another work by the Dane, which develops in broad outline a theory of practically effective philosophy, and which therefore is valuable to us above all else. Kierkegaard had it published under the title *Point of View for my Work as an Author*. In it he demonstrates (among much else) how education in the second understanding turns out to be the very art of listening. This educated (*gebildeten*) listener he calls "his teacher." And we have good reasons to recognize in this sort of teacher the philosophical practitioner incognito. What is the crucial difference that distinguishes this "other" sort of teacher from the "ordinary" one? An "educated" teaching, according to Kierkegaard, does not presume to be dealing with 'an ignorant person' who must be led 'in the know,' but [knows] that there is no 'empty vessel that one could fill,' no 'blank slate on which to inscribe' at will. Rather, what he is dealing with is one caught up in thoughts, and these thoughts must first be made uncertain to him, before anyone can succeed in gaining access to him. Kierkegaard then goes on to characterize this "other" sort of teacher, the philosophical practitioner-to-be:

> For to be a teacher does not mean simply to affirm that such a thing is so, or to deliver a lecture, &c. No, to be a teacher in the right sense is to be a learner. Instruction begins when you, the teacher, learn from the learner, put yourself in his place so that you may understand what he understands and in the way he understands it, in case you have not understood it before. Or if you have understood it before, you allow him to subject you to an examination so that he may be sure you know your part. This is the introduction. Then the beginning can be made in another sense.[27]

Much is to be gained for Philosophical Praxis if we understand that this mindset is to be acquired through education, and if we expect it of the philosophical practitioner. This may be reinforced by borrowing two more passages from Kierkegaard's *Point of View for my Work as a Author*, that simultaneously anticipate a next, third, and final conception of that education that has become indispensable to Philosophical Praxis. First the two quotations, which follow without ado from what has been stated so far. "If real success is to attend the effort to bring a man to a definite position, one must first of all take pains to find him where he is and begin there."[28] He then elaborates upon this recommendation as follows:

> This is the secret of the art of helping others. Anyone who has not mastered this is himself deluded when he proposes to help others. In order to help another effectively I must understand more than he—yet first of all surely I must understand what he understands. If I do not know that, my greater understanding will be of no help to him. If, however, I am disposed to plume myself on my greater understanding, it is because I am vain and proud, so that at bottom, instead of benefiting him, I want to be admired. But all true effort to help begins with self-humiliation: the helper must first humble himself under him he would help, and therewith must understand that to help does not mean to be ambitious but to be patient, that to help means to endure for the time being the imputation that one is in the wrong and does not understand what the other understands.[29]

The important point here, found in the shortest possible version in a note by Goethe (quoted previously) from *Elective Affinities*: "To share of oneself is nature, to take what is shared as it was given is honorable."[30] But by quoting this aphorism, a *third viewpoint on education*, as announced, is already opened up. Education in this third sense (perhaps essential, but in any case indispensable with regard to Philosophical Praxis) is an acquired *mindset*, a *habitus*; not merely the content of possible knowledge, but the very *constitution* of a person. In short, insofar as Philosophical Praxis comes down to education, it does not depend much, certainly not only, on what the philosophical practitioner knows or thinks, but on *who he is*—more precisely: on *who he has become*. Such becoming, however, is the result of education.

Here it is fitting to note, that, at least as a word and concept, *Bildung* is originally a very German affair. What else has the German language bequeathed to other languages as a foreign word? Thanks to Fröbel, the word '*Kindergarten*' is famous. And I hear that '*Rucksack*' has been carried to foreign lands. Well and good. But above all, *Bildung*, education, the word and concept that has centrally occupied us here. One might wonder how it originally found its way into the German language. In fact, it was through Meister Eckhart,[31] who formulated his doctrine of stages and held that the highest stage attainable by man was the sixth in which man "unbuilds" [*entbildet*] himself in order to be "built over" again [*überbildet*] in God's likeness. But this is a highly demanding doctrine theologically, which defies brief treatment. So I will go no further into it here.

Instead, I would like to revert to what I have called the third viewpoint on education, probably the most ambitious and challenging idea of education. And let me add: Philosophical Praxis, if it is serious about its cause and genuinely wants to earn the distinction of being a *philosophical* practice, must now become heir to this most demanding concept of education. This ideal of *Bildung* originates with Wilhelm von Humboldt, the preeminent founder of the university in Berlin that today bears his name.

What is *Bildung* to Humboldt? The fulfillment of the "ultimate task of our existence," and that is: "to achieve as much substance as possible for the concept of humanity in our person."[32] The end goal, however, is "that Bildung, wisdom and virtue" add to the "inner worth" of an individual "to such an extent that the concept of humanity, if taken from this one example alone, would be of a rich and worthy substance."[33]

The purpose and measure of education, as proposed by Humboldt, I essay to clarify to myself by means of a wholly imaginary, rather curious, yet thought-provoking story. Conceived as an address to an imaginary audience, it reads as follows: Picture a spaceship, against all odds, that one day lands on earth, sent out for purposes of exploration by the superior inhabitants of a distant planet. And now these aliens take you aboard, as the one single specimen of humankind, in order that, back on their home planet, their conspecifics can get an idea of humanity. Now you must ask yourself whether you can, with a clear conscience, be convinced that those aliens made a good choice when they decided to pick you; that, in other words, humanity is most highly represented in your person, so that humanity may glory in you for its sake. If you ask yourself *this* question in *this* way, you are asking yourself, in Humboldtian fashion, about the quality of your own education.

We notice from this fictitious tale how 'wickedly complex' the answer to this question would need to be. Any one-sidedness here would be an injustice—hard to believe that humanity would see itself validly represented in, say, a molecular biologist, or circus trapeze-artist. And I too would just as much refuse my consent if a selection committee had come up with the shameless and curious idea to offer the extraterrestrials a world beauty queen or a male supermodel as humanity's emblem. As exemplar of humanity, I would prefer by far one who—to quote Socrates—had a "beautiful soul"—and I should pick, despite his imposing ugliness, the old gnome and fox of the Athenian Agora himself.

Above all, our standard-bearer would have to display all the fine qualities that we traditionally call the virtues. He would need to be judicious and wise, prudent in the choice of his means toward reasonable ends, lenient in the judgment of others, affectionate in dealing with intimates, open to everything worthy of our interest, serene in the face of an imponderable fate. True to his word, he would be trusting when lacking reason to mistrust. His convictions would have been duly deliberated, experience garnered on paths most forked. His judgment ripened in silence would be equitable, for in all things he seeks the best outcome of things, and not his own advantage only. He would know what he wants, and before that, because he shrinks from overblown self-estimation, he knows what he can get done; such would be his practice of humility.

His character would be plain and forthright, so that he could be counted on. He would take the best as his example, and so would scorn to excuse the slipshod, and be wary, lest he veer into mediocrity. What must be demanded, he demands first from himself, not from others. His speech would be candid, his sentiment sincere. Kind would be his heart, tidy his thinking. His hopes would be a promise, his fears justified; and, in view of the brevity of life, he would know how to help himself along through humor. Thus he would be of a cheerful disposition, as a rule in good spirits, and, all in all, he would be at one with himself and with his fate, which in the good times would be cause for gratitude, even if he could not say succinctly to whom.

Has this small selection and short enumeration sufficiently illustrated what I have been driving at? Of course, the account that I attempted could yet be extended *ad ultimo* as well as rendered more exactingly. But probably it is quite unnecessary. Surely by now it has likely become quite clear what I mean by *Bildung*, or education in the third sense, this *acquired mindset*, as well as how thoroughly in agreement it is with the justly famous idea of human education as conceived by Humboldt. And so it suffices after this sketch, to return again to the question: is Philosophical Praxis a matter of education in this third sense? Put differently, does the justification and success of Philosophical Praxis depend upon philosophical practitioners being so bold as to measure themselves against this most demanding of standards? My answer is: *Yes!*

Finally, in these three conceptions of education, as I have endeavored to present them in successive steps, Philosophical Praxis finds still another measure, its goal, so to speak, its "wither-to" in its conversations with guests and visitors. In other words: Neither health nor cleverness, neither the ringing success in business nor popularity with the masses—to consider alternatives—are what Philosophical Praxis is all about. Rather, it seeks to promote the education of those who turn to it in their need. Its most brilliant success would be, if it would finally release those who turn to it as equal to life, as *Lebenskönner*. For the new word for education is: *Lebenskönnerschaft*. It contains what today could be called 'education.'

NOTES

1. Immanuel Kant, *Anthropologie im pragmatischer Hinsicht*, 619 (= A 246). Picard translation. For a mediocre translation of this passage, see *Anthropology from a Pragmatic Point of View.* Trans. by Mary J. Gregor (The Hague: Martinus Nijhoff, 1974), 145 fn.

2. Friedrich Nietzsche, *Unfashionable Observations*. In *The Complete Works of Friedrich Nietzsche*, II. Trans. by Richard T. Gray (Stanford, CA: Stanford University Press, 1995), 246. Used with permission.

3. The German word *Bildung* is notoriously impossible to translate; and in academic works it is therefore occasionally left untranslated. Here, despite its limitations, the word 'education' is used for *Bildung* throughout, with few exceptions, namely for the most part in quotations from existing translations of sources that use other words (such as 'culture' or 'image' or 'form'). 'Self-formation,' 'nurture,' or 'enculturation' have more suitable connotations in many contexts, but consistency seemed important. These alternate valid renderings make clear what becomes evident though this chapter, that 'education' is by no means to be taken narrowly as formal education or accreditation. Also, see the chapter 7 above on 'Philosophical Praxis as a Profession.'

4. Achenbach note: This chapter is the revised text of lecture with which I opened the 7th International Congress on Philosophical Praxis in Copenhagen in 2004. The name of conference was "Philosophical Practice—A Question of *Bildung*?" The original version was published under the title "Philosophische Praxis und Bildung" in Achenbach, *Zur Einführung der Philosophische Praxis* (Köln: Dinter, 2010), 253–265.

5. One will note the allusion here to Kierkegaard's 1841 dissertation, published in English translation under the title, *The Concept of Irony With Continual Reference to Socrates.* Trans. by Howard and Edna Hong (Princeton, NJ: Princeton University Press, 1989). (Achenbach cites a German translation.)

6. Gracelessly graceless—*heillos heillosen Bewußtsein.*

7. *Auskennen.* Relevant here is Ludwig Wittgenstein's redolent remark: "A philosophical problem has the form: "'I don't know my way about,'" *Philosophical Investigations*, §122 (Oxford: Basil Blackwell, 1958). In the German original: "Ein philosophisches Problem hat die Form: Ich kenne mich nicht aus."

8. The words 'cultured citizen' do disservice to the connotations of '*Bildungsbürger,*' despite being close to literal. The question that immediately follows in the German is: "Doch wieso 'Bildungsbürger'?" The broad context is difficult to make plain. Achenbach is alluding here to a distinction that goes back a long way in the history of the word '*Bildung*': a distinction between *Bildungsbürger* and *Bildungsmenschen*; i.e., between the civic/political aims of education on the one hand, and its self-formation or self-cultivation aims on the other. (Relevant here is Wilhelm von Humboldt's "Theorie der Bildung des Menschen," mentioned later.)

9. Friedrich Nietzsche, *On the Genealogy of Morality*, Essay III/8 Trans. by Carol Diethe. Revised Student Edition (CUP, 2007), 79.

10. Søren Kierkegaard, *Two Ages: The Age of Revolution and the Present Age. A Literary Review.* Ed. and trans. Howard V. Hong and Edna H. Hong (Princeton,

NJ: Princeton University Press, 1978), 9 fn. (with minor adjustments). Kierkegaard was discharged Nov. 4, 1830, three days after having been drafted.

11. Regarding this quotation Achenbach cites Kierkegaard's *Concluding Unscientific Postscript* (in German), but this is an error. The correct attribution is apparently to his Tagebücher, his *Journals and Notebooks,* of 1849 (specifically, under Siglum X1 A 258). Unfortunately, I have not been able to locate the passage in the relevant volume of the Princeton University Press edition of *Kierkegaard's Journals and Notebooks*, so have myself translated the German in Achenbach.

12. Friedrich Nietzsche, *Unpublished Fragments from the Period of Thus Spoke Zarathustra* (Summer 1882–Winter 1883/84), 14. Transl. by Paul S. Loeb and David F. Tinsley (Stanford, CA: Stanford University Press, 2019), 60 (§ 168).

13. The German reads: "Beide, Kierkegaard wie Nietzsche, hatten noch das feine Ohr, das aus dem Wort 'Zeitung' 'Zeit' und aus 'Journalismus' 'le jour' heraushörte."

14. The German chapter title is "Der sich entfremdete Geist. Die Bildung." Bailie and Miller also translated *Bildung* here as 'culture.'

15. G. W. F. Hegel, *The Phenomenology of Spirit*. Translated by Peter Fuss and John Dobbins (Notre Dame, IN: University of Notre Dame Press, 2019), 260. Achenbach chops up and re-arranges a single sentence in the original, which in English runs: "Thus really the sole concern of such judging and speaking is to overwhelm everything in this the real world with its candidness and indomitable spirit."

16. Hegel, *Phenomenology*, 262.

17. G. W. F. Hegel, *Hegel's Lectures on the Philosophy of Religion: The Lectures of 1827.* Trans. by Brown, Hodgson, Stewart, and Harris (Berkeley, LA: University of California Press, 1988), 76 (marginal pagination).

18. Hegel, *Philosophy of Religion*, 76.

19. Hegel, *Philosophy of Religion*, 76.

20. Friedrich Nietzsche, "On the Utility and Liability of History for Life," in *Unfashionable Observations*, trans. by Richard T. Gray (Stanford, CA: Stanford University Press, 1995), 109.

21. Friedrich Nietzsche, "On the Utility and Liability of History for Life," in *Unfashionable Observations*, 120. Achenbach quotes Nietzsche sparingly here, removing context more familiar to German readers. In Nietzsche, there is implicit reference and critique (or rather mockery) of the "Eternal Feminine," which at the end of Part Two of Goethe's *Faust* "draws us upward." The full Nietzsche quotation is provided here: "We are dealing with a race of eunuchs; and for a eunuch, one woman is just like any other, just a woman, woman-in-herself, the eternally unapproachable—and hence it makes no difference what you do, as long as history itself remains 'objective' and is preserved by those who themselves can never make history. And since the Eternally Feminine can never draw you upward, you drag it down to your level, and since you are neuters, you consider history to be a neuter as well. But lest someone be led to believe that I am earnestly comparing history to the Eternal Feminine, let me state clearly that, quite to the contrary, I believe it to be the Eternal Masculine. But for those who are 'historically cultivated' through and through it cannot make much difference whether it is one or the other; for they themselves are neither

man nor woman, nor even hermaphrodite, but instead always only neuters—or, in more cultivated terms, simply the Eternally Objective."

22. Nietzsche, *Unfashionable Observations*, 120.

23. Nietzsche, *Unfashionable Observations*, 120.

24. Nietzsche, *Thus Spoke Zarathustra*, Part 2, "Of Scholars," 147–148. Hollingdale translation.

25. Nietzsche, *Thus Spoke Zarathustra*, Part 2, "Of the Land of Culture," 142. Hollingdale translation.

26. Arthur Schopenhauer, On learning and the learned, Ch. 21, §247 in *Parerga and paralipomena: short philosophical essays,* 2. Trans. by Del Caro and Janaway (CUP, 2015), 511 (marginal pagination).

27. Søren Kierkegaard (1848). *The Point of View for My work as an Author.* Reprinted in *A Kierkegaard Anthology* (Robert Bretal, editor) (Princeton, NJ: Princeton University Press, 1946), 355.

28. Kierkegaard, *Point of View*, 333.

29. Kierkegaard, *Point of View*, 333–334.

30. Honorable—*Bildung.* Goethe, *Elective Affinities.* From Ottilie's Journal, Part 2, Ch. 4. Laura V. Adrian translation. See related note in Conversational Mastery.

31. Meister Eckhart, "Of the Nobleman," in *Meister Eckhart: The Essential Sermons, Commentaries, Treatises, and Defense.* Transl. by Edmund Colledge, OSA and Bernard McGinn (Paulist Press, 1981), 242. The relevant passage reads: "The sixth stage is when man becomes free of images and is transformed into the image of God's everlastingness and has attained to a complete and perfect oblivion of this transient life in time, and has been drawn and wholly changed into a divine image and has become God's child." The words 'image' and 'form'—even 'draw'—do the work done in German by cognates of "*Bild.*" Blakney's translation truncates the first Eckhart line quoted above, rendering it as follows: "In the sixth grade he is 'disformed' and transformed in the divine eternal nature, having achieved full perfection." See *Meister Eckhart: A Modern Translation.* Transl. by Raymond Bernard Blakney (New York: Harper Torchbooks, 1941), 76.

32. Wilhelm von Humboldt, "Theory of *Bildung.*" A translation by Gillian Horton-Krüger of "Theorie der Bildung des Menschen," in *Teaching as a reflective practice: The German Didaktik tradition* (London: Lawrence Erlbaum, 2000), 58. This "substance," Humboldt goes on, is to be achieved, "both during the span of our life and beyond it, through the traces we leave by means of our vital activity. This can be fulfilled only by linking the self to the world to achieve the most general, most animated and most unrestrained interplay."

33. Humboldt, "Theory of *Bildung,*" 59. The quotation has been slightly altered to fit the grammatical context. The concern in praxis is the individual level, but the "inner worth" of which Humbodlt speaks is also what is demanded of "a nation, an age, of entire mankind, if it is to occasion respect and admiration."

Chapter 9

Philosophical Praxis and the Virtues

> Humans are creatures to whom one can only do justice by overtaxing them. They are creatures that only come to their senses when one demands more of them than simply what is customary among speaking apes. . . . In a related sense Kierkegaard would later instruct his readers that whoever wishes humans well must place obstacles in their path.
>
> —Peter Sloterdijk[1]

I take the liberty of opening with a thesis:[2]

> For a philosophical practitioner, daily work life is but a 'special case' of regular life (of 'private' life, as we say), because the probity required at his work differs in no essential ways from what is required of him in the prose of everyday life. True, the philosophical practitioner in counseling is clearly challenged in a 'special' way, but how he meets this special challenge is not fundamentally different from his proficiency to deal with life problems and difficult situations—at any rate: it *should* not be different from it. Put otherwise, the philosopher is expected to make no distinction between himself as a private person and himself as a working person, which is otherwise customary in the regular working world—as also in the working world of science.

The same point can also be made this way: As the philosophical practitioner leads his life, so he is available in praxis. I add: that is how he *needs* to be available to visitors in his praxis. But why? Because the people who seek him out in praxis have on their mind precisely the same question that the philosophical practitioner must in his own way answer for himself in terms of his own life—and that question is: 'How shall I live?' or, 'How am I actually living?'

Our visitor, however, who commonly cannot come to grips with *his life*, and who now entrusts *himself* to me, is entitled to the legitimate expectation that the philosopher he sits down with will address his problems with convincingly life-proven deliberations, i.e., not with 'mere' thoughts the relevance of which for life remains unconsidered. As a philosopher, therefore, whose advice in urgent life-questions is sought, I must always also answer 'with myself'—even when reflection makes clear that I was not myself able to verify it in my life; for then the visitor has a right to know, at what point the developing thought, which I put forward for him to consider, was not yet possible for me personally to carry out, and why therefore I am only able to reason about it as a 'mere' thought. For, to give a recommendation that I as a philosopher (i.e., as a conscious human being) am not prepared to follow, or with which I myself would not be able to comply, would be tantamount to fraud, or at least to deception.

Compactly put: Just as the person in praxis is an instigation to me, so for my part I can only be an instigation to my guest.[3] And just this makes the question about the conduct of my own life so important, for it is the very form that I have managed to give to the problem that I myself am, both for myself and for others. The virtues, in consequence, are of the first importance for the philosophical practitioner, because the condition of his life cannot in philosophical counseling be set aside as a so-called 'private matter,' but substantially shapes the course of his praxis.

The situation is aggravated by the fact that, for visitors to my praxis, I am, in a particularly formidable sense, exactly the imposition [*Zumutung*] that I present to other people generally. As a rule, those who are already themselves overburdened with their problems lack the imperturbability or the power of resistance to withstand without harm further problems that another person now causes them—in this case the philosopher in praxis.

So, to summarize these first considerations: Virtue as an acquired and lifelong craft of life leadership belongs at the very center of Philosophical Praxis. For this is what visitors to the practice seek for themselves—the know-how to lead life well, or at least better—which the philosopher-practitioner likewise seeks, if that search does not already constitute philosophy as such in its utter seriousness. And so it has been since Socrates. It was so (historically halfway from Socrates to us) for my friend, Michel de Montaigne: "Our great and glorious masterpiece is to live appropriately. All other things—ruling, hoarding, building—are only little appendages and props, at most."[4] And, to cite a highly respected contemporary witness, it is still so today, as the philosopher Hilary Putman attests offhandedly: "the central philosophical question is *how to live*."[5]

Given such stipulations, one may by rights worry that philosopher practitioners would be robbed of all the protections enjoyed by specialists, experts and other service providers, and left perpetually *overextended.* For whose life has such an exemplary form that it could open itself to be honestly seen?

And this worry might yet be fortified by allusion to the large number of life failures amongst so-called 'philosophers,' who would evidently have been unequal to the demands that Philosophical Praxis would have made upon them. Let us also admit that, to the committed eye, these figures—often gray, crouched, crestfallen people—are rather miserable creatures: hunkered down in their seminars amid their tomes, or perhaps drifting through corridors, spiritualized away like droll intellectual ghosts. To imagine such life-averse scholastics as these dispensing their counsel, doling out life-enriching guidance to others, is no less than to picture a farce and an unintentional comedy.

With this, we may for the time being take as justified our intention to deal with 'virtue' [*Tugend*] and 'virtues' as regards their meaning *in* and *for* Philosophical Praxis.

But now an objection ought to be considered: the word 'virtue' [*Tugend*], like its opposites, 'vice' or 'folly,' seems to have fallen so far out of linguistic usage that to speak of it as if it still had prestige would be an inexcusable naivety. "Virtue" is a word, Nietzsche once said, with which one can no longer think anything, "an old-fashioned word that makes people smile—and it is worse if you do not smile, since that means you are a hypocrite."[6] And Paul Valéry concluded that 'virtue' and 'virtuous' are nowadays found only "in catechism, in farce, in the academy, and in operetta."[7] Recall that 'virtue' suffered a fate similar to that of another pivotal term of any ethics oriented to practical life: 'morality' [*Sittlichkeit*] and 'moral' also seem to have withdrawn from linguistic traffic. Already Schopenhauer found 'moral' [*sittlich*] to be "a tame and feeble expression, difficult to distinguish from 'polite,' which in popular language is called 'prissy.'"[8] I could entertain us for a long time citing similar quotations, for I collect such charming passages. But let me be curt: the 'prestige' of the term is unthinkably bad. Norbert Hinske, in his "Reflections on Virtue Ethics," admitted at the outset that the word 'virtue' arouses "associations today that obscure rather than clarify the matter at issue."[9] Indeed, the once thoroughly serious term, he says, has "become a sottise."[10]

No doubt other voices can be cited who, with courageous levelheadedness,[11] unconcerned by prevailing thought-dictates, appeal for an understanding of the urgent currency of virtue—Hermann Lübbe, for example:

> The more modern we become, the more emancipated we are, the more important virtue becomes for our lives—namely, our savvy [*Könnerschaft*] in managing the rigors of self-determined living. The gauntlet thrown down by the modern world is to make a purposeful use of freedom. Questions as to how to lead life answer themselves very simply when hardship with its blunt imperatives presses

> upon us. But virtue, or the capacity of self-determination through worthwhile deeds, is dependent on *freedom*.[12]

Also Amitai Etzioni, one of the progenitors of American communitarianism, concluded an interview with the (to my taste simplistic and overbold) assertion: "the citizens of societies all over the world long for a virtue debate."[13] It is cause too for thought that in France a book on virtues by philosopher André Comte-Sponville became a bestseller (*Petit traité des grandes vertus*); but it also gives pause for thought that the German publisher found it appropriate to emphasize the presumed untimeliness of this "small breviary of virtues and values" right in the title in the form of courageous defiance: on the cover of the German translation, the title reads, *Ermutigung zum unzeitgemäßen Leben*; or: 'Exhortation to an Untimely Life.'

It behooves us to ask why the most erudite advocates of virtue think it must first be defended against the condemnation by the spirit of our age?[14]

Norbert Hinske, in line with the best traditions, declares the virtues to be those "qualities which every human being needs in order to tap into his or her specific possibilities in the long run and thereby, despite the unpredictability of fate, to lead a fulfilled life"; or, as Hinske adds: they are the "qualities through which one finds oneself."[15] Must we not ask how such an understanding of the virtues could ever have become obsolete?

Are we dealing here perhaps with a mere misunderstanding, with philosophically untutored ignorance, so that it would suffice to point out to people their own preconceptions for them to find their way back to the ancient reverence for virtue as life-mastery?

The answer is no. On the contrary, I assume that the hit to virtue's reputation is deeply bound up with a truly *revolutionary*, but often overlooked, transformation in human self-understanding that occurred when we entered modernity. Put plainly, modern man thinks of himself quite differently than premodern man did—namely, in a way that is inconsistent with the basics of any understanding of virtue. Let me explain this assumption briefly—'briefly,' that is to say, with the audacity of reckless simplification.

The basis of any understanding of virtue, it might be said, is the validity of the conviction expressed most pithily by Arnold Gehlen: man is the being "that does not live, but *leads* his life."[16] Brilliantly reduced to its essentials, this is the premodern principle, more precisely, the precept of *antiquity*. There it held true: one only becomes what one is destined to become if one endeavors to become it. This means that an accomplished life was understood to be the achievement of work upon oneself. It meant too that insofar as sagacity and prudence, insight and distance from oneself, reason and the wisdom of experience are not the actual and ultimate arbiters of how a human life should be led (bluntly: absent the acquisition of virtues), life itself must fail or remain poor and stale, flat and banal. It falls prey to the momentary demands of affects, is torn to and fro, and finds neither form nor composure. The accomplished and honorable [*ansehnliche*] life, on the other hand, is of the creation of the reason-oriented conduct of life, of an examined life, worthy of respect, which we honor deservedly, enshrine as exemplary, and to which we rightly pay respect. I propose to call this human self-image the 'proud' one. For this is the pride of man: that he owes to himself *his* prowess and virtue, to *his very self*, and to his *care for himself*.

But after ancient times, under the sign of Rome and under that of baptism, instead of the philosopher, the priest now advanced to the position of spiritual director, like a transfigured Charon.[17] Humankind stands on Heaven's reserve and is entrusted to grace; for the good life cannot be mastered on our own. By nature, man is the sad and sick animal, and that "bit of heavenly light"—"he calls it Reason"—he only uses it "to act more beastly than beasts ever do."[18]

Ergo: on his own he can do nothing; for the human being, precisely *because* he is human, is a sinner, the fallen creature, expelled from paradise, corrupted and lost, in need of merciful redemption. A brave reactionary whom I hold in high esteem, Nicolás Gómez Dávila, put this image of man in aphoristic terms: "human nature is the problem for which there is no human solution."[19] It cannot be said more succinctly. Pride is broken, humility is the answer, but our dependence still connects us with the very highest place. Such as we are, we may amount to little, but all the same we are 'children of God.' The accomplished life is the life devoutly *dedicated*, the one we owe and betroth to the Father in Heaven.

This human self-image I propose to call the 'humble' one.[20] Christian humility is to trust, not haughtily in oneself, but in God and His grace. The consciousness of *leading one's own life* is supplanted by the faithful confidence of *being led*.

But now Rousseau enters the stage. Incidentally, the metaphor of the *stage* seems to me indispensable, for Jean-Jacques steals the scene with his decidedly "theatrical" appearance. In vignette: the forebear of everyone contemporary, or anyhow modern, pipes up. And what he proclaims to us is truly epoch-making 'good news.' I will try now to decode.

Whereas in ancient times the individual *himself*—personally called to excellence [*Vollkommenheit*]—*directed* his life himself; and while the Christian trudge over the earth *under the eye of God* with confidence in His guidance; according to Rousseau—and here I quote Ernst Cassirer—"responsibility [is assigned to] a point where no one before him had looked for it." Jean-Jacques invents "a new *subject* of responsibility, of 'imputability'"—no longer "the individual human being, but human society."[21]

Let me expand: "society," this brand new locus of "imputability" to which the responsibility for our lives now falls is a concept of such generous breadth and expandable openness that it is ripe for transformative appropriation. Let us therefore confine ourselves to noting that it is no longer the individual, each one for himself, who bears responsibility; still less is it left to the grace of God; responsibility now lies with the ensemble of *relations*. The reigning truth now is that the individual is neither the achievement of a self-responsible self-leadership of life, nor the well-led child of heaven; rather he finds himself to be a product of circumstance. And so he begins to ask who and what it was that made him become the way he has become. Thus begins the story of modern man's *endless curiosity about himself*. Henceforth man's attitude towards himself is in the main *theoretical*: "How was it possible that I became who I am?" Peter Sloterdijk diagnosed it as a symptom of the contemporary "who-am-I-neurosis."[22]

The prevailing idea becomes that life, as long as it runs undisturbed, i.e., 'normally,' will of itself issue in achievements. In other words, if it fails to, something must have prevented these achievements from occurring. This no doubt is the far-reaching implication of Rousseau's hypothesis of the "naturally good man": if he discovers that he himself is bad, somehow not right, then something must have spoiled him. In this way he sees himself as a victim, analyzes himself as one who is traumatized, neurotized—to put it crudely—'screwed by the system.'[23] He suspects that something must have happened that hindered his goodness, that made him lose his goodness, that threw him off the rails. So he begins to search for the circumstances that have prevented him from becoming what certainly he would have become on his own: namely, a normal, good, correct, healthy, hard-working, life-loving, orgasm-happy, peaceful and gentle man, friendly to all, and flush with complacency. Inevitably, our man now gets back on track by chasing down heteronomies so he may free himself from them; for freedom he now confuses with liberation from the impositions that do not allow him to live autonomously. He comes to see himself as a being alienated from himself. He recognizes himself as a being deprived of himself by others. And accordingly his work will be to remove layer by layer—negation of negations—all that is alien in himself in the hope that, beneath all the sedimented biographical strata and psychological tectonic faults, the real me—the true, liberated, *healthy* self—will finally greet the day. The aim and mission of life is finally 'to come to oneself' after a long and arduous detour; in other words, . . . it is the psychologists' turn! Just as the proud man admonished himself; just as the pious man knelt humbly in the confessional; so modern man lays his body down on the couch of his psychotherapist. But what shall we call this image of man that has made the proud incomprehensible and the humble obscure to us? Perhaps the 'sad' one? Maybe the 'obstreperous' one? Both amount to the same. Following a note of Nietzsche, I could call it the 'undignified' image of man: "*The most general sign of modern times*: man has lost an incredible amount of *dignity* in his own eyes."[24]

He begins to sicken of himself; nausea set in; he has lost respect for himself, and as a result also for other people. He grouses and grumbles, but does not know how to help himself. He is somehow suffering, depressed somehow, somehow not well, but he has no idea what well is, and certainly not what might help him. Plainly his plight is that he 'lacks' something—but what, he knows not. One is tempted here to recount Nietzsche's disquietingly grandiose prophecy of the "last man," who discovers happiness and makes everything small, invents his little pleasures for day and for night.[25] But I resist.

For—despite all due reservation towards such grand narratives—what I was seeking has been found: namely, a possible explanation for the fact that virtue has such bad press these days, for why people today cannot even begin to relate to virtue.

Yet it is one thing to suppose that virtue has become an incomprehensible notion to people, and quite another thing to question whether this obliviousness is a boon. Our inquiry about the relation of virtue to philosophical praxis would acquire a certain urgency if indeed it could be shown that the atrophy of the virtue-perspective, far from being a boon to people, is instead a bane, the very origin of their complaints and despondency. It shares in the cause of the sufferings they report to us in praxis. And our theme would even prove itself to be of utmost importance if one could assume that regaining the perspective of virtue would be beneficial in praxis—helpful for those who visit us and helpful for us. And that indeed is what I assume.

By way of parenthesis, it is even conceivable to regard the emergence of Philosophical Praxis itself, and the interest in it that has been gradually building, as an indication that some few people have begun to suspect the connection, and are now looking for a way out of their 'undignified' self-conception by beginning to disdain the long-celebrated relief from self-responsibility. And that indeed is my impression.

To show that the "loss of virtue"[26] is in fact not a liberating gain for life, but the root in life of tremendous trouble, I should like now to share several paraphrased fragments from conversations in praxis. I do so without preparatory comment, except for the assurance that this small selection bears on our theme:

At decisive cusps in conversation, one visitor blurts out something like: 'That is out of the question; my pride forbids it.'

Or another, for example, comes across like this: he has thought it often himself, and he won't deny that it is right and convincing. But, to be honest, if he has to admit it, at bottom he just couldn't care less. 'Perhaps,' he adds,

'I am simply too comfortable, you know, or, if you'd rather, too lazy. But who leaps over his own shadow?'

Yet a third visitor relates: he has in fact 'just hung around' in his life, and if he did anything, it was because he enjoyed it: 'Well, just watching TV, playing computer games, and so on; or when friends come over, we go somewhere where there's something going on; girls, of course . . . '—etc.

A female visitor reports: It is truly terrible, she freely admits, but when she gets real ticked off, there is just no stopping her. She loses all composure and 'flips out.' Passed the point of no return, she gets carried completely away, and just doesn't give a shit. 'You really have no idea,' she says as an aside, 'because I'm just chatting about it now very casually; but you should see me. . . .' In sum, she is wholly beside herself. The last time, she took a wedding gift she had received from his parents (who always show up with such outrageously expensive stuff, like the big Chinese vase, which of course had cost a small fortune) and with cold—indeed, ice-cold—calculation, smashed it on the ceramic tiles in the kitchen in front of him. 'I tell you, it was a boom, as if the thing had exploded,' she affirms. And then she pauses a moment before adding: 'I know I'm making his life hell. Of course I am. But how about *me*? How am *I* doing? Is my life so great? Let him stew in the same juices!'

Another woman says: "You know, I hate him sometimes. He basks in his triumphs, lives life to the fullest. Every door opens to him, then he acts so generous, annoying everyone with his appalling composure, which comes so easily to him. Yes, of course, in his situation I too could adopt his laid-back style, everything nice and calm, think first, and rattle off his whole litany: 'but look . . . ,' 'only think . . . ,' 'shouldn't we rather . . . ,' and so on. Nothing breaks his calm. You wouldn't believe how much this posturing gets under my skin! I'll tell you what it is: he is so sure of himself that no one can reach him. You break your teeth on him. I'm going crazy, I tell you!"

Finally, one guest in consultation, facing a life situation that demanded a decision from him, says: 'I'm not even thinking about it! Do you understand? I don't think about it at all!'

Now I would like, with one small, final detour, to say at last what I have been up to with this small nosegay culled from assorted consultations. While reflecting on the loss of virtues, it gradually dawned on me that their loss goes along with that of their opposites, namely, the loss of vices. One might well ask whether one can even speak of virtues if one remains mum about the vices. Are there still any virtues at all, for a consciousness of which there are no longer any vices?

But now a different question arises, whether in fact it is only the *consciousness* of vices that has disappeared, leaving the *actual* vices free and unencumbered? The same might be said of the devil, who is not at all interested in anyone 'believing' in him, or even 'recognizing' him as such. Baudelaire, who may well claim to be a connoisseur in this field, nailed the situation in this gem-like line: "The most beautiful ruse of the devil is that he persuades us that he does not exist."[27]

In order, then, to avoid doing a favor to the Evil or Wicked One, who would prefer to remain unrecognized and unnamed, I therefore allow myself to ask whether the seven capital or deadly sins,[28] even if incognito, are not discoverable in these fragmentary vignettes from Philosophical Praxis; six of those vices being (neatly in the order of their appearance, and beginning with the capital vice *par excellence*):

Superbia—pride, hubris, arrogance[29]
Acedia—sloth, indolence, listlessness
Luxuria—lust, fornication, addiction to pleasure
Ira—wrath, anger, hatred
Invidia—envy,[30] resentful covetousness, vainglory
Aphrosyne—imprudence; rashness; non-judiciousness

Let us calmly venture this thesis: the vices, of which these days[31] there is no longer any talk—of them even less than of the virtues—run wild as long as they are overlooked. In a botanical image: unattended, they take over like weeds.

Must the philosopher in praxis not become a gardener? He makes room for the virtues by pushing back the overgrown undergrowth. However, he does not 'cut down,' nor does he uproot: the implement he uses is called elucidation [*Aufklärung*], a honing of consciousness, a calling out of what would gladly remain concealed. In this way, he draws attention to what has been discreetly overlooked. What the darkness has reserved for itself is brought to light.

NOTES

1. Peter Sloterdijk, *God's Zeal: The battle of the three Monotheisms*. Trans. by Wieland Hoban (Cambridge, UK: Polity, 2009), 134–135. Used with permission. In the original text, the final sentence quoted in the epigram occurs before the others.

2. Achenbach note: This text is based on the lecture given at the opening of the 4th International Conference on Philosophical Practice, which took place in 1998 at the birthplace of Philosophical Praxis, in Bergisch Gladbach, Germany.

3. In this context, I render the important word *Zumutung* as 'instigation.' Colloquially, it might be rendered as a 'bother,' and illustrated not only by what is bothering people and bringing them to praxis but also quite differently by philosophy itself, as when people find philosophical questions to be a bother. Clearly the multivalent

German word applies in different senses to the guest and to the practitioner. For the latter, one might compare a loving imposition and respectful challenge set by a loving parent or a caring coach, a rousing burden that demands growth.

4. Michel de Montaigne, *The Complete Essays of Montaigne*, trans. by Donald M. Frame (Standford, Standford University Press, 1958), 851. The original citation is the German translation by Tietz (Zürich: Diogenes, 1992), vol. 3, 428.

5. The immediate context is noteworthy and contains a qualification, specifically an attribution, that Achenbach suppresses. Putnam writes: "for James, as for Socrates, the central philosophical question is *how to live*" (italics in original). But from the broader context it is clear that Putnam himself endorses the view he here attributes to others. The sequel is also worth quoting: "But for James, as for Socrates and his successors, the opposition between philosophy which is concerned with how to live and philosophy which is concerned with hard technical questions is a false opposition." Hilary Putnam, *Pragmatism: An open question* (Oxford: Blackwell, 1995), 22.

6. Friedrich Nietzsche, *Unfashionable Observations*, Vol. 2 of The Complete Works of Friedrich Nietzsche. Trans. by Richard T. Gray (Stanford, CA: Stanford University Press, 1995), 178, lines 20–21.

7. Paul Valéry, from a speech before the Académie Francaise. Achenbach quotes the speech in German from Josef Pieper's *Über das christliche Menschenbild*, 4th ed. (Freiburg: Johannes Verlag Einsiedeln, 2018), 18. Picard translation from the Achenbach text.

8. Arthur Schopenhauer, *On the Basis of Morality*. Picard translation. The Payne translation of Schopenhauer (not unreasonably) renders *sittlich* and *unsittlich* as "customary" and "non customary." This rendering (unsuitable in the present context) reflects Schopenhauer's rejection of these Germanic terms, in favor of the "scientific" word, *moralisch*, with its Greek and Latin cognates. Yet Payne's own version of the line Achenbach cites is nevertheless worth quoting in full (in its immediate context) for the parenthetical glosses Payne gives on the terms in question. Schopenhauer in Payne: "*sittlich* is a tame and feeble expression and is difficult to distinguish from *sittsam* (decent, demure, bashful), the popular term for which is *zimperlich* (prim and prudish). We must make no concessions to Germanomania." *On the Basis of Morality* (Indianapolis: Hackett, 1995), 131, fn 8. Achenbach cites page 552 of Bd. III of Lütkehaus's edition of Schopenhauer's *Werke in Fünf Bänden*.

9. Norbert Hinske, Welche Eigenschaften braucht der Mensch? Überlegungen zur Tugendethik in *Forschung und Lehre* 7/98, 348–350.

10. Norbert Hinske, "Welche Eigenschaften." The lovely French word '*sottise*,' meaning a failure of intelligence, or a piece of stupidity, occurs in the original German.

11. Levelheadedness—*Besonnenheit*. Here the Greek *sophrosyne* (moderation, self-restraint) is in mind.

12. Hermann Lübbe, "Tugend tut not," in *Die Zeit*, 37 (10.9.93), 44. Picard translation.

13. Amitai Etzioni, "Hart im Sinkflug. Über den Zwang zu Werten in der Gesellschaft," *Spiegel*, 3 (4.3.1996), 348.

14. Allusion to Friedrich Daniel Ernst Schleiermacher, *Uber Religion. Reden an die gebildeten unter ihren Verächtern* [1799]. See *On Religion: Speeches to Its Cultured Despisers*. Trans. and ed. by Richard Crouter (Cambridge University Press, 1988).

15. Norbert Hinske, "Welche Eigenschaften," 348.

16. Arnold Gehlen, *Anthropologische Forschung. Zur Selbstbegegnung und Selbstentdeckung des Menschen* (Reinbek: Rowohlt, 1961), 38: The idea, "to speak with GOETHE," that we have to master the "feat" of our life, becomes understandable only "from that basic fact of the human being: who does not live, but leads his life, out of experiences and achievements, which he himself has created and brought up. . . . " From the essay therein: Vom Wesen der Erfahrung (1936). [Achenbach note.]

17. Last four words added during translation.

18. Johann Wolfgang von Goethe, *Faust*. Trans. by Martin Greenberg (New Have: Yale University Press, 2014), 12. (From the Prologue in Heaven; it is Mephistopholes who is quoted.)

19. Achenbach note. Nicolás Gómez Dávila, "Auf verlorenem Posten," Vienna 1992, p. 267: "To be a reactionary is to realize that humankind is a problem without a human solution." [Picard note:] The original in Spanish is: "Ser reaccionario es comprender que el hombre es un problema sin solución humana" (*Nuevos escolios a un texto implícito*, Tomo II, p. 123). Thanks to Juan Fernando Mejia-Mosquera for assistance with Dávila.

20. The contrast is between the 'proud' (*stolze*) vs. the 'humble' (*demütige*) self-image (or *Menschenbild*); to which the 'undignified' (*würdelose*) is about to be added.

21. Ernst Cassirer, *The Question of Jean-Jacques Rousseau* Trans. by Peter Gay (New York: Columbia University Press, 1954), 75. Again a single passage has been broken up by Achenbach and made into his own sentence. Italics follow Achenbach's German, not Cassiser's English. Also, I have substituted "individual human being" for "individual man" in Gay's translation. It is noteworthy that the "dilemma" that Rousseau is attempting to solve here, according to Cassirer, is that "we can neither trace evil back to God not find its cause in the character of human nature."

22. Peter Sloterdijk, *Critique of Cynical Reason*. Trans. by Michael Eldred (Minneapolis: University of Minnesota Press, 1987), 375.

23. The German is "was euch kaputt macht." It is an allusion to the slogan "Macht kaputt, was euch kaputt macht!" Or: Wreck what wrecks you. There exists (still on YouTube) a famous German song with the title "Macht kaputt was euch kaputt macht," released in 1970 by the proto-punk band Ton Steine Scherben.

24. Friedrich Nietzsche, *The Will to Power*. Trans. by R. Kevin Hill and Michael A. Scarpitti (Penguin, 2017). The German reference is to KSA, XII, *Nachgelassene Fragmente Ende 1886—Frühjahr 1887*, Der Wille zur Wahrheit, Fragment 7 [3].

25. Achenbach alludes here to the section 5 of the Prologue of Friedrich Nietzsche's *Thus Spoke Zarathustra*, part of which appears in Kaufmann's translation as: "we have discovered happiness." I have superadded phrases from the original in Nietzsche to Achenbach's laconic text in order to make clear the implicit content of the allusion, which may be less familiar to English readers. I imitate Kaufman once in translating

erfinden as "discovers" (because it is funnier), but revert to "invents," the more natural translation, in the very next phrase.

26. "Verlust der Tugend"—the German title of an influential 1981 book by Alasdair MacIntyre. See *After Virtue: A Study in Moral Theory*, 3rd ed. (Notre Dame, IN: Notre Dame Press, 2007).

27. Achenbach quotes Baudelaire via Denis de Rougemont, *Der Anteil des Teufels* (Munich: Matthes und Seitz Verlag, 1999), 19. De Rougemont cites Baudelaire, *Les petits poèmes en prose*, XXIX Le Joueur Généreux: "la plus belle des ruses du diable est de vous persuader qu'il n'existe pas!" De Rougement's work also appeared in English translated by Haakon Chevalier, though I have not seen it, and have translated the Baudelaire line directly from the French. See Denis de Rougemont, *The Devil's Share* (New York: Pantheon Books, 1944). Achenbach also makes mention of Leszek Kolakowski, *Gespräche mit dem Teufel. Acht Diskurse über das Böse* (Munich: Serie Piper, 1963), 60 and following.

28. Achenbach mentions "eight classic vices," rather than the seven deadly sins, as they are more popularly known in English. However, he only lists six "Laster," leaving out gluttony (gula) and greed or avarice. The exact number and list varies historically.

29. Max Scheler, Reue und Wiedergeburt, in *Vom Ewigen im Menschen*, 3rd ed. (Berlin: Der neue Geist Verlag, 1933), 21: "Man is hardened and obdurate far more from pride and arrogance than from the fear of punishment born of his concupiscence, and he is all the more so the deeper the guilt sits in him and the more it has become, as it were, a part of his self. It is not confession but first of all self-exposure before himself that is so difficult for the hardened man."

30. Achenbach note: "Max Scheler once very wisely remarked that envy, at its worst and most inwardly poisonous, took the form of 'existential envy.'" See Max Scheler, "Das Ressentiment im Aufbau der Moralen," in *Gesammelte Werke*, III (Bern: Francke-Verlag, 1955). Editorial addendum: An English translation of the German text of 1915 has been made by Lewis B. Coser, on page 9 of which one reads: "The most powerless envy is also the most terrible. Therefore *existential envy* which is directed against the other person's very *nature*, is the strongest source of *ressentiment*. It is as if it whispers continually: 'I can forgive everything, but not that you *are*—that you are *what* you are—that I am not what you are—indeed that I am not you.'" Max Scheler, *Ressentiment.* Translation by Lewis B. Coser (Milwaukee, WI: Marquette University Press, 1994), 9.

31. Written in 1998. In regard to some of the vices listed, the point remains true today. Yet since then there has been considerable focus in the philosophical literature on certain vices at least.

Chapter 10

What Matters? What Is Important in Truth? What Is Crucial in the End?

Guiding Perspectives in Philosophical Praxis

> In the history of philosophy, the general rule holds good: Tell me what you think of Socrates, and I'll tell you what kind of philosophy you have.
>
> —Odo Marquard[1]

I would like to discuss three questions, questions that are similar to the members of a family, so that we could say that they are in a way one question.[2] And then I would like to show to what extent the answer to these three or this one question will result in guiding perspectives for Philosophical Praxis.

Since the wording of these questions is so extraordinarily important, however, I take the liberty of presenting them here first in the original German language: *Worauf kommt es an? Was ist wahrhaft wichtig? Was ist letztlich entscheidend?*

Those familiar with German will appreciate the nuance that is hard to translate fully. If, remaining aware that a complete translation might prove difficult, we nevertheless attempt an English rendition, we might say: *What matters? What is important in truth? What is crucial in the end?* Another translator looking at my title might propose instead a somewhat less formal version: *What matters most? What is really important? What is ultimately essential?*

Let me now venture a first thesis: these questions not only provide guidelines for our practice, but I maintain that they are *original questions* of philosophy—at least of philosophical tradition. Indeed, it is this that qualifies them for Philosophical Praxis and which at the same time also legitimizes our practice as a philosophical endeavor.

Let me elaborate.

Asked for our philosophical forebear, who would we name? Most of us, without a doubt, would point to Socrates, and we would do so rightly. Cicero called Socrates the "father of all philosophy"[3] and said of him that "Socrates was the first who brought down philosophy from the heavens, and established it in cities." He even "introduced it into families," and "obliged" people "to examine into life and morals, and good and evil."[4]

Do we notice here how Cicero, with regard to Socrates, makes an essential distinction [*Entscheidung*] or, if you will, says what matters? "Inquiry into . . . the stars"[5] is not our first concern. Instead, we are to take an interest in what matters to people down here, in the polis.

But the crucial point is this: Socrates, the proto-philosopher, did not get involved himself in the questions and worries that his dear fellow humans had in their rather scattered [*Zerstreuungen*] everyday lives.

No, he is convinced that they, for the most part, lived like somnambulists and fussed over things that are not worth the bother. In a way they lived their lives as though continuously putting on a scene from Shakespeare's *Much Ado About Nothing*. Thus, they did *not* ask themselves what really mattered. Instead, they were preoccupied with lots of minor matters, with bits and bobs, as the Brits say, and they hardly ever seemed to care for what mattered most. That is why Cicero said that Socrates had "obliged" people to confront questions they wanted no part of. Socrates confronted his fellow Athenians with thoughts they either *did not* have or, if they had them, did everything they could to *avoid* and even *escape* them.

What is the result of this?

The result is that, right from the start, philosophy has been *inconvenient*, to some even *annoying*. Others perceive philosophy as a disturbance of the much beloved routine of their everyday lives. *Philosophy*, in other words, *engages in sabotage*. And I should add: philosophy that no longer disturbs and discomforts is not worthy of our attention.

The German philosopher, Robert Spaemann—a companion of Philosophical Praxis from the beginning—stands in the Socratic tradition when he lucidly declares that philosophy does not exist to "provide easy solutions, but to make the tasks and our questions more difficult."[6]

Today, of course, most people rather seem to wish to have the difficulties of their lives simply lifted from them without having to raise a finger. What Socrates knew so well, Spaemann knows too, and so do I.

In light of this fundamental trait of philosophy—let me put it this way: philosophy has a way of respectfully overburdening people, instead of being at their service. Now, I would really love to name all those who have taken that stance, but time does not allow it. So I shall only call on one more key witness of this principle and I happily point out that he was a Southern American—by the way, he has been an insider tip amongst intellectuals in Germany for quite a while now—I am referring, of course, to the late Columbian Nicolás Gómez Dávila. Entirely in the spirit of Philosophical Praxis, this grandiose maverick declared: "The sick soul does not heal itself by suppressing its petty conflicts, but by plunging into noble conflicts."[7] This indeed is what matters: to open a path for people so that they begin to ask themselves what is truly important in the end. For, if we can tempt them to ask themselves these questions in a profound way, then they are already beginning to free themselves from their meaningless, often irrelevant, erratic lives, from their mundane muddling through.

Again: *how* people answer the question regarding what matters is at first not most important. What is important is *that they at all ask themselves that question*. Asking ourselves what matters to us adds weight to our lives—or, as Dávila put it: plunges us into "noble conflicts." For example it is one thing to "want" this or that—it is something else entirely to ask ourselves *what we really, really want*. Then we do not simply "want," but make our "willing" the subject of discussion. That is, our thinking is then no longer at the service of our desires, but our will and desires must submit to our thinking and contemplation. This often leads to a critique of the desire-imperative,[8] which as a rule so many of us hold dear.

Now the following is important—and here I return to our philosophical master, to Socrates. Getting *others* to interrogate themselves in the spirit of those questions is not enough. It is much more important that we ourselves recognize the meaning of these questions and that we live *our own lives* in their light. There is a very important reason for this and it will become clearer to us when we consider the life of Socrates.

But in order to explain it, I must go far afield, which I shall now do.

We first note the following: Socrates notoriously annoyed his fellow men with his apparent ignorance and, usually after an arduous discussion, he ultimately wrung the confession from his interlocutors that they did not know as much as they had thought at first. Socrates' irony was to appear as if it were he who needed teaching. The same Socrates, however, in the decisive moment, that is, during his plea in court, knew exactly what really mattered. And he knew it without wavering or doubting. He knew it as certainly and as adamantly as one can know anything. To what am I referring here? I am referring to Socrates' dying request to the Athenians. He asks them to please him after his death by doing unto his sons as he had done unto the Athenians he had met at the Agora. Do you remember what he asked of the people who sentenced him to death?

> Punish my sons when they grow up, men, paining them as I have pained you, should they appear to you to care for money or anything else more than virtue. And if they are reputed to be something, though being nothing, reproach them as I have you—that they do not care for the things they should and that they think they are something when they are worth nothing.[9]

But not only this! In fact, Socrates "knows" a lot in his apologia before the Athenians, and he is unshakable in his knowledge. But most importantly: he knows it, not on account of having established it argumentatively or dialectically in his all too familiar way; rather, it is plain and simply his "conviction" (*lógo*), for he has it because it "on reflection seems best to me."[10] That is how it always was with him, he tells us.

But: what are such "convictions"? Truly the most fundamental matters—such as . . . well, let us consider the question he asks himself: should one fear death? What is his answer? He has "no adequate knowledge of the underworld,"[11] of Hades, but there is one thing he knows for certain: "to do injustice and to disobey someone better than oneself, whether god or human being, I know is bad and shameful."[12] And if he were accused of having "engaged in the sort of pursuit from which you are now in danger of dying,"[13] he would answer: "You are wrong, sir, if you think that a man who is any good at all should take into account the risk of life or death he should look to this only in his actions, whether what he does is right or wrong, whether he is acting like a good or a bad man."[14]

Ergo? Socrates *knows* what is right and what is exemplary. He also "knows" things, by the way, which most of us today would probably see and judge in a decidedly different way: different times, different customs. Nevertheless, let us indulge ourselves in the pleasure of hearing him out. He "knows," for example, that Achilles was right to "avenge the death of [his] comrade, Patroclus"[15] as it would be a disgrace "to live a coward who did not avenge his friends."[16] And he knows: "wherever a man has taken a position that he believes to be best, or he has been placed by his commander, there he must . . . remain and face danger, without a thought for death or anything else, rather than disgrace."[17]

But I shall here refer to the one sentence, which the German philosopher Franz Vonessen called *the* sentence of Socrates. What sentence? I quote from the *Apology*: "neither will Meletus nor Anytus harm me, [they] would not be able to, for I do not think it is possible for a better man to be harmed by a worse."[18]

This Socrates says to his Athenian judges, telling them that, if they kill him, they will harm, not him, but themselves. A few lines later, Socrates explains his attitude[19]—and this proposition is all about *attitude*!—"Certainly [Meletus] might kill me, or perhaps banish or disenfranchise me, which he and maybe others think to be a great harm, but I do not think so. I think he is doing himself much greater harm doing what he is doing now: attempting to have a man executed unjustly."[20]

It is clear what this conviction—at once profound and all-surpassing—is based upon; namely, that indubitability with which Socrates concludes his conversation with Gorgias: "But among so many arguments this one alone survives refutations and remains steady: that doing what is unjust is more to be guarded against than suffering it, and that it is not *seeming* to be good but *being* good that a man should take care of more than anything else, both in his public and in his private life."[21]

And now I would like to ask: Are we to concede that these convictions are truly *fundamental*, that they are foundational principles, guiding maxims of a sort that express in a most wished-for clarity exactly what mattered most to Socrates, what to him was singularly and finally important; or, what in the last resort was the clincher? Such convictions are not beliefs that one just "has" in the same way that one has a hat, or money, or some random opinion. Recall that for Socrates it is worse to do wrong than to suffer wrong. Now, such a profoundly held belief or conviction, by which we measure and judge the world, bathes one's whole view of the world, of human beings and their place in it, in a totally new and clarifying light. Something literally 'clears up' in the true sense of the word and begins to shine. By contrast, the regular maxim of getting off easily plunges the world into a diffuse twilight.

This then is the thesis that it is not important *what* Socrates said to people; rather, what is important is *who* he himself was. I have asserted this thesis in order to elucidate another, namely: what we say to those who come to visit us in our practice is secondary; far more crucial is what we ourselves have 'let be said' to us.[22]

This raises the question, how does Socrates come to think the way he does? If he claims to *know* what he does, then I must ask: on what basis does he *know*? Does he have any 'reasons' for saying so? Are there 'arguments' that have brought him to his stance? The answer is: *no, no, no!* Instead: he *stands for* it. *He himself* stands up for his belief. The foundation of his philosophical remark to the judges is the philosopher himself, is Socrates himself, as he lives and breathes. It is *his* avowal, his ultimate credo, to have lived by this adage and to want to live by it to the end. This is how he affirms that this attitude is *the only one that is worthy* to live by.

By the way, we must not forget: It was *this* that moved convinced the disciples of Socrates—and what disciples he had, and how very diverse! Not his often outlandish argumentation, his discussions that went back and forth, which would subsequently be called 'dialectic'; and it was certainly not the so-called 'proofs' he composed for his conclusions—all of which we must consign to Socrates' unique 'irony.' To choose one example—let us ask ourselves: Have his arguments for the immortality of the soul ever convinced even one of us? Have any amongst us become believers in immortality because he says and avows, 'Yes, it is so'? I don't think so.

Clearly, something else is at work in Socrates' approach when with a few dialectic ruses he unsettles his fellow Athenians and their opinions, and when, as a result, all of a sudden nothing is any longer as obvious as it was, but everything has been called into doubt and 'hangs in the air.' This is exactly what happens when he declares in court that to fear death "is no other than to think oneself wise when one is not more than to consider yourself wise when you are not," because it means "to think one knows what one does not know. No one knows "whether death is not the greatest blessing for humans, yet people fear it as if they knew it is the greatest of all evils."[23]

As we all know, this is how it usually goes with that old codger and Satyr, as Alcibiades called him. But it is all mere rhetorical mumbo-jumbo and irony—for what is important to Socrates—and his followers were well aware of it—what is truly important to him, is that he not degrade himself before his accusers, whom he sees were in the wrong, by begging for his life.

It is important to me that I get this crucial distinction across and that we do not confuse matters here: no dialectic discussion of death has any bearing whatsoever on the fact that Socrates evidently fears other things more than he fears death. Thus, what *counts* is his fearlessness before the tribunal that sentenced him to death, the calm and serenity with which he explained to his accusers that they harm themselves more than they can harm him; because it is they who burden themselves with injustice, and that *that* is the worst thing someone can do to themselves.

This moreover is what convinced the disciples of Socrates; this is what overwhelmed them and left them sleepless; and this is what finally seduced them to philosophy. For they were certain: on someone so capable of being calm and serene in so grim a situation, philosophy itself must have conferred a fortitude and a vivifying, invigorating certainty, which they were eager to acquire for themselves. *This* and nothing else—such is my thesis—was *the practical impact* of Socrates, the earliest of all practitioner-philosophers at the Agora. This was the lesson his followers understood, in contradistinction, by the way, to most later academics, seated upon their chairs. And indeed, they have still not understood it, which is why I consider this charm offensive necessary now.

After all, many later philosophers saw the affinity between our Socrates and that other person whom was executed as the supposed "King of the Jews," whose prodigious words, speaking of his tormentors and mockers, "Father, forgive them, for they know not what they do."[24] These other words are in fact akin to the attitude of Socrates.

Now, since I have just named him, and drawn him into play, let me add that that carpenter and son of Mary is in many other ways a spiritual twin of those early philosophers whose goal and aspiration was to be truly wise, especially in terms of the question what matters most and what is truly important. Think of when Jesus tells his disciples of the famous Parable of the Rich Fool in order to explain to them that one's life does not consist of the abundance of one's possessions. Is it not remarkably parallel to the convictions of the Athenian and his later disciples? The Parable tells us the story of a rich farmer whose land was highly productive and who therefore thought to himself, 'What shall I do, for I have nowhere to store my crops?' And he said, "I will do this: I will tear down my barns and build larger ones, and there I will store all my grain and my goods. And I will say to my soul, 'Soul, you have ample goods laid up for many years; relax, eat, drink, be merry.'" But God said to him, "Fool! This night your soul will be required of you, and the things you have prepared, whose will they be?' So is the one who lays up treasure for himself and is not rich toward God."[25]

Has it by now become clearer what I am trying to get at?

What about those who were a nuisance to Socrates and a thorn in his side? That is, those who take the decidedly different view that it be would yet better if there were no suffering at all, though in the worst case, they could succeed in enduring it if it were someone else's suffering. Every man for himself, as the English vernacular says.[26] Or those who say that life 'naturally' is foremost about succeeding and having lots of money and power and prestige, and a good reputation and, if fate has so ordained, some glitz and glamour as icing on the cake? Can you seriously believe that 'irrefutable arguments' could persuade anyone who buys into such convictions?

In view of the Lord's parable I just referred to, could you, with good arguments, dissuade anyone from their conviction that they would gladly forego the so-called "richness toward God," if only thereby they get a good life in this world and can enjoy their well-invested wealth and profits? In general—says the pocket-sized Faust—he thinks not at all of lowering his sights here on earth in the vague hope for a heavenly compensation one day. With this trick, he reckons, priests have long enough pulled the wool over poor souls' faces.

Let those who wish to, lose themselves in such argumentation! In the end, when nothing is accomplished, the point will have to be accepted: what matters most is entirely different. Namely, what matters is how *he himself* stands in relation to these questions. Nor will it help to quote cunning or wise sentences from the works of philosophy to make an impression—Schopenhauer summed this up in a great metaphor: "One cannot nourish others with undigested waste, but only with the milk that has secreted itself from one's own blood."[27]

Let me give you an example. Imagine someone comes to you seeking for help, eaten up by an addiction for 'success.' This is someone who has always tried to please everybody and who, to gain their approval, like a camel, has threaded the eye of every needle—not indeed in order to earn his way into heaven, but in order to get that position or job he is aiming for. Thus, imagine a person who has never found the courage to show backbone, who has never learned to stand upright, who would not even know what it means to stand by his word. This is someone who considers trustworthiness obsolete and a cliché, and to whom integrity is but an antiquated ideology. This is someone who has always only tried to get by, to belong by any means necessary, not to get booted out, not to be left behind. Imagine that someone like that—and you know how likely it is to meet a human being of that type—comes to us, to our praxis; exhausted, burned out, disappointed, but still admiring those who have 'made it,' who have 'arrived' at the top, the successful people, the few in the spotlight, the much-sought-after, the envied, the happy—as your guest calls them.

Well? What would you do? What would you tell your guest?

I think this much is certain: none of you who leer at success and at continuous and instant gratification, none of you who fear that your guest could leave you or could bear a grudge against you would be able to pull anyone out of this trap. Quite the opposite. Ideally our imagined guest would find someone who knows the temptations this person has fallen prey to, but who has been able to pass through those temptations thoughtfully[28] and consciously, thus you should be someone who has freed yourself from these temptations and left them behind like a childhood illness that we must suffer through in order to be immune to it for the rest of our lives.

So what would I do, and what say to him?—Well, I would maybe venture a little attack that might put my guest to the test, just to ascertain whether he has any sense of humor, that is, whether he can be seduced into laughing at himself, or at least to crack a smile; which would at least be a start. And provided I had any hope that he might be able to amuse himself for once, I would, for this purpose, recite to him a poem—*nota bene*: a philosophically highly educational poem. Written by Robert Gernhardt, its title is "Always" (*Immer*), and it is so entertaining that I cannot withhold it from you all:

> Always someone swifter than you
> You crawl
> He walks
> You walk
> He runs
> You run
> He flies:

There's always someone yet swifter than you.
Always someone more gifted than you
You read
He learns
You learn
He seeks
You seek
He finds out:
There's always someone yet more gifted than you.
Always someone more famous than you
You're in the papers
He's in the encyclopedia
You're in the encyclopedia
He's in the legends
You're in the legends
He's a monument:
There's always someone yet more famous than you.
Always someone richer than you
Your book is reviewed
His is being read
Your book is being read
His is devoured
Yours is treasured
His is being bought:
There's always someone yet richer than you.
Always someone more popular than you
You are praised
He is loved
You are honored
He is adored
They lie at your feet
They carry him on their shoulders
There's always someone yet more popular than you.
Always someone better than you
You are ailing
He languishes
You die
He passes
You are judged
He is redeemed
There's always someone yet better than you
Always
Always
Always.[29]

What a poem! But now the rider that is due here: in this choice to recite, everything hinges on whether I myself have already actually learned what this poem has to teach us, and whether our imaginary guest convincingly notices and can witness this learning in me.

Let me summarize, in conclusion of what has been said so far. Those who come to us philosophical practitioners are not looking for philosophical instruction. They are looking instead for someone who has become judicious and philosophically thoughtful [*nachdenklich*]. In the sense of Kierkegaard, we could borrow an uncommon expression and say that they seek a philosophically up-built person.[30]

Now, of course, I know that in all this I have not said very much so far, but I think that I have said something that is truly important to us in Praxis, or such is my *conviction*. Let me put it this way. As is widely known, research on therapy has found time and time again that, in terms of the effectiveness of therapy, what matters is not the type of therapeutic theory that is being applied, but the therapist, which is to say: what kind of human being the therapist is. What then usually follows these findings by way of explanation fits perfectly the context of psychotherapies: there follows talk of 'empathy' and sensitivity, of a friendly commitment to understanding, etc. We already know this often-recited litany which bears little to no content . . .

Nevertheless, in one respect—and by no means an inessential respect—we can say the same thing about Philosophical Praxis. What matters most is not *which philosophies* play a role in the background of the practitioner's thinking, but rather, the *philosopher him or herself*, in other words, the *character* of the person the guest meets. Thus the lead question of Philosophical Praxis is no longer, 'What is philosophy?' but rather, 'Who is a philosopher?' As philosopher in praxis, I do not 'represent' any specific philosophy, am not a 'spokesperson' of any philosophical direction, trend or school. Instead, my acquaintance with philosophy, and with those philosophers who have become standard bearers for me and my own spurs to philosophy, must have in some measure become my very flesh. *The philosopher*, whom the guest *of the Philosophical Praxis* hopes to meet, *is philosophy as institution in a specific case*: he is philosophy 'incarnated'—to employ terminology that was thought up by[31] and belongs to theology.

But now, in conclusion—partly as an expression of respect for this 'summit meeting' of philosophical practitioners from all over the world[32]—I would like to do something that I have always strictly avoided until now. Up to now it has been said that I have always and most scrupulously shunned the term 'method,' just as Paul Feyerabend also avoided it. But just this once I shall be unfaithful to myself and say a few words as to 'how' precisely we may tempt our guest to—perhaps even seduce them into—exposing themselves to questions that, as that guest might say, are 'alien' to them.

For this purpose, I consider a thought that I recently found in a lecture from 1971 by Georg Picht, an important German philosopher and student of Heidegger. It is a very plain yet penetrating thought: "A person is educated [*gebildet*] if they understand what they themselves say."[33]

Well, do we understand what this sentence is saying to us? It brings to expression the deep insight that everything we say or think, that everything we are 'aware' of, finds its ground in an infinite profundity and fullness that is unconscious, 'un-thought-of' and not understood. One could speak of unconscious spirit, of misconceived *logos*, or even of uncognized concepts. Do you see what I am driving at? Every single word that we speak, every term has its own history, its own implications and carries with it an abundance of thoughts thanks to which the word has gained its meaning and form. Every single one of our judgments is made possible by a long history that could perhaps be traced all the way back to prehistoric times—and even everyday chatter that concerns itself with what is *en vogue* or *à la mode*, even such chitchat we are able to understand only if we comprehend how a phrase has come to be, or perhaps had to come to be, and what has made it possible or popular.

I am not afraid to cite a very trivial example: who can understand how people have come to call something 'cool'? (Amongst German youths this phrase was extremely popular, and it was on almost every tongue.) Do we trust ourselves to explain this habit in such a way that our interlocutor understands the 'worldview' to which the usage belongs and that is represented by it? Do they see how this particular worldview also shapes the judgments that decide what matters most, what is truly important and what is ultimately essential? For, clearing this up *is* the part played by Philosophical Praxis; it is emphatically enlightenment [*Aufklärung*].

I hope to have cleared this up with these intimations as to what Picht meant by his extraordinarily clever sentence when he said that only the person who understands what they themselves say is educated. For it is true: in every sentence we utter there is contained infinitely many other propositions, thoughts, judgments, assessments, perspectives, etc., which for the most part lie concealed like unclaimed treasures. The task of the philosophical practitioner is to raise and retrieve them.

A sublime, highly ambitious goal is thus set for Philosophical Praxis; one in which the Socratic heritage is both embraced but also modified. Let me summarize my thoughts as follows: Philosophical Praxis is all about getting people to understand what they are themselves *saying*. This takes place, however, only when they begin an acquaintance with the spirit revealing itself 'behind' (or 'in') their sentences, initially veiled there. If we succeed in bringing that spirit to light, thereby exposing it to the scrutiny of our guests, they will face directly what has decided for them what most matters, what is important in truth, and what in the end is crucial. Only then can the revision begin.

And us?

We shall accompany and support our guest on their path and we shall do so according to what has become our own measure by which we live. Often what we require the most here is courage, the courage to trust our own convictions. For my part, I am convinced: the discouraged do not reach far, and certainly they cannot reach guests who turns to them.

NOTES

1. Odo Marquard, *Der Einzelne. Vorlesungen zur Existenzphilosophie* (Stuttgart: Reclam, 2013), 149. Picard translation. Used with permission.

2. Keynote speech at the opening of the 15th International Colloquium on Philosophical Practice in Mexico City on June 25, 2018. The lecture was delivered in English, in a very capable translation by Johannes Litger, which was used (with permission) as an excellent starting-point for the present version, which contains my own revisions (many merely cosmetic). It is perhaps worth mentioning that it was at this conference (specifically, at the workshop Achenbach offered in the days before the conference itself) that the author and the translator of this book first met.

3. Cicero, *The Nature of the Gods*, XXXIV. *Cicero's Tusculan Disputations: Also Treatises on the Nature of the Gods, and On the Commonwealth.* Trans. by C. D. Yonge (New York: Harper & Brothers, 1877). Accessed July 2, 2023, at https://www.gutenberg.org/files/14988/14988-h/14988-h.htm.

4. Cicero, *Tusculanae disputationes*, 5, IV. Achenbach quotes a German translation, *Gespräche in Tuskulum*. Here he has broken apart a single passage into short phrases. The English version in the Mexico City keynote was apparently the work of the original translator, as no references were provided. I have sought instead to insert existing English translations of cited classical sources whenever possible. Here I have again quoted (slightly altered) from *Cicero's Tusculan Disputations,* trans. by C. D. Yonge (New York: Harper & Brothers, 1877).

5. Cicero, *Tusculan Disputations*, 5, IV. Yonge translation.

6. Robert Spaemann. "It cannot be the business of philosophy to make the solutions easier, but the problems harder." (Literal translation by Picard.) Die zwei Grundbegriffe der Moral, in *Grenzen: Zur ethischen Dimension des Handelns* (Stuttgart: Klett-Cotta, 2001), 78. I have left the English translation of the quotation as it was.

7. Achenbach cites Gómez Dávila in a German translation: Nicolás Gómez Dávila, *Einsamkeiten*, (Wien: Karolinger, 1987), 111. Günther R Siegl translation. The English translation used here is due to Dr. Juan Fernando Mejia-Mosquera. The original Spanish reads: "El alma enferma no se sana suprimiendo sus conflictos mezquinos, sino arrojándose entre conflictos nobles." The quoted line appears on page 161 of the second volume of *Escollos a un texto implícito* (Bogotá, Instituto Colombiano

de Cultura, 1977). This work has been translated into English by Roberto Pinzón as *Scholia To An Implicit Text*. Bilingual Selected Edition. (Benjamin Villegas Editores, 2013). Special thanks to Juan Fernando Mejia-Mosquera for his invaluable assistance on Gómez Dávila.

8. Desire-imperative—*Wunschprinzip*. Allusion to Hans Jonas.

9. Plato, Apology, 41e. Trans. by Mark Kremer (Newbury, MA: Focus Publishing/R. Pullins, 2006), 28.

10. Plato, Crito, 46b. Trans. by G. M. A. Grube in *Collected Works* (Indianapolis/Cambridge: Hackett, 1997), 37–48. "I am the kind of man who listens to nothing within me but the argument that on reflection seems best to me."

11. Plato, Apology, 29b. Trans. by G. M. A. Grube. In Plato, *Collected Works*, 17–36. Note that here I switch to a Grube translation of Plato's *Apology*. Here and below I select the translation that best suites the context in Achenbach.

12. Plato, *Apology*, 29b. Kremer translation.

13. Plato, *Apology*, 28b. Kremer translation.

14. Plato, *Apology*, 28b. This is Grube.

15. Plato, *Apology*, 28c. Grube.

16. Plato, *Apology*, 28c. Grube.

17. Plato, *Apology*, 29a. Grube

18. Plato, *Apology*, 30c–d. Kremer translation.

19. Attitude—*Haltung*.

20. Plato, *Apology*, 30d. Grube.

21. Plato, Gorgias, 527b. Trans. by Donald J. Zeyl in *Collected Works* (Indianapolis/Cambridge: Hackett, 1997), 791–869.

22. There is an allusion is to *Eingelassenheit*; see chapter 4.

23. Plato, *Apology*, 29a. Minor modification is made to this Grube translation.

24. Luke 23:34. King James Version.

25. Luke 12:13–21. I have let the close paraphrase stand as it appeared in the received Litger English translation.

26. This is somewhat loosely translated, but I leave it as is. The German "vernacular" Achenbach quotes is "Jeder ist sich selbst der Nächste" (Everyone is his own neighbor.)

27. Arthur Schopenhauer, On learning and the learned, Ch. 21, §247 in *Parerga and Paralipomena: Short Philosophical Essays*, 2. Trans. by Del Caro and Janaway (CUP, 2015), 511 (marginal pagination).

28. Thoughtfully—*nachdenklich*.

29. Robert Gernhardt, Immer. Original appeared in *Frankfurter Allgemeine Zeitung*, 53. (3.3.2007), 44. Also in *Gesammelte Gedichte, 1954–2006* (Frankfurt am Main: S. Fischer Verlag, 2008). The English translation is by Johannes Litger, slightly adapted by Picard.

30. Achenbach note: I speak here of an 'up-built' philosopher, in allusion to Kierkegaard's *Edifying Discourses*, which in English translation are called *Upbuilding Discourses*. See for instance Søren Kierkegaard, *Upbuilding Discourses in Various Spirits*. Ed. and trans. Howard V. Hong and Edna H. Hong (Princeton, NJ: Princeton University Press, 1993).

31. Thought up by—*vorgedacht*. Literally, pre-thought.

32. 'Summit Meeting' because it took place in Mexico City, which is high above sea level.

33. Georg Picht, Enzyklopädie und Bildung, in *Merkur* 25 (279), 1971, 633. Original: "Gebildet ist ein Mensch, wenn er das versteht, was er selber sagt."

Chapter 11

Character and Destiny

Philosophical Praxis Has Much to Learn from Schopenhauer

> It is not enough simply to will something, or even to be able to do it; a human being must also *know* what he is willing, and *know* what he can do: only then does he begin to show character, and only then can he achieve anything properly.
>
> —Arthur Schopenhauer[1]

Those who in moments of repose have indulged themselves in a deep reading of Schopenhauer (and I have always had the impression that reading Schopenhauer was precisely an 'indulgence'); those who, thanks to a concomitant interest in Philosophical Praxis, have allowed this perusal to open singular new vistas, know very well that any philosophy that is obliged to prove itself in practice can expect from this philosopher not only reinforcement and backing, but equally to be thrown by him into doubt.[2]

In this context, the doubts that may arise for philosophical practitioners from Schopenhauer's peppery, polemical settling of accounts with "university philosophy" have the very least role to play. That noted, it should be lost on no one that his celebrated critique of university-chair philosophy hits Philosophical Praxis even harder, due to its particular argumentation. For, as is well known, he accused the former, firstly, of being beholden to non-philosophical interests,[3] even serving them compliantly; but, above all, also of being in the pay of clients who well knew why they underwrote the intellectual enterprises of the philosophers. Schopenhauer's worry was that Truth would degenerate into a "whore"[4] as soon as venerable philosophy was "degraded to a way of earning one's bread."[5] Since, as the preface to the second edition of his main work says, "the rule has always applied, 'Whose bread I eat, his song I sing,' earning money with philosophy was for the ancients the characteristic mark of the sophist."[6]

And really it was Schopenhauer's pathos, which he himself considered an indispensable condition without which Truth would not grant access, that "the matter itself [*die Sache selbst*] must also be pursued for itself. Otherwise it cannot succeed. For foresight is everywhere a threat to insight."[7]

There is a yet weightier misgiving that Schopenhauer casts in the path of our self-examination. This was so important to him that he mentioned it in the already quoted 1844 Preface to the second edition of *The World as Will and Representation,* in the beginning of which he writes: "this is just the curse of this world of misery and need: everything must serve and slave for them."[8] And he goes on: "the world is not built to permit any noble or sublime striving—such as a striving towards light or truth—to thrive unchecked or to exist for its own sake."[9]

It is the extreme precaution of his assessment of the world and its need for truth that drove Schopenhauer to advise constant resignation: "nobody who seriously takes on and pursues a problem . . . can count on the sympathy of his contemporaries."[10]

So let me now say this: if Schopenhauer is right; if philosophy, in order not to debilitate itself, is required to remain an outsider in this world, it would need to render itself unassailably distant from what makes the world go round, so as not to sell out and become common. At first glance, this requirement would appear extremely hard to reconcile with the project of Philosophical Praxis, namely to open the doors of philosophy to everyone, and to bar in advance no concern brought to it or left at its step. At any rate, it can not be lost on anyone that philosophy, as Philosophical Praxis, mixes it up with the world, does not shy away from the public, and by all means engages in contemporary debates, and in the public sphere with the questions of the day. It is undoubtedly less ascetic, less withdrawn from the world than Schopenhauer would have insisted of it in the interest of an uncontaminated allegiance to truth.

So much for these first misgivings that philosophical practitioners will meet in the encounter with the philosophy of Schopenhauer—questions that, once raised, demand a thorough-going response and resolution if the mission of Philosophical Praxis is to be undertaken without naiveté.

On the other hand, it will not have eluded anyone conversant with Schopenhauer's philosophy that in his work, as in that of few others, we come across on almost every page groundbreaking deliberations that strengthen us and provide invaluable intellectual bolstering of our work.

For instance—in direct connection with the misgivings just cited from the start of his 1844 Preface—take Schopenhauer's account of the only sort of philosophizing in any position to prove helpful to others. I am keen to insert this quotation, as it exactly describes what can only be regarded as an indispensable condition of any philosophizing orienting itself in conversation:

> But it is a strange fact about philosophical meditations that only what someone has thought through and investigated for himself can later be of use to someone else; not what was intended for others from the start. The former has the recognizable character of complete honesty, because people are not trying to fool themselves or offer themselves empty shells; this banishes all sophistication and word-mongering.[11]

That all 'word-mongering' be banished is indeed of utmost importance in Philosophical Praxis, for what convinces others is never what *can* be thought, nor what once *was* thought by somebody else; but only, if at all, what *is being* thought, and that the one thinking the thought is also able to vouch for it. Reminders to keep to this principle of Philosophical Praxis continually suggest themselves whenever Schopenhauer comes up. For, from what other philosopher is to be gleaned such a bounty of unfailingly useful quotables that tend to confer a graceful, dignified polish upon the conversations held in Praxis? Let me quickly adduce an example from a recent conversation, in the course of which it became necessary to work towards the acceptance of age-related changes in life. To that end, I had recourse to a passage—from a literary perspective, among the most stunning—drawn from Schopenhauer's "Aphorisms on the wisdom of life," namely from its final part, which deals with "The Difference Stages of Life."

> If the character of the first half of life is an unsatisfied longing for happiness, that of the second is dread of misfortune. For, with the second half, the recognition has more or less occurred that all happiness is chimerical, whereas suffering is real. Now the more sensible characters at least will strive rather for mere freedom from pain and an undisturbed state than for pleasure. When the door bell rang during the years of my youth, I was happy, since I thought that now it was coming. But in later years my feeling on the same occasion rather resembled alarm: I thought, 'Here it comes.'[12]

"There are," he goes on, "two contradictory *feelings* towards the human world":[13]

> during one's youth, one often has the feeling of being *abandoned* by the world; in later years, one often has the feeling of having *escaped* from it. The former, an unpleasant one, rests on the lack of acquaintance with the world, the latter, a pleasant one, on being acquainted with it.—As a result, the second half of life contains, like the second half of a musical period, less striving, but more peace than the first.[14]

And yet, those who in conversation would venture such a gem of Schopenhauerian circumspection—as I in this case did—must very strictly interrogate themselves as to whether in fact their own life has attained a perspective that discloses the stages of life *as* they are here represented. For only then should one dare to borrow these words from the old sage. In that case, of course, nothing speaks against such borrowing: it does not detract from our own warrant that someone else, with such fathomless humor, knew how to frame the conviction in a manner worthy of being handed down.

With all that has been said so far, I have merely intended by way of introduction to highlight certain misgivings to be found at every turn in Schopenhauer's writings that complicate our work in Philosophical Praxis in the most appropriate and desirable manner; and also to point to the abundance of hints and helps that can support us in innumerable ways in conversations with our visitors—presuming once more that have grown into them, and that our progress in life validates what would otherwise degenerate to mere "word-mongering."

My thesis is formulated in the subtitle I have given to this chapter: Philosophical Praxis has much to learn from Schopenhauer. I can now start to unpack it, and to corroborate it by recalling some pertinent passages from his principal work, the two-volume *The World as Will and Representation*. To that end, we shall be interested above all in the fourth and final Book of Volume One, the subject of which (as Schopenhauer writes at its opening), "one would call, to express things in the usual terms, practical philosophy."[15] Among other things, this fourth Book also develops in the clearest terms what I have taken for my title: the relationship between 'Character and Destiny.' But before getting to that, I would like to draw your attention to something that, before all else, philosophical practitioners have very good reason to bear in mind.

What I have in mind is a striking feature of the first Book of Volume One. "To express things in the usual terms," one could call it *epistemology*. It offers[16] a "First Consideration" of "The World as Representation," discussing both "Representation as Subject to the Proposition of the Sufficient Ground" and "The Object of Experience and Science." Nevertheless, Schopenhauer concludes this first Book not in epistemology, but with a pointed engagement with the *practical philosophy* of reason of the Stoics.

Now this engagement with the Stoics' ideal life conduct (later prosecuted further in more exacting terms in "On the Practical Use of Reason and Stoicism," the 16th chapter of Volume Two) reveals with utmost clarity its contrast to the outline of Schopenhauer's own practical philosophy. As such, it provides an almost indispensable backdrop against which Schopenhauer's unique philosophical legacy stands forth. For this reason, I will briefly discuss Schopenhauer's idiosyncratic critique of the Stoa, which I do with particular pleasure, since a frequently encountered assumption[17] is that Philosophical Praxis has taken upon itself the task of rehabilitating Reason as a corrective authority for life-orientation, and life-guidance, expecting from it the power and virtue that overcomes all suffering and unhappiness.

> The *Stoic sage* presents in an ideal form the most complete development of *practical reason* in the true and authentic sense of the word, the highest peak a human being can attain using only reason, where the distinction between humans and animals shows itself most clearly. For originally and essentially Stoic ethics is not a doctrine of virtue at all, but simply a guide for rational living: its end and aim is the achievement of happiness through spiritual repose, and virtuous conduct is included only as it were accidentally, as *a means rather than an end.*[18]

What Schopenhauer goes on to cite (the consequences for the Stoics of this "peak") is readily recognizable to us in the compendium of *therapeutic* recommendations that remain in vogue today. I quote a few of them, as formulated by Schopenhauer, because it is Schopenhauer we are concerned with, rather than the Stoics:

> The Stoic insight was that privation and suffering do not follow immediately and necessarily from not-having. . . . It followed from this that all happiness depends on the proportion between what we claim and what we receive. . . . In keeping with the end and spirit of the Stoics, *Epictetus* begins with one idea and constantly keeps returning to it as the core of his wisdom. The idea is this: we should ponder very carefully indeed and distinguish between what depends on us and what does not. If we take no account at all of the latter, we can be sure to remain free from all pain, suffering and anxiety.[19]

To the founder of Stoicism, Zeno of Citium, Schopenhauer also attributes the imperative, which enjoys widespread familiarity today: namely, that "to attain the highest good, i.e., blessedness through spiritual repose, one must live in harmony with oneself."[20] He proceeds to wrap up his presentation of Stoic practical philosophy with the following appreciation:

> Taken as a whole, Stoic ethics is in fact a very valuable and estimable attempt to adapt that great privilege, reason, to an important and salutary [*heilbringenden*] end, namely that of raising us above the suffering and pain that every life encounters. . . . And this allows us to participate to the highest degree in that dignity which attaches to us as rational beings distinct from animals (in fact there is no other sense in which we can talk of dignity).[21]

So much, then, for Schopenhauer's agreement with the Stoa, which many contemporary practitioners will no doubt be eager to quote, those at least who feign to situate Philosophical Praxis in the tradition of Hellenistic life instruction and infer, from such proximity, that the efforts they undertake intending to help may rightly be called *philosophical*. Yet Schopenhauer does not allow the Stoic ambition to stand without opposition. On the contrary, to me at least, the opposition he mounts seems far more momentous than the generous partial approval he previously voiced:

> It is rather completely contradictory to want to live without suffering, a contradiction also contained in the common expression 'a blessed life' [*seliges Leben*]. . . . This contradiction is also revealed in the ethics of pure reason itself, since the Stoics are forced to include in their guide for a blessed life . . . a recommendation for suicide in the case of excessive and incurable [*unheilbar*] bodily suffering incapable of being philosophized away with principles and inferences, just as oriental despots include a fine vial of poison among their splendid jewels and utensils. In this case, bliss, the only purpose of life, has been thwarted and suffering can now only be evaded through death, which should itself be undertaken with indifference, like any other course of medication.[22]

So this is Schopenhauer's first objection, which today displays an "untimely" sort of explosiveness, since the abolition of suffering seems to be one of the last self-evident truths. Indeed, it is on the basis of this self-evidence that one deems oneself entitled to decide what is to be done when people complain and look for ways to throw off the burdens that oppress them.

But Schopenhauer's second objection, it seems to me, is yet more momentous: it is directed against the very image of the ideal Stoic sage—and it is almost as if one could already hear Zarathustra's mockery: "But he who is the wisest amongst you, he also is only a discord and hybrid of plant and of ghost. But do I bid you become ghosts or plants?"[23]

Schopenhauer thus:

> The inner contradiction, mentioned above, that affects Stoic ethics even in its basic idea, can also be discerned in the fact that the Stoics were never able to present their ideal, the Stoic sage, as a living being with inner poetic truth: he remains stiff and wooden, a mannequin that no one can engage with and who does not himself know what to do with his own wisdom. His perfect composure, peace and bliss really contradict the essence of humanity, so that we are unable to form any intuitive representation of him.[24]

Then Schopenhauer, concluding the first book with this, adds a decisive hint by contrasting the wooden mannequin of Hellenistic-Stoic wisdom with the "Christian saviour, that splendid figure, full of depths of life, of the greatest poetic truth and highest significance, but who, with perfect virtue, holiness and sublimity, nevertheless stands before us in a state of the utmost suffering."[25]

There—in that last half-sentence—is laid bare what Schopenhauer regarded as the deepest defect in the Stoic program of averting suffering. The Stoics indeed knew that:

> nobody would get upset about some misfortune, some aggravation and lose his temper if reason constantly reminded him what the human being really is: a creature in the greatest need of help, subject to countless misfortunes both small and large, every day and every hour, 'the most miserable creature,' and who must therefore live in constant worry and fear.[26]

And indeed they probably also correctly saw what was called an ultimate resort, Epictetus' "endure and forego,"[27] and that "what the application of reason to practical matters achieves in the first instance is [to reunify] what is one-sided and fragmentary in mere perceptual cognizance [and secondly to use] the contrariety afforded by the latter as mutual correctives; thereby [obtaining] the objective correct result."[28]

And yet, as Schopenhauer adds in a later place, if we seek in the writings of the Stoics "the ultimate reason for the imperturbable equanimity that is continually demanded of us, we find nothing other than the cognition that the way of the world is completely independent of our will and consequently that the troubles we encounter are unavoidable."[29]

This comes down to nothing more than the advice that we ought so to govern our desires and demands that they no longer clash with the way of the world. Expect no more from the world than it can deliver. What it deprives you of, forego. What it exacts from you, endure. Expect from yourself only what is entirely under your power.

It was with these principles that the Stoics first started down the therapy path. For in supposing—again I quote Schopenhauer—that "our suffering always springs from a mismatch between our wishes and the way of the world," they quite logically concluded that "one of these must be changed and made to fit the other." And, "since the way of things is not under our power . . . we must adapt our willing and wishing to the way of things: because the will alone is under our power."[30]

To say it loose and carefree: the suffering of people was here for the first time construed as an invitation and guidance on how to *work on themselves*. The sufferers are presented an object to overhaul: namely, their very selves. On the whole, there is nothing to achieve—and yet there is so much to do: one commences to grapple with oneself. And—what is the result? "When we look closely and seriously," Schopenhauer sums up, we recognize in Stoic *ataraxia* "a mere hardening and insensibility to the blows of fate."[31]

The question arises: What is *missing from this picture*? Only by asking this question, it seems to me, can we entice the philosopher Schopenhauer to voice his protest against this way of working off suffering, thereby also his opposition to today's therapeutic endeavor to focus man upon himself, or: to distract himself with himself.

Schopenhauer's answer: Stoic serenity remains utterly bereft of the "metaphysical tendency."[32] Put differently, the meagerness of life had not yet become a scandal to them, so they fell short of the highest potentiality for human being. That, however, is not to bear evils bravely, nor to withstand one's affects, nor even to care for the self; for that—seen from an appropriate distance—is far too small a concern, all too limited in its scope, if not actually blinkered. Rather, Schopenhauer regarded this *metaphysical need* as the very best and most worthy, the most venerable and the deepest human possibility, given this world such as it is.

And so Schopenhauer succeeded chapter 16 of Volume Two, devoted to Stoicism and its practice of reason, with the seventeenth chapter, which decidedly surpasses anything that even occurred to the practically engaged Stoics as a question. Its title is: "On Humanity's Metaphysical Need." He regards it as a mark of greatness that existence in general has become a question and a riddle for a person, even a completely incomprehensible quandary: "a human being is, accordingly, an *animal metaphysicum*."[33]

> If there is anything in the world to be desired, so much so that even crude and dull brains, in moments of lucidity, value it more highly than silver and gold, then it is that a beam of light should fall on the obscurity of our being and offer us some sort of key to this perplexing existence in which nothing is clear except its misery and its nothingness.[34]

Schopenhauer here offers what is potentially a radical repudiation of all spiritual exercises, of all determination to work upon oneself—for even the dull and vulgar rabble, as he says, are sensitive to a problem that the Stoic and therapeutic determination to oblige the suffering to work upon themselves is oblivious to or (to use a common phrase) draws a blank on. Determination to practice thus falls under suspicion of defrauding humanity of all that is best for it: for therapeutic 'soul-work' turns out to be anti-metaphysical.

I want to be clear. What makes Schopenhauer's admonition indispensable for the practitioner philosopher is his objection to a reason-based praxis that is able to prove itself only as effort toward a smart, well-arranged reasonableness in the conduct of life. For to believe that people will be helped by getting rid of their worries, by lifting the burdens that oppress them, by making easy what is difficult for them, or perhaps by taking it lightly—to believe all that is to enter an unholy alliance with superficiality, which today has nothing better to offer than the recommendation to kindly divert oneself and to put questions for which there is no solution out of mind.

The questions brought by those who come to practice, however, are by no means (or in any case not only), 'What should I do?' or 'What is to be done with me?' Rather, to venture an impossibly short formula, they are: 'Yes, that's it. But, what is that? How can I understand this? How is this possible? How can this be?' These are questions that find no ready answer by being transmuted into directives how to act or into advice to do this or that; and they are not to be straightened out by a decision to change oneself. They are questions that deserve a thorough-going philosophical discussion, thoughtful awareness, and much pondering; to be exact, they require more philosophical questions, more decisive questions, perhaps more advanced questions. Only then will the *seriousness* that is due to them be recognized. This indeed, in my impression, is what matters most. And the importance of Schopenhauer is to remind us of it.

This prepares the way for what I would like to put before you in the remainder, namely some annotated excerpts from the Fourth Book (of Volume One) of *The World as Will and Representation*. To summarize in the briefest terms possible, which can only be provided by careless use of terms, here in advance are the subjects that Schopenhauer treats in the four Books making up that volume: the First Book develops epistemology, the Second natural philosophy, the Third aesthetics, while the Fourth is devoted, as already mentioned, to "practical philosophy"; and of this latter some mention shall now be made.

And yet I recognize that, even among philosophers, Schopenhauer's main work is more legend than secure acquisition made familiar by thorough study; so just in case I will quote the opening sentences of his extraordinary Fourth Book, which I think ought to interest philosophical practitioners going forward:

> The final part of our discussion declares that it will be the most serious, since it deals with human actions, which are of direct concern to everyone; no one is unfamiliar with or indifferent to such a topic. In fact, it is so natural for people to relate everything to action that they will always consider that part of any systematic discussion which concerns deeds to be the culmination of the whole work, at least to the extent that it is of interest to them, and will accordingly pay serious attention to this part, if to no other.[35]

There follows the turn of phrase quoted at the beginning, that this final Book—"according to the usual way of expressing oneself"—is about "practical philosophy." But immediately thereafter there follows a qualification that, at first sight, seems to run counter to all efforts towards Philosophical Praxis:

> In my opinion, philosophy is always theoretical, since what is essential to it is that it treats and investigates its subject-matter (whatever that may be) in a purely contemplative manner, describing without prescribing. On the other hand, for it to be practical, guide action, shape character—these are longstanding demands, and mature insight should encourage us to give them up once and for all. Because here, where the worth or worthlessness of an existence, where salvation or damnation is in question, the issue cannot be resolved with dead concepts, but only by the innermost essence of the man himself, the daemon that leads him and has not chosen him but rather has been chosen by him (as Plato would have it), or his intelligible character (as Kant says).[36]

But this "intelligible character" philosophy, in so far as it wants to become active practically, is utterly powerless to reshape or transform. For:

> Virtue is as little taught as genius: indeed, concepts are just as barren for it as they are for art, and useful for both only as tools. It would be just as absurd to expect our systems of morals and ethics to inspire virtuous, noble and holy men as it would be to think that our aesthetics could create poets painters and musicians.[37]

And now the caveat which, in my opinion, is at the same time also to be read as a work order for Philosophical Praxis:

> Philosophy can never do more than to interpret and explain what is present, to bring the essence of the world—that essence which speaks intelligibly to everyone *in concreto*, which is to say as *feeling—to the clear and abstract cognition of reason, and to do so in every possible respect and from every point of view*.[38]

What follows from this? "In this ethical [Fourth] Book no prescriptions, no doctrine of duties is to be expected."[39] And "there will be no talk of an '*unconditioned ought*.' . . . We will not talk about 'oughts' at all: that is how you talk to children and to nations still in their infancy, not to those who have acquired all the culture [*Bildung*] of a mature age."[40] And summarizing: "Our philosophical efforts can extend only to an interpretation and explanation of human action and the innermost essence and content of the very different and even conflicting maxims which are its living expression."[41]

Schopenhauer's resolute rejection of all well-meaning determination to change the world, and of all intentions to improve loved ones, is exceptionally dear to me, and concerns no one more than the philosophical practitioner, who will likely be very tempted to act out such practical ambitions *in praxis upon others*.

However, against this ambition to change people for their own good we need continual warning—and Schopenhauer has sounded his. The rationale of this warning, moreover, is the testimony of such a subtle understanding of people that one is hard-pressed to find a comparably refined description of the consequences of well-meant moralizing, even in psychological literature. In chapter 19 of Volume Two, "On the Primacy of the Will in Self-Consciousness" (which contains the grandiose anticipation of psychoanalysis that Schopenhauer is so often credited with), it is said in no uncertain terms that no ethics is even possible:

> This is in fact why it is impossible to have an ethics that forms and improves the will itself. For any teaching can affect only *cognition*: and this never determines the will itself. That is, the *fundamental character* of willing, but merely its application to circumstances at hand.[42]

What does this imply? Once more a caveat—or as might as well be said again, a work order, to which instead and exclusively our attention [*Aufmerksamkeit*] ought always to be turned:

> An amended cognition can modify action only in more accurately showing the will the objects available to it and allowing it to judge them more correctly; in this way the will can gauge its relation to things more correctly, can see more clearly what it wills, and consequently will be less likely to make a mistake in its choice. But the intellect has no power over willing itself, over its basic direction or fundamental maxims.[43]

Schopenhauer now gives the justification for this obligation to a self-limiting reticence in our practical aspirations. It elaborates on the *consequences* of not respecting those limits:

> Anyone who, either through experience or the reproofs of others, has recognized and regretted a fundamental failing in his character might well make a firm and honest resolution to improve himself and cast off the failing: but in spite of this, the failing is once again fully in evidence at the very next opportunity. New remorse, new resolution, new offence. When this has happened several times, he becomes conscious of the fact that he is incapable of improving himself, that the failing lies in his nature and personality, indeed that it *is* his personality. Now he will curse and condemn his nature and personality, he will experience a painful feeling that can rise to the level of a pang of conscience: but he can do nothing to change this. Here we see that what condemns and what is condemned come cleanly apart: we see the former as a purely theoretical capacity to construct and resolve upon a praiseworthy and desirable course of one's life; but we see the latter as something real, existing and immutable that pursues quite a different course, in spite of the former; and then we see the former remaining behind again with impotent remonstration against the constitution of the other, with which it identifies itself again, and by means of this very affliction. Here will

> and intellect are broken very cleanly apart. In the process the will shows itself to be the stronger, indomitable, unchangeable, primitive and at the same time essential as well, the one on which everything depends; the intellect bemoans the will's failings but takes no comfort in the correctness of its *cognition*, as its proper function.[44]

What conclusion are we to draw from this? I say it is this: in Philosophical Praxis our first responsibility is not in fact to the thinking, the judging, or beliefs of a person, but rather to *this individual human being before us*, which is to say, to someone of a *determinate* character and with a *particular* will. These are the realities that demand recognition. Yet this will, which constitutes our very being, cannot be freely disposed either at will or according to insight. In yet other words: we face a human being *who is a destiny unto himself.* And the only appropriate attitude for us to bear toward this special character is to *recognize* it and appreciate it as the basis of all our further common undertakings—because: it *is* that basis.

At this point, in order to develop and promote this proposed principle, it would be indispensable to take up Schopenhauer's notion of the "intelligible character," which, as the first and last destiny of man that accompanies his life, reveals itself (at least enough to be surmised) in the "empirical character." That task, however, is impossible within the confines of this chapter. It remains for me for now only to assume the matter as justified, in order to conclude with the question as to the consequences that follow as regards the design of a philosophical consulting praxis.

Wouldn't Schopenhauer's thinking deprive its followers of any possibility to be effective or gain practical influence? Must they not rather revoke any ambition to establish philosophy as praxis?

No. On the contrary, what results from the recognition of Schopenhauer's doctrine of character is its *call for particularized attentiveness*[45] which has guided me in my work for a long time.

In order to make this perspicuous, it is necessary to go into Schopenhauer's *third determination of character*, which he presents under the title "*acquired character*." To say it upfront and briefly, this "acquired" (and moreover only "to be acquired") character deserves the attention of the philosopher in praxis. For it is only in relation to this third determination of character that the philosopher finds his bearings on that for which he is useful and may be need, even helpful. Let us first look at the passage in which talk of the "acquired character" is introduced:

> Besides the intelligible and empirical characters, we can mention a third that is distinct from those others, the *acquired character*, which is only acquired over the course of a life and through contact with the world. That is what people

> have in mind when they praise someone as a man of character or censure him as lacking in character. Of course, someone could say that empirical character is unalterable since it is the appearance of the intelligible character, and, like every phenomenon in nature, internally self-consistent; and as a result, a human being must also appear internally consistent and self-identical and thus cannot need to acquire a character artificially, through experience and reflection. But this is not how it seems to that person, and although people might always be the same, they do not understand themselves at every moment; in fact, they frequently misunderstand themselves until they have acquired a certain degree of genuine self-knowledge.[46]

After this, Schopenhauer, with the help of an image, goes on to explain how such a self-misknowing presents and betrays itself. Ideally, life proceeds in the form of a straight line, which reveals along the way just who it is that walks that line. Without yet having attained insight into one's own being, one will always be tempted to "act like children at a fair, grabbing at everything that tickles our fancy without stopping to make up our minds."[47] Thus "*we would zigzag all over the place without getting anything* done."[48]

In this image, I dare say, many a complaint presented by visitors to Philosophical Praxis may be summarized. But what then is the mission of the philosopher? Understanding and interpreting, as was said at the beginning, and then: to shed light, *to think further and beyond*[49] to help others inch toward wisdom and insight. For, according to Schopenhauer (and I agree with him):

> It is not enough simply to will something, or even to be able to do it; a human being must also *know* what he is willing, and *know* what he can do: only then does he begin to show character, and only then can he achieve anything properly. Prior to this he is indeed lacking in character, despite the natural consistency of the empirical character, and although in general he must be true to himself and run his course, he will not set off on a straight line but rather take a shaky, crooked line, deviating, wavering, turning back, and setting himself up for pain and remorse: and this is all because he sees before himself in matters both great and small, everything that human beings can and do achieve, and does not yet know what portion of this is appropriate or practicable or even just enjoyable for himself. He will envy other people for positions and circumstances that are suited only to the other people's characters, not to his own, and in which he himself would be unhappy, or even unable to cope. Just as fish do well only in water, birds in the air, and moles underground, everybody can do well only in the atmosphere they find congenial.[50]

Since it is in the interest of the still young Philosophical Praxis to assemble what are, in some measure, 'main and reference texts' for initial orientation, I would like here to reproduce the passage immediately following the one just quoted. In my view, it ought to be appreciated as a reference text for all Philosophical Praxis:

> Many a person has no insight into these matters and will make all sorts of failed attempts, doing violence to his character in many small respects and being forced to yield to it again overall: and what he achieves so painfully and against his nature will not give him any pleasure; what he learns in this way will remain dead; even from an ethical perspective, if someone performs a deed that is too noble for their character, that does not arise from a pure and direct impulse but instead from a concept, a dogma, then subsequent egoistic remorse will rob it of all value, even in the person's own eyes. *Velle non discitur*. We realize only through experience how inflexible other people's characters really are, and until then we harbour a childish faith that we can move them with irrational ideas, with pleas and entreaties, with examples and noble actions, and make some one of them abandon his type, alter his way of acting, forgo his way of thinking, or even widen the scope of his abilities; and we do the same with ourselves. We must first learn from experience what we want and what we can do: until then we do not know it, we lack character, and we will frequently have to be driven back onto our own true path by sharp blows from the outside. But if we finally learn this lesson, we will have achieved what the world calls character, *acquired character*.[51]

And so it is that we find Schopenhauer, whom we had at first assumed would refuse to concede any interest in Philosophical Praxis, doing quite the opposite and assigning to it a field of work as justified as it is necessary, work that indeed demands from Philosophical Practitioners quite theoretical competences—principally: understanding, perceptiveness, and elucidation—that are nevertheless of extraordinary practical relevance, not least for those who travel a precarious path *because and so long as they lack the insight* that allows them *to know what they are doing*.

If, however, anyone should wish to raise the objection that this cannot be everything and the whole of what a philosopher in praxis has to offer to people seeking advice, then I would add that, given the outline just provided of the challenges that await him there, the limit of his engagement is by no means circumscribed, even in Schopenhauer's sense. On the contrary, it can go beyond that—indeed, very far beyond that—in rare and favorable cases, the door may open onto wider vistas, and the view will become free from the still condoned bondage [*Verhaftung*] of the individual, this very character, who cannot escape as his destiny.

As is well known, Schopenhauer's actual intention was to abolish our inner enslavement, the collapse back into ourselves, our cleaving to individuality as the form in which Will brings itself to fruition, takes its stand, prevails. His intention, in a word, was to *abolish*[52] *egoism*, to overcome its narrowness, its ruthless self-realization; for—and this is Schopenhauer's profound insight—all suffering and misfortune has its reason and the basis of its continued existence[53] in the *principio individuationis*.

But to follow him there is no longer possible: to let him take me there would entail a further and more ambitious program than I had planned for this place. And so I take leave of Schopenhauer by letting him speak once more and now for the last time. Drawing together what follows from his teaching, he writes that "character can never be altered partially; instead, with the consistency of a law of nature, character must realize itself as a whole in the particular individual whose appearance it is; but this very whole, the character itself, can be fully abolished by the alteration in cognition."[54] Yet this abolition can only occur on condition of a fundamental change in cognition in general: in cognition, it is our bondage [*Verhaftung*] to ourselves that we should have to overcome.

NOTES

1. Arthur Schopenhauer, *The World as Will and Representation*, 1. Transl. by Judith Norman, Alistair Welchman, and Christopher Janaway (CUP: 2010), 358. Used with permission. Note that here and throughout I quote the Norman/Welchman/Janaway translation (hereafter, the 'CUP translation'), except where otherwise indicated. Page numbers in citations to Schopenhauer refer to the marginal pagination in this translation, and thus to the pagination of the Hübscher edition of the *Sämtliche Werke* (Brockhaus, 1988).

2. Lecture given in 1994 in Tübingen at the 9th Colloquium of the Society for Philosophical Praxis (GPP e.V.).

3. See "On university philosophy," in Volume I of *Parerga and Paralipomena* (CUP: 2014), 125–176. (Marginal pagination, also based on the Hübscher *Sämtliche Werke.*) Schopenhauer's alarm concerned established religion, but his objection readily applies to present circumstances.

4. Arthur Schopenhauer, *The World as Will and Presentation*, I. Trans. by Richard E. Aquila, with David Carus. (New York: Pearson Educational, 2008), xviii. "Truth is no whore who throws herself on the neck of those who do not desire her. Rather, she is so shy a beauty that even one who sacrifices everything to her can still not be certain of her favor." In this instance the wording is taken from the Aquila/Carus translation—note the distinct English title. Aquila/Carus translation works better in several instances (as here); but the CUP translation is to be assumed unless explicitly indicated.

5. Schopenhauer, *World as Will*, I, xix. "However could that philosophy which has been degraded into a way of earning one's bread fail to degenerate into sophistry?" Aquila/Carus translation. CUP does away with the bread metaphor, relegating it to a footnote, so I follow Aquila/Carus here.

6. Schopenhauer, *World as Will*, I, xix. CUP does away with the bread metaphor, relegating it to a footnote. Again, I follow Aquila/Carus here, as Achenbach quotes the bread metaphor.

7. Schopenhauer, *World as Will*, I, xvii. As in Aquila/Carus. The CUP version preserves the pun (*Absicht-Einsicht*) only in a footnote: "intent is always dangerous to insight."

8. Schopenhauer, *World as Will*, I, xvii.

9. Schopenhauer, *World as Will*, I, xvii.

10. Schopenhauer, *World as Will*, I, xvii.

11. Schopenhauer, *World as Will*, I, xx. This is the CUP translation except for the very last word (in German, *Wortkram*), which CUP renders as 'verbiage.' The Aquila-Carus "word-mongering" is more suited to Achenbach's purposes.

12. Arthur Schopenhauer, *Parerga and Paralipomena*, I, 512. I have altered the CUP translation slightly, putting "more sensible" in place of "more rational" for "*vernünftigeren*."

13. Arthur Schopenhauer, *Parerga and Paralipomena*, I, 512. Emphasis added.

14. Arthur Schopenhauer, *Parerga and Paralipomena*, I, 512. Note that here the "world" [*die Welt*] clearly refers to other people, to the social world.

15. Schopenhauer, *World as Will*, I, 319. I choose Aquila/Carus for the wording, but I have taken the unusual liberty of re-ordering the grammatical elements of this quotation, to lay emphasis where it is needed, and set up what is to come.

16. The quoted phrases that follow are section titles from the first Book of Schopenhauer's *World as Will and Representation.*

17. Indeed, Philosophical Praxis is sometimes associated with the recent revival of sorts of Stoicism. See for instance: Massimo Pigliucci, *How to Be a Stoic: Using Ancient Philosophy to Live a Modern Life* (Basic Books, 2018); Jules Evans, *Philosophy for Life and Other Dangerous Situations: Ancient Philosophy for Modern Problems* (New World Library, 2013); Ward Farnsworth, *The Practicing Stoic: A Philosophical User's Manual* (Godine, 2018); Donald Robertson, *Stoicism and the Art of Happiness: Practical Wisdom for Everyday Life*, 2nd ed. (Quercus, 2018).

18. Schopenhauer, *World as Will*, I, 103. This is the CUP translation, except that '*Giestesruhe*' is rendered "spiritual repose" (as in Aquila/Carus) rather than "peace of mind." Also, the italics follow Achenbach.

19. Schopenhauer, *World as Will*, I, 104–106.

20. Schopenhauer, *World as Will*, I, 106. Aquila/Carus

21. Schopenhauer, *World as Will*, I, 107.

22. Schopenhauer, *World as Will*, I, 108.

23. Nietzsche, *Zarathustra*, Prologue, 42.

24. Schopenhauer, *World as Will*, I, 108–109.

25. Schopenhauer, *World as Will*, I, 109.

26. Schopenhauer, *World as Will*, II, 164–165.

27. Schopenhauer, *World as Will*, II, 165. As in CUP. Schopenhauer uses the Latin '*sustine and abstine*,' rendered "endure and renounce" in Aquila/Carus. For references, see related notes there and CUP footnote.

28. Schopenhauer, *World as Will*, II, 165. The Aquila/Carus adapts itself somewhat more readily to Achenbach's grammar here.
29. Schopenhauer, *World as Will*, II, 172.
30. Schopenhauer, *World as Will*, II, 173. I have eliminated the Greek words in the original passage or replaced them with the English given in a CUP footnote.
31. Schopenhauer, *World as Will*, II, 174.
32. Schopenhauer, *World as Will*, II, 174.
33. Schopenhauer, *World as Will*, II, 176. Note: I restore the Latin here, which Schopenhauer's translators retain in a footnote.
34. Schopenhauer, *World as Will*, II, 180.
35. Schopenhauer, *World as Will*, I, 319.
36. Schopenhauer, *World as Will*, I, 319.
37. Schopenhauer, *World as Will*, I, 320.
38. Schopenhauer, *World as Will*, I, 320. Italics as in Achenbach. Also, I have restored the Latin from a CUP footnote.
39. Schopenhauer, *World as Will*, I, 320. I switch here to Aquila/Carus translation for grammatical reasons.
40. Schopenhauer, *World as Will*, I, 320.
41. Schopenhauer, *World as Will*, I, 321.
42. Schopenhauer, *World as Will*, II, 251.
43. Schopenhauer, *World as Will*, II, 251.
44. Schopenhauer, *World as Will*, II, 251–252.
45. Call for particularized attentiveness—*eine spezifizierte Aufmerksamkeits-Anforderunng*.
46. Schopenhauer, *World as Will*, I, 357.
47. Schopenhauer, *World as Will*, I, 358.
48. Schopenhauer, *World as Will*, I, 358. Italics as in Achenbach's text. The image of a line comes up in this same context in Schopenhauer, who writes: "For, just as our physical path on earth is always only a line, not a surface, so in life, if we would seize upon and possess one thing, we must leave countless others lying, left and right, renouncing them." The zigzag path is a vain attempt to make a surface of a line.
49. The word '*weiterdenken*' has been inserted here, where it nicely belongs. It reflects Achenbach's view that the philosophical practitioner need not 'know the answers' or 'what to think,' but only how to think on, to think further and beyond (Laura V. Adrian's rendition).
50. Schopenhauer, *World as Will*, I, 358–359. The CUP translation is here altered very slightly. I have preferred "lacking in character" to "characterless" for the German "*charakterlos*"; the point seems to be, not an absence of identifying features altogether, but an absence of moral distinction. Aquila/Carus have "without character."
51. Schopenhauer, *World as Will*, I, 359. For consistency, I have once again altered this CUP translation slightly, preferring "lack character" to "characterless" for the German "*charakterlos.*" Here too Aquila/Carus have "without character."
52. Here and below (also in CUP), 'abolish' stands in for *Aufhebung*, which is of course a key term in the philosophy of Hegel, whom Schopenhauer held in such low

regard. Achenbach is suggesting that Schopenhauer, despite himself, is showing a proximity to Hegel at this culminating moment in his philosophy.

53. Achenbach note (quoting Schopenhauer): "We saw earlier that hatred and malice are conditioned by egoism and that these are based on cognition caught up in the *principium individuationis.* We also found that seeing through that *principium individuationis* is the origin and essence both of justice and, when it goes further, of love and nobility at the very highest levels. This [amended or altered cognition] alone, by eradicating the distinction between one's own individual and that of others, explains and makes possible the perfect dispositional goodness that goes as far as the most disinterested love and the most generous self-sacrifice for the sake of others." *World as Will*, I, 447. [Editorial insert: I have dared to revise CUP, specifically the difficult final sentence, with the double aim to simplify the English grammar and to make plain its relation to the present context.] Accordingly, the foundation of morality on Schopenhauer's view is the "intuitive cognition that recognizes in another individual the same essence as in its own" *World as Will*, I, 435.

54. Schopenhauer, *World as Will*, I, 477. 'Cognition' is '*Erkennen*' and 'abolished' is '*aufgehoben.*' See note 52, this chapter.

Chapter 12

Philosophical Praxis as Alternative to Psychotherapy and Pastoral Care

The only way to see things *humanly* is to see them individually.

—Thomas Mann[1]

This chapter looks at Philosophical Praxis as an alternative to psychotherapy and pastoral care.[2]

Pastoral care, psychotherapy, and Philosophical Praxis are all three mutually distinct, and each needs to be clearly set off against the others. That is, each of these three modes of thoughtful relations with people allows itself, by comparative differentiation, to be distinguished from the other two. Pastoral care would then gain form by clarifying in which way it is *not* psychotherapy and *not* Philosophical Praxis. For its part, psychotherapy could come to terms with its own concepts and activities through its advocates explaining to us how the soul has lost its heavenly home and now has to find its way without a guiding star; in what way its forsakenness is now to be read as illness, and grace as health; that its 'father' is now only the earthly one, the mother the one who bore it, and its brothers and sisters, not those of the spirit, but those of the nursery. And of course an initial understanding of Philosophical Praxis would be possible as well, since through comparison and distinction we often gain in determinativeness.

In the same way, it would further be possible to demonstrate what pastoral care, psychotherapy and Philosophical Praxis have in common, to what extent—despite their different modalities and their thoroughly different intentions—they might also nevertheless initiate somewhat similar transformations.

Clearly, then, the relations amongst the three could further be analyzed with a view to their unity and commonality—and some will perhaps think that we arrive in this way at what is essential, and that whatever is left out is merely secondary.

I wish to proceed differently. I would like to put pastoral care, psychotherapy and Philosophical Praxis in a different light by regarding them *historically*, since a historical perspective allows us to perceive commonalities and differences at once. And since I am constrained by the limited space of a single chapter, I must risk airily telling it as a crudely outlined short story. This presupposes your active cooperation insofar as you will need to forgive me for some exaggerations and overly bold emphasis by kindly attributing them to the shortness of the presentation.

No doubt our tersely drawn historical overview is *not* initiated by pastoral care—not at least in the high-cultural milieu—but rather it is philosophy that emerges first. And it makes its appearance as the pursuit of a judicious and reasonable way of life[3]—and by no means as a purely theoretical interest in World-Knowledge, unconcerned with life and its fulfillments.

Exactly correspondingly, 'wisdom' was also at the very center of attention in Greek antiquity. Wisdom, which had to prove itself not only as the truth of knowledge, but above all as the fulfillment of one's life, as judiciousness [*Besonnenheit*] in the conduct of life, as—in the words of Socrates—"the examined life."

And so from the very beginning philosophy was not only but in fact *primarily* praxis: the *exercise* of impactful practical insight, *askesis*, an early form of philosophizing which Pierre Hadot ranks under the heading "Spiritual Exercises of Wisdom."[4]

Not today only but since the times of Chrysippus the Stoic, the title and task of the "*therapeutikos*" fell to philosophy. Philosophy was held in high esteem as *medicina mentis* already when Socrates lived, and it was 'master of the soul' in Hellenism up to Seneca and the emperor Marcus Aurelius. If now—in place of many names not mentioned—I name Plutarch, it is mostly in order to work in two points that impose themselves on me against the background of the experience collected so far in my Philosophical Praxis.

As may be noted, I am recalling philosophers who nowadays are not exactly the center of attention of officialdom in philosophy. Seneca was not rehabilitated until Diderot, in a brilliant work of his old age.[5] Plutarch—still highly honored by Goethe, and esteemed by Erasmus as the only author whose writings, next to the Bible, deserved the designation "sacred"—was also, as is well-known, indispensable to a man like Montaigne.

I mention these details to hint at my first point: philosophical praxis will teach us to revise our customary appreciations of the philosophical tradition. Hitherto relatively under-appreciated thinkers will appear in a different and new light. With a single quotation from Plutarch I will try to give you an idea of this. In his treatise, *Contentment*, it is pithily said: "Nothing in human life is pure and unalloyed."[6] I say: anyone to whom it would be given to unpack the total meaning of this sentence would achieve fully authorized access to the foyer of Philosophical Praxis.

But I was going to make *two* remarks. So here is the second. All the experience gathered from the multitude within the philosophical tradition teaches us that the great founding philosophies, inclusive of their basic options, have all been discredited by other later founding philosophies, and have had their objective validity claims quashed. Put differently, the truth-claims of Knowledge have not endured. Intended for eternity, they have, without exception, lapsed into time—or, in Hegelian terms, they have been reduced to a mere moment in the history of philosophy.

By contrast, the orientation-cues of practical philosophy have fared quite differently: they have proved to be extraordinarily *resistant to obsolescence*[7]—compared to those of theoretical philosophy. Whoever wants to illustrate this perception may once again read Descartes' "provisional moral code."[8] Whereas Descartes himself thought that he had not yet found an enduring foundation for practical philosophy, so that he felt compelled to make do with a "tentative" and "provisory" orientation in important practical matters, today's reader will undoubtedly come to the conclusion that what Descartes believed to be beyond doubt soon turned up doubtful—what he only dared to impart provisionally, by contrast, turned out to be enduring and unsurpassed. Put differently: the supposedly certain became uncertain, and some supposedly uncertain things have remained current, alive and unaged [*unveraltet*]. So much for the two remarks I have allowed myself as an insertion.

And now, to pick up where we left off, which was to outline for starters in a short story the *historical* relations of practical philosophy, pastoral care, psychotherapy and Philosophical Praxis. With the appearance of Christianity, philosophy forfeited its undisputed position as a "guide of the soul."[9] This loss can be traced clearly in a paradigmatic biographical episode from Augustine's *Confessions*. It was not philosophy that proved to be the healer of his melancholy, but faith: hope is placed in the "Savior," "for this disease Thou alone curest."[10]

In "Pastoral Care," a highly worthwhile article in a classic reference work, *Religion in Geschichte und Gegenwart*, one finds an explanation of this transition from practical-philosophical to pastoral life-guidance care, in the form of a casual though pretty remark: "In educated homes, the pastor took the place of the domestic philosopher."[11] A case of *recasting*[12]: the priest assumes the role of the philosopher.

Today, however, it is in all likelihood too much for contemporaries to fully grasp what has happened. Most of them will hardly succeed in perceiving more than a 'change of personnel' in this process. Typically, it is the *psychological* perspective that obscures the radical nature of that upheaval in spiritual history; for instance, by supposing that faith in faith had simply proved to be more 'effective' than faith in reason—for a while, for at least a few centuries; but then the Enlightenment took hold, and with it faith in 'faith in faith' was withdrawn, and so on.

Thus, to the psychological view, the difference in substance always disappears behind the difference in its assessment—nothing remains but so many views and matters of opinion, about the truth of which nothing is said. Only the condition [*Befinden*] of the psyche can be judged, depending on whether it has come to this or to that opinion.

Allow me then to insert at this point a digression which seems to me necessary in order to make understandable even a little that transition from practical philosophy to pastoral religion—for understanding can not be achieved if the *psychological prejudice—the prejudice of our era*—is not first irritated.

Imagine two people, united by the bond of marriage, have arrived in your practice. In the everyday life of marriage, in the routine of living together, the two of them have failed, at first imperceptibly, then more and more obviously. At some point in their life together fissures grew, into which the most immediate interests of the two isolated individuals—past all mediation—have gradually seeped. Lately the two have armed themselves against each other with lawsuits, and finally they mutually admit the disaster to each other. They are at their last resort: that's why they are with you in your practice.

And now imagine further that *one* of these two children of fate, having been brought up strictly in the Catholic faith, believing in the sanctity of marriage, regards it as a "sacrament" and "established by God," and therefore as indissoluble, in accordance with faith; that it was concluded before God, begun under his blessing, sealed with the promise that they will remain faithful to the union entered into "for better, for worse, for richer, for poorer, in sickness and in health," till Death dissolve the bonds of marriage. Obviously, given this conviction, the divorce petition of the other was not consented to.

On the contrary, marital miseries are interpreted as temptation, and the severity of the misery as a trial through which one must prove oneself. By contrast, the other half of the marriage (who no longer identifies as 'the other half') is absolutely convinced that—but we may spare ourselves the portrayal of the other appraisal of the situation, as it is far too boring to relate; it is familiar to one and all. Here and there it may take on a little individual color; on the whole, however, it just represents the generic and usual thinking as it presently is.

According to this thinking, all there is to be seen here is a difference of opinion, two views—if you like, imprintings—the *origins* of which, if need be, could be further explained, so that it could then be said why one thinks and feels one way, the other a different way—e.g., the one had a very strict, very orthodox, very Catholic upbringing, while the other had grown up in a liberal atmosphere . . .

To be sure, such interpretations could be made far more subtle, more fine-grained, so to speak, and therefore much more satisfying intellectually than is done here. But this is not what matters. To the contrary, what is decisive in this context is that the essential question at stake (i.e., the dispute at the *heart of the matter*—the question, *what* is marriage) is in this way sidelined. It disappears behind the question of *how marriage is thought of*, and where this opinion originates and what follows from it. Nothing else is possible for the *psychological* view; because for a psychologist to want to decide about 'the thing itself' would be to come off as 'dogmatic.'

What escapes the psychologist—in all probability—is the insight that he himself has already decided this matter dogmatically, and is a party to it. For the question in dispute for the two spouses is whether marriage is a matter of opinion or not. Is it the individual subject who falls under the jurisdiction of marriage, and is judged according to whether he or she satisfies its demands; or is it, on the contrary, the marriage that falls within the jurisdiction of the individual subject, and is to be judged according to whether or not it satisfies his or her demands?

I hope that by now you see why I decided to include this digression. I wanted to show by way of example that the meaning of the transition from the Hellenistic philosophical elevation of the *art* of living to the religious care for the soul (for its salvation and its eternity, for damnation or grace, for its will to stand before the highest judge) cannot be understood if it is interpreted *psychologically*, i.e., if it is 'understood' in the usual way it is today. For the pride of this understanding is precisely *not* to understand. And we know where this has led us: today pastoral care itself is in pretty bad shape. Theology has lost the condition of its possibility, without which it becomes a farce, namely: faith. To express myself in philosophical terminology: the preconditions of all metaphysics have been lost.

This I should now like to clarify from a singular perspective, which at the same time will illustrate once again the power of religion to outdo philosophy.

No doubt reason too was able to offer counsel and to cultivate conduct throughout life that afforded equanimity and mental tranquility through adversity and hardship; yet however one might console oneself, it was, seen from the perspective of faith, a bleak consolation. One might have learned to expect death calmly, and finally to die with Stoic dignity; but in regard to the ultimate issue—Death itself, the scandalous fact that degrades man to finiteness and to an incident—nothing at all has changed. Only faith, insofar as the heart turns toward it, was able to achieve peace of heart, not indeed from its own exercise, but from the consoling certainty that the thorn of death had indeed been blunted, Death itself killed, its kingdom overthrown.

All weight now hung on *one* question: whether the Truth is the *truth*. And yet, it is not our favor [*Befinden*] and our judgment that decides, but the other way round: it is the Truth that judges [*befindet*] our favor and our judgment. In yet other words: in faith, man knows himself to be held under reserve; he knows that he will be judged, *his* rectitude is in question. But for the person who has emancipated himself from faith, this relationship is reversed: it is now he who makes claims subject to reservation, and it is also he who, for his part, judges the rectitude of faith. In brief: it is he who administers the claims. The question now is not whether man can still stand before his God, but whether the good Lord still exists 'for us.'[13] Since then, God lives—as far as the will of man goes—by the grace of Man. Thus the ground for the pastoral care is taken away. And the ground for psychotherapy is prepared. For the preconditions that have rendered faith in faith impossible are the same ones that now give rise to faith in psychotherapy.

The process in spiritual history that I have outlined here is so powerful, however, that these days, as it seems to me, pastoral care and pastoral theology, under pressure to be *effective*, have long since oriented themselves by psychotherapy. This I have noticed not only in numerous conversations with Protestant clergy, but especially in conversations with Catholic priests. The officially believed and familiar God is no longer taken seriously. Priests have problems, not with their God, not religious or theological problems, only problems of a worldly character with their church. Questions of legitimacy or legality take precedence—legal interests are paramount—and celibacy is judged in terms of health strategy or psychic hygiene—if not simply according to what is trending. That one who breaks his vows avoids being 'inhibited' and a life of forced inhibition—this is taken as the pivotal fact. No longer can the idea even be grasped that such self-authorization *is* the very rebellion against God, a mortal sin, a 'sin against the Spirit.' So the question becomes: What has happened?

What has happened—so far hardly noticed—is *a revolutionary breakdown of the prevailing conception of man*, in other words: people think differently of themselves, and indeed *fundamentally* different.[14]

At first, it held true: one only becomes what one is destined to become if one strives to become it. This means that an accomplished life does not fall into anyone's lap, but is understood as the repayment for work upon oneself. It meant too that insofar as sagacity and prudence, insight and distance from oneself, reason and the wisdom of experience are not the actual and ultimate arbiters of how a human life should be led, life itself will fail or remain poor and stale, flat and banal. It falls prey to the momentary demands of affects, is torn to and fro, and finds no form. It was under these conditions that philosophers became mentors and life-advisers.

Then later something else held sway, creating conditions that justified and made necessary the pastoral ministry of souls—namely, that humankind stands on Heaven's reserve and is entrusted to Grace; for the good life cannot be mastered on our own. On his own he can do nothing, for man, as he lives and breathes, as he is by nature, is above all a sinner, a fallen creature, lost, corrupt and therefore in dire need of redemption. In Nicolás Gómez Dávila, one of the most important contemporary reactionaries, I found an aphorism that concisely expresses this conception: "the human being is the problem for which there is no human solution."[15]

The modern age—Rousseau was one of its pioneers—invalidated this conception of man. It was burdensome and too much of a bother; also it offended the vanity of people, who would rather believe that, the way they are in the world, they are already all right, just the way happenstance made them. Thus they have fallen prey to the idea that, as long as everything goes 'normally,' life of itself will issue in achievements; then, if it fails to, it is because something hindered it.

The modern conviction is: Man is good, and if he is not good, he has been damaged, victimized, traumatized, neuroticized. If therefore something has happened that hindered him in his goodness, then circumstances must be sought that prevented him from becoming what certainly he would have become on his own: namely, the normal, good, right, healthy, fun-loving, peace-loving and gentle man, friendly to all and flush with complacency.

I hope that the recasting [*Umbesetzung*] of dependencies that was brought to fruition with modernity has become clear—after all, we usually owe our perception of freedom to the rearrangement of our dependencies.

Thus the human being, for the purposes of achieving autonomy, sets off on a search-and-destroy mission for heteronomy—and thus has already entered upon the path of psychotherapy. He sets out from an understanding of himself as one alienated by others,[16] as one deprived of himself by others, in order then to remove by degrees—layer by layer, negation of negations—all that is alien in himself in the hope that, beneath all the tectonic subductions, the real me—the true, liberated, *healthy* self—will finally come to light. The underlying and guiding idea of most therapies may well be 'to come to oneself.' Yet this idea is a hope whose justification is bound up with the fact that human nature—after the alien incursion is disposed of—*is good.*

Let me however abruptly relate this now back to the beginning: this new conception of human nature, which now anchors and governs the self-evident, stands in polar opposition to the earlier certainty, once expressed by Arnold Gehlen in this way: man is the being "that does not live, but *leads* his life."[17] Where this older conception prevailed, the question that naturally arose was how to acquire the wherewithal necessary to leading one's life, i.e., how one could set oneself up to lead life in a worthwhile way. The old practitioner-philosophers were helpful in this.

The modern self-assessment of man also stands in no less sharp contrast to past religious premises: that was the knowledge that man could be saved only by repentance, only by renouncing his immediate nature; that is, by way of redemption and remission of sins.

Both conceptions, however, only look backward. And you will ask—quite rightly—how Philosophical Praxis, as the junior alternative, now stands in relation to the selectively highlighted modalities of pastoral care and psychotherapy just sketched in historical progression.

You will have noticed, in the first place, that my assessment is that the ancient tradition (for instance: stoically cultivated soul equilibrium and cosmic homogeneity) cannot simply be reinstated, even if philosophy amounts in the end to the resolution to maintain the presence of the past, thus opposing the arrogance of the superiority of the modern. Yet what has been tested and proved—at the individual level—as the so-called 'art of living' is by no means deprived of all plausibility.[18]

As an aside: granted that, at present, the intellectual contours of Hellenism once again present themselves as plausible ways of leading life, at least for particular, minority elites; nevertheless, if it treats the ancient models as undamaged goods applicable today, Philosophical Praxis relies on ignorance.

And now, after this side remark, back to the question of the relationship of Philosophical Practice to pastoral care. The topic is complex. I will nevertheless try to say at least a little about it.

I have many times in consultation been in a situation that (like that of Kierkegaard) I had become acquainted with through reading. The content and severity of faith, perhaps the sharpness of an either-or, can most easily be impressed upon someone who—stuck in distant doubt—has himself been unable to break through to the seriousness of existence, but who at the same time seeks no refuge in shallow reassurances. To put a point on it: Philosophical Praxis became the alternative in some cases to pastoral care, not on account of a tone prevailing in it of cheerful or depressive unbelief, but thanks to a spirit that won't let faith fall, even if it does not find its way to it. In Philosophical Praxis, faith lives on under difficult conditions, those of doubt and a thousand questions. Meanwhile, an earnest and easy-going faith, a spiritual life of unquestioning security and pious certainty, appears today to the religiously more sensitive person as inexcusable naivety in serious matters. It lacks the ear to really hear our cares as cares [*Sorgen*], and to dignify them, which is the beginning of all thinking-through.[19]

With this let me return also to the other question raised: to what extent and in what way could Philosophical Praxis be an alternative to psychotherapy? Against the background of what has been presented so far—mostly in a historical perspective—one might now expect that philosophical practitioners would articulate another, an alternative, revived image of human nature and on this basis lay the groundwork of a transformed way of relating to people who turn to philosophy with unsolved problems. And indeed much on this head has been attempted by me—although only in rudiments and so far mostly scattered. Yet as an example let me refer to character and destiny (see chapter 11).

I might also recall Michael Schefczyk's resolute attempt to rehabilitate our obligation to justify our conduct,[20] a duty in danger of getting lost by the focus on psychological motive-hunting. He places emphasis on "conceptual fates," destinies determined by thought and understanding, which, relative to the "drive fates,"[21] have hitherto been under-appreciated in their significance for life.

But here and just now I should like to place the emphasis elsewhere. First of all, Philosophical Praxis is characterized by an in-principle inexhaustible surplus of *negations*. Following Hegel, everything particular takes its validity to be general, but has its status elucidated *as* a particular (i.e., as limited and bounded), at best as a relative and provisional validity. But particularities are what give established therapies each their identity and orientation.

For Philosophical Praxis, by contrast (not to spare the polemical spice) the opposite applies: its enemies are the smalled-minded and the know-it-alls, who unmistakably betray themselves through their stiffening of the particular.

This extends to the recognition of methods, which—in sharp contrast to Philosophical Praxis—is routinely taken as a precondition of self-respecting psychotherapeutic work. However, every method teaches us to see something, but by the same token also to *overlook* something else. Philosophical Praxis, in consequence, does not work *with* methods, but *upon* methods. Method subordinates each particular; but the method-critical perspective of Philosophical Praxis ensures the particular retains its right to correct the method.

This undoubtedly complicates understanding and denies the easily manageable idea of what Philosophical Praxis is all about. But this is to be endured. I'll tell you with a comparison why this is inevitable.

One might compare a conversation played out in accordance with rules of procedure to a novel written according to previously established rules dictating how a 'good novel' should be written. The result at best would be a trivial novel, and certainly no work of art.

Indeed, it is only *within the individual consultation* that the rules, like emergent 'inner laws,' gradually give a consultation its distinctive individual face. This already suggests the comparison with a work of art, which does not conform to the rules; it casts them—not in stone—but *in the individual case*, or lends them plausibility in a given instance.

As a rule, rules on how to understand people undermine the understanding of people.

On the contrary, it is the very striving to understand that sets in motion the preconditions of understanding itself. The rule is not to be allowed to impose an image of human being, but the very human being before you to be understood must be provided sufficient latitude to amend the rules of understanding. We only begin to understand a person when we realize that we are compelled to revise the presuppositions of our understanding. To understand a person, according to Paul Feyerabend, is to be able to understand a "historical mini-tradition."[22]

La Rochefoucauld could be named as a worthy precursor of this conviction: "It is easier to know man generally than to know a particular man."[23]

All this, of course, can only be made absolutely clear in the individual case, which is not after all a 'case.' Adorno's dictum guides us here: where Philosophical Praxis actually succeeds, it is not a matter of philosophizing about the concrete, but out of the concrete.[24]

Let me show you, from a different direction, why Philosophical Praxis would in principle be betrayed and misconstrued the moment it definitively or *positively*[25] expressed itself, why it must persevere in disappointing the usual demand for information.

If you let yourself be misled into wanting to say in some definitive way just what Philosophical Praxis is (how it works; what its procedures, its interests and its goals are; what vistas it anticipates opening, what it intends to achieve) then you would not only make yourself laughable, but philosophy too.

For just as philosophy always takes on a definite and determinable character only in the individual work, so Philosophical Praxis does only in the individual consultation.

This same point can be made by reference to one of the undisputed classical works of philosophical literature, by a tip of the hat to Hegel's *Phenomenology of Spirit*. Imagine if this author and this work, moving itself from standpoint to standpoint, were to be asked: from what standpoint is this work constructed? "Consciousness," perhaps, or "Sense Certainty"? Skepticism or Stoicism? Enculturated Spirit, the Religious . . . ? How could the author possibly pick one?[26]

Those who by this hint have understood me will also understand when I add: it is therefore the aspiration of Philosophical Praxis that what isn't finished by half be halfway finished, and what was wrongly concluded gets going again. Thus—once again speaking in an image—Philosophical Praxis keeps on the way. Its drive is to bring home—but its power is to persevere on the way. Philosophical Praxis thus maintains the relationship to truth that negative theology found to God: it does not know it, but does not leave it. In the well-known formulation: its knowing is its not-knowing, *docta ignorantia*.

NOTES

1. Thomas Mann, *Reflections of a Nonpolitical Man*. Trans. by Walter D. Morris (New York: Frederick Ungar, 1983), 352. Originally published in German in 1918. Republished 2021 by the New York Review of Books. Used with permission.

2. This chapter was originally presented as a lecture presented at the 10th Colloquium of the *Gesellschaft für Philosophische Praxis*, held in Hannover in 1995.

3. A judicious and reasonable way of life—*besonnen-vernünftige Lebensform*.

4. Pierre Hadot, *Philosophy as a Way of Life* (Oxford: Blackwell, 1995), Ch. 3. Achenbach note: Hadot later put out two other books that emphatically illustrate the thesis just quoted: *The Inner Citadel: The Meditations of Marcus Aurelius*, rev. ed. (Harvard, 2001) and *What Is Ancient Philosophy?* (Belnap, 2004).

5. Denis Diderot, *Essai sur la vie de Séneque le philosophe, sur ses écrits, et sur les regnes de Claude et de Néron* (Paris: chez Letourmi le jeune, Á Tours, an 3 de la République française [1795]). I have not been able to locate an English translation. Achenbach refers to this work in German translation: Essay über die Herrschaft der Kaiser Claudius und Nero sowie über das Leben und die Schriften Senecas—zur Einführung in die Lektüre dieses Philosophen, in *Philosophische Schriften*, II. Ed. by Thomas Lücke (Berlin: Verlag Das Europäische Buch, 1984), 239–584.

6. Plutarch, Contentment, 474A. In *Essays*. Trans. by Robin Waterfield (Penguin, 1992), 230. In Greek, the title of this essay is *euthymia*, which, as Waterfield notes in the Introduction to the essay, both Seneca and Cicero translated as *tranquillitate animi*, a notion mentioned by Achenbach elsewhere in this book (see, e.g., Ch. 2). Seneca also has a work of this title.

7. Resistance to obsolescence—*veralterungsresistent*.

8. "Une morale par provision." Rene Descartes, *Discourse on Method*, Part Three. In *The Philosophical Writings of Descartes*, I. Trans. by John Cottingham, Robert Stoothoof, and Dugald Murdoch (CUP, 1985), 122–126.

9. The "guide of the soul" or *psychopomp*, is originally a mythic figure like Hermes, who guides departed souls. The idea of philosophy as psychopomp is related to the spirit or *daimon* of Socrates, who guided Socrates while he was yet alive. The principle takes on a greater role in Neoplatonism. In this regard one may recall Achenbach's allusion in the Prelude to Apollo Musagetes.

10. Augustine, *Confessions*, 4.3.5. Trans. by E. B. Pusey (Oxford: J. H. Parker, 1838).

11. Galling, *Religion in Geschichte und Gegenwart*, V. 3rd ed. (Tübingen: Mohr Siebeck, 1965), 1641. The title in English of this classic work would be *Religion in History and the Present*. There is since 2007 a "completely new revised" fourth edition that runs past 9,000 pages.

12. *Umbesetzung*. Recasting or redeployment; rendered by Blumenberg's translators as 'reoccupation.' "'Reoccupation' means that different statements can be understood as answers to identical questions." Hans Blumenberg, *The Legitimacy of the Modern Age*. Trans. by Robert M. Wallace (Cambridge, MA: MIT Press, 1985), 466.

13. 'Nicht ob der Mensch vor seinem Gott bestehen kann, ist jetzt die Frage, sondern ob der Herr vor uns besteht.' In the German, the same verb is used in both parts of the sentence.

14. Achenbach note: The following section presents—along with a plea for indulgence—a three-step "metaphysical short story" (from philosophy via pastoral care to psychotherapy), which I reworked three years later in "Philosophical Praxis and the Virtues" (reprinted as chapter 9). That version added names for three corresponding "images of man": the "proud," the "humble," and the "undignified" modern man. Here, in the lecture at the earlier colloquium, I was still lacking these identifying titles.

15. Nicolás Gómez Dávila, *Auf verlorenem Posten: Neue Scholien zu einem inbegriffenen Text.* German translation by Francisco Pizano de Brigard (Vienna: Karolinger, 1993), 267: "To be a reactionary is to realize that man is a problem without a human solution." The original in Spanish is #2375: "Ser reaccionario es comprender que el hombre es un problema sin solución humana." *Nuevos escolios a un texto implícito*, II (Colombia: Procultura, 1986), 123. Thanks to Professor Juan Fernando Mejia-Mosquera for correcting and improving my English translation.

16. Alienated by others—*von Fremden fremd gemacht.*

17. Arnold Gehlen, *Anthropologische Forschung. Zur Selbstbegegnung und Selbstentdeckung des Menschen* (Reinbek: Rowohlt, 1961), 38. Picard translation.

18. Gerd Achenbach, Lebenskunst. Sieben Annäherungen an ein vergessenes Wissen. In Aleida Assmann (ed.), *Weisheit Archäologie der literarischen Kommunikation*, III (Munich: Wilhem Fink Verlag, 1991), 231–238.

19. Thinking-through—*nachdenken.* Achenbach note: The posture meant here, which made faith into a conversation, can be found—not in Kierkegaard only—but especially clearly in Dostoevsky, who confessed in his *Diary of a Writer* that he possessed a "faith not like a child, but my *hosanna* has passed through the *great purgatory of doubt*, as in my last novel the devil says of himself." Today the same stance is represented by, for example, Martin Walser, who prefers the self-disclosure that he does not believe in God, though he "misses" him. In just this way Julian Barnes opened his 2008 novel *Nothing to be Frightened of*: "I don't believe in God, but I miss him" (Vintage Canada Edition, 2009). Jordan Peterson recently found this fine variation: "I'm not a believer, but I fear that God exists" ("Also sprach Jordan Peterson," *Spiegel* 49, 1/12/2018, p. 131). Editorial addendum: Achenbach quotes a German translation of Dostoevsky; I have simply translated the German. An English translation by Boris Brasol appeared as F. M. Dostoevsky, *The Diary of a Writer.* New York: Charles Scribner's Sons, 1949. Achenbach quotes Julian Barnes in English. I have translated the Jordan Peterson quotation from the German.

20. Obligation to justify our conduct—*Begründungspflichtigkeit.*

21. Michael Schefczyk, Philosophische und psychologische Individualberatung, *AGORA* No. 10/11 (1991). Here Schefczyk distinguishes 'drive fates' or

Triebschicksale, a notion in Freud, from a novel idea, 'conceptual fates' or *Begriffsschicksale.* Freud's paper, *Triebe und Triebschicksale*, appeared in 1915. It is translated as 'The Instincts and their Vicissitudes' in Vol. 14 of *The Standard Edition of the Complete Psychological Works of Sigmund Freud* (London: The Hogarth Press, 1957), 109–140.

22. Paul Feyerabend, *Erkenntnis für freie Menschen.* Frankfurt a M: Suhrkamp, 1980 (11th edition, 2016). On "historical mini-traditions," see note 11 in chapter 7.

23. La Rochefoucauld, *Maxime.* Maxim #436. Picard translation. "It est plus aisé de connaitre l'homme en général, que de connaître un homme en particulier."

24. Theodor W. Adorno, "We are not to philosophize about concrete things; we are to philosophize, rather, out of these things." *Negative Dialectics* (New York: Continuum, 1973), 33. E. B. Ashton translation.

25. 'Positive' is here used in the sense of 'explicitly laid down,' 'explicit, express, definite, precise'—as per the OED—rather than its most common English use, meaning happy or cheerful. Relevant in this regard is Achenbach's above-mentioned "surplus of negations," as well as the allusion in the final paragraph below to the necessity of a *via negativa* in philosophy. Positivism too resists theory, but in favor of brute fact; which is a motivation very distinct from Achenbach's insistence on the level of the human individual with his or her own "historical mini-tradition."

26. Some explanatory points have been added to the original to clarify the intent of this allusion to Hegel. The standpoints named are headings found in Hegel's classic 1807 work.

Bibliography

Achenbach, Gerd B. *Philosophische Praxis. Schriftenreihe zur Philosophischen Praxis*, 1. Köln: Verlag für Philosophie, 1984; 2nd ed., Dinter, 1987.

Achenbach, Gerd B., and Macho, Thomas H. *Das Prinzip Heilung. Medizin, Psychoanalyse, Philosophische Praxis. Schriftenreihe zur Philosophischen Praxis*, 2. Köln: Verlag für Philosophie/Dinter, 1985.

Achenbach, Gerd B. "Lebenskunst. Sieben Annäherungen an ein vergessenes Wissen." Opening Lecture of the 4th GPP Colloquium, October 1986 in Klagenfurt. Appeared in *Weisheit: Archäologie der literarishen Kommunickation,* III. Edited by Aleida Assmann. München: Wilhelm Fink Verlag, 1991, 231–238. Reprinted in revised form as Lebenskunst in *Zur Einführung der Philosophischen Praxis*, 329–339.

Achenbach, Gerd B. *Das kleine Buch der inneren Ruhe*. Freiburg/Basel/Wien: Herder, 2000; revised and expanded edition, 2016.

Achenbach, Gerd B. *Lebenskönnerschaft*. Freiburg/Basel/Wien: Herder, 2001; Köln: Dinter, 2010.

Achenbach, Gerd B. *Zur Einführung der Philosophischen Praxis: Vorträge, Aufsätze, Gespräche und Essays, mit denen sich die Philosophische Praxis in den Jahren 1981 bis 2009 vorstellte. Eine Dokumentation*. Köln: Dinter, 2010.

Achenbach, Gerd B. *Kleine Chronik der Philosophische Praxis, 1981–1995*, 3rd ed., 2011. Accessed July 15, 2023, at https://www.achenbach-pp.de/papers/archiv_chronik_philosophische_praxis_1981-1995.pdf.

Achenbach, Gerd B. "Aussichten auf ein Ende des kalten Krieges im Reich der Medizin. Philosophisches Plädoyer für eine praktische Weisheit, die den Streit der Theorien schlichtet," in *Patientenorientierung und Professionalität*, 2nd expanded ed., edited by Peter F. Matthiessen. Bad Homburg: Verlag Akademishe Schriften, 2011.

Achenbach, Gerd B. *Vom Richtigen im Falschen: Auf Wegen philosophisch inspirierter Lebenskönnerschaft*. Freiburg/Basel/Wien: Herder, 2003; Köln: Dinter, 2014.

Achenbach, Gerd B. "Der Patient und sein Arzt," in *Ärztekammer Nordrhein: Kommunikation*, 117. Deutscher Ärztetag. Düsseldorf: 2014, 67–92.

Achenbach, Gerd B. *Philosophie der Philosophische Praxis. Einführung*. Baden Baden: Alber Verlag and Nomos Verlag, 2023.

Achenbach, Gerd B. *On Right in Wrong*. Translation by Michael Picard of *Vom Richtigen im Falschen*. Lanham, MD: Lexington Books, forthcoming.

Adorno, Theodor W. *Philosophische Terminologie*, I. Frankfurt am Main: Suhrkamp, 1973.

Adorno, Theodor W. *Negative Dialectics*. Translated by E. B. Ashton. New York: Continuum, 1973.

Adorno, Theodor W. "Philosophie und Lehrer," in *Gesammelte Schriften*, X/2. Frankfurt am Main: Suhrkamp, 2003.

Adorno, Theodor W. "Why still Philosophy?" in *Critical Models: Interventions and Catchwords* (1998), 5–17. Translated by Henry W. Pickford. New York: Columbia University Press, 2005.

Alain (Émile Chartier). *Propose sur le bonheur*, in Cahiers du Capricorne, 1. Paris: 1925. Also appeared with Éditions Gallimard in Paris in 1928. German translation by Albrecht Fabri, *Die Pflicht, glücklich zu sein*. Frankfurt a.M.: Schmitz, 1979.

Aristotle, *Eudemian Ethics*. Translated by Michael Woods. Oxford: Clarendon Press, 1982.

Augustine. *Confessions*. Translated by E. B. Pusey. Oxford: J. H. Parker, 1838.

Barnes, Julian. *Nothing to Be Frightened of*. Toronto: Vintage Canada, 2009.

Baudelaire, Charles. *Petits Poèmes en prose*, in *Œuvres complètes de Charles Baudelaire*. Paris: Michel Lévy frères, 1869. Accessed online at https://fr.wikisource.org/wiki/Petits_Po%C3%A8mes_en_prose.

Benjamin, Walter. "The Story-teller," in *Illuminations: Essays and Reflections*. Translated by Harry Zohn. New York: Schocken, 1969.

Benjamin, Walter. "Goethe's Elective Affinities," in *Selected Writings, 1913–1926*, vol. 1, 297–360. Cambridge, MA: Harvard/Belknap Press, 1996.

Benjamin, Walter. *Selected Writings*, II, Part 2, 1931–1934. Edited by Michael W. Jennings, Howard Eiland, and Gary Smith. Cambridge, MA: Belknap Press, 1999.

Binswanger, Ludwig. *Being-in-the-World: Selected Papers of Ludwig Binswanger.* Translated by Jacob Needleman. New York: Basic Books, 1963.

Bloch, Ernst. "Über den Begriff Weisheit," in *Philosophische Aufsätze zur objektiven Phantasie*, *Gesamtausgabe* Bd. X. Frankfurt am Main: Suhrkamp, 1969.

Blumenberg, Hans. *The Legitimacy of the Modern Age*. Translated by Robert M. Wallace. Cambridge, MA: MIT Press, 1985.

Blumenberg, Hans. "Die Frage, an der Plato starb." *Frankfurter Allgemeine Zeitung*, April 4, 1996, 33.

Boss, Medard, and Heidegger, Martin. *Zollikon Seminars*. Frankfurt am Main: Klostermann, 1987.

Brem-Gräser, Luitgard. *Handbuch der Beratung für helfende Berufe*, 3 vols. Munich-Basel: Reinhardt, 1993.

Bubner, Rüdiger. "Was kann, soll und darf die Philosophie?" *Neue Rundschau*, 1976, 228–229.

Cassirer, Ernst. *The Question of Jean-Jacques Rousseau*. Translated by Peter Gay. New York: Columbia University Press, 1954.

Cicero. *Cicero's Tusculan Disputations: Also Treatises on the Nature of the Gods, and On the Commonwealth*. Translated by C. D. Yonge. New York: Harper & Brothers, 1877. Accessed July 2, 2023, at https://www.gutenberg.org/files/14988/14988-h/14988-h.htm.

Descartes, René. *The Philosophical Writings of Descartes*, I. Translated by John Cottingham, Robert Stoothoof, and Dugald Murdoch. Cambridge: Cambridge University Press, 1985.

Diderot, Denis. Essai sur la vie de Séneque le philosophe, sur ses écrits, et sur les regnes de Claude et de Néron. Paris: chez Letourmi le jeune, Á Tours, an 3 de la République française, 1795.

Diderot, Denis. *Philosophische Schriften*, II. Edited by Thomas Lücke. Berlin: Verlag Das Europäische Buch, 1984.

Diels, Hermann. *Fragmente der Vorsokratiker*, 2. Auflage, 2. Band, 1. Hälfte. Berlin: Weidmannshce, 1907.

Domizi, Donata. "Philosophische Praxis. Eine Standortbestimmung," *Information Philosophie*, Heft 4 (2019), 86–94.

Dörner, Klaus. *Der gute Arzt. Lehrbuch der ärztlichen Grundhaltung*, 2nd ed. Stuttgart: Schattauer, 2003.

Dostoevsky, F. M. *The Diary of a Writer*. Translated by Boris Brasol. New York: Charles Scribner's Sons, 1949.

(Meister) Eckhart, Johann. "Of the Nobleman," in *Meister Eckhart: The Essential Sermons, Commentaries, Treatises, and Defense*. Translated by Edmund Colledge, OSA, and Bernard McGinn, 240–247. Mahwah, NJ: Paulist Press, 1981.

(Meister) Eckhart, Johann. "The Aristocrat," in *Meister Eckhart: A Modern Translation*. Translated by Raymond Bernard Blakney, 74–81. New York: Harper Torchbooks, 1941.

von Engelhardt, Dietrich, and Schipperges, Heinrich. *Die inneren Verbindungen zwischen Philosophie und Medizin im 20. Jahrhundert*. Darmstadt: Wissenschaftliche Buchgesellschaft, 1980.

Epictetus. *Discourses, Fragments, Handbook*. Translated by Robin Hard. Oxford University Press, 2014.

Etzioni, Amitai. "Hart im Sinkflug. Über den Zwang zu Werten in der Gesellschaft," in *Spiegel*, 3 (4.3.1996), 348.

Evans, Jules. *Philosophy for Life and Other Dangerous Situations: Ancient Philosophy for Modern Problems*. Novato, CA: New World Library, 2013.

Farnsworth, Ward. *The Practicing Stoic: A Philosophical User's Manual.*, 3rd ed. Boston, MA: Godine, 2018.

Feuerbach, Ludwig. *Sämtliche Werke*, II. Leipzig: Otto Wigand, 1846.

Feuerbach, Ludwig. *Principles of the Philosophy of the Future*. Translated by M. Vogel, with introduction by T. E. Wartenberg. Indianapolis, IN: Hackett, 1986.

Feuerbach, Ludwig. *Grundsätze der Philosophie der Zukunft*. In *Gesammelte Werke*, IX, 264–341. Stuttgart: De Gruyter Akademie, 1990.

Feyerabend, Paul. *Against Method*. London: Verso, 1978.

Feyerabend, Paul. *Science in a Free Society*. London: New Left Books, 1978.

Feyerabend, Paul. *Erkenntnis für freie Menschen*. Frankfurt am Main: Suhrkamp, 1980 (11th edition, 2016).

Feyerabend, Paul. *Philosophical Papers*, II: *Problems of Empiricism*. Cambridge: Cambridge University Press, 1981.

Foucault, Michel. *Histoire de la sexualité*, vol. 1: *La volonté de savoir*, 1976, vol. 2: *L'usage des plaisirs*, 1984, vol. 3: *Le souci de soi*, 1984. Paris: Éditions Gallimard.

Foucault, Michel. *The History of Sexuality*. New York: Vintage, 1980.

Foucault, Michel. *The Use of Pleasure*. Translated by Robert Hurley. New York: Vintage, 1985.

Foucault, Michel. *Care of the Self*. Translated by Robert Hurley. New York: Vintage, 1986.

Freud, Sigmund. "Instincts and their Vicissitudes." Reprinted on pages 109–140 of *The Standard Edition of the Complete Psychological Works of Sigmund Freud*, 14. Translated by James Strachey. London: The Hogarth Press, 1957.

Galling, Kurt (ed.). *Religion in Geschichte und Gegenwart*, V. 3rd ed. Tübingen: Mohr Siebeck, 1965.

Gehlen, Arnold. *Anthropologische Forschung. Zur Selbstbegegnung und Selbstentdeckung des Menschen*. Reinbek: Rowohlt, 1961.

Gehlen, Arnold. *Moral und Hypermoral. Eine pluralistische Ethik*. Frankfurt am Main: Klostermann, 1969.

Gernhardt, Robert. "Immer." *Frankfurter Allgemeine Zeitung*, 53 (3/3/2007), 44. Reprinted in *Gesammelte Gedichte, 1954–2006*. Frankfurt am Main: S. Fischer Verlag, 2008.

Goethe, Johann Wolfgang von. *Meister Wilhelm's Apprenticeship and Travels*, 2. Translated by Thomas Carlyle. London: Robson, Levey, and Franklyn, 1858.

Goethe, Johann Wolfgang von. *Torquato Tasso*. Translated by J. Cartwright. London: D. Nutt, 1861.

Goethe, Johann Wolfgang von. *Elective Affinities*. Translated by R. J. Hollingdale. London: Penguin Classics, 1978.

Goethe, Johann Wolfgang von. *Goethes Werke, Weimarer Ausgabe*, IV Abteilung, Briefe, vol. 4. Munich: Deutscher Taschenbuch, 1987.

Goethe, Johann Wolfgang von. *Wilhelm Meisters Lehrjahre*, Vol. 7, 12th ed. Munich: C. H. Beck, 1989.

Goethe, Johann Wolfgang von. *From My Life: Poetry and Truth*, Part 3. Vol. 4 of *Goethe: Collected Works*. Translated by Robert R. Heitner. Princeton, NJ: Princeton University Press, 1994.

Goethe, Johann Wolfgang von. *Faust: A Tragedy*. Translated by Martin Greenberg. New Haven and London: Yale University Press, 2014.

Gómez Dávila, Nicolás. *Escollos a un texto implícito*, 2 Vols. Colección Autores Nacionales, 21. Bogotá: Instituto Colombiano de Cultura, 1977.

Gómez Dávila, Nicolás. *Nuevos escollos a un texto implícito*, 2 vols. Bogotá: Procultura, 1986.

Gómez Dávila, Nicolás. *Einsamkeiten*. Translated by Günther R. Siegl. Vienna: Karolinger, 1987.

Gómez Dávila, Nicolás. *Auf verlorenem Posten: Neue Scholien zu einem inbegriffenen Text.* Translated by Francisco Pizano de Brigard. Vienna: Karolinger, 1993.

Gómez Dávila, Nicolás. *Notas*, 2nd ed. Bogotá: Benjamin Villegas Editores, 2003.

Gómez Dávila, Nicolás. *Scholia to an Implicit Text.* Bilingual Selected Edition. Translated by Roberto Pinzón. Bogotá: Benjamin Villegas Editores, 2013.

Grossner, Klaus. *Verfall der Philosophie. Politik der deutschen Philosophen.* Hamburg: Reinbek, 1971.

Habermas, Jürgen. "Does Philosophy Still Have a Purpose?" (1971) in *Philosophical-Political Profiles*. Translated by Frederick G. Lawrence, 1–19. Cambridge, MA: MIT Press, 1985.

Hadot, Pierre. *Exercices spirituels et philosophie antique*. Collection des études augustiniennes. Série antiquité; 88. Paris: Etudes augustiniennes, 1981.

Hadot, Pierre. *La citadelle intérieure. Introduction aux Pensées de Marc Aurèle.* Paris: Fayard, 1992.

Hadot, Pierre. *Qu'est-ce que la philosophie antique?* (Folio essais; 280). Paris: Gallimard, 1995.

Hadot, Pierre. *Philosophy as a Way of Life*. Translated by Michael Chase. Oxford: Blackwell, 1995.

Hadot, Pierre. *The Inner Citadel: The Meditations of Marcus Aurelius*. Translated by Michael Chase. Cambridge, MA: Harvard University Press, 1998.

Hadot, Pierre. *What is Ancient Philosophy?* Translated by Michael Chase. Cambridge, MA: Harvard University Press, 2002.

Han, Byung-Chul. *The Expulsion of the Other; Society, Perception and Communication Today*. Translated by Wieland Hoban. Cambridge: Polity, 2018.

Hegel, Georg Wilhelm Friedrich. *Hegel's Lectures on the History of Philosophy*, 2. Translated by E. S. Haldane and Frances H. Simson. London: Routledge and Kegan Paul, 1968.

Hegel, Georg Wilhelm Friedrich. *Vorlesungen über die Philosophie der Religion*, II. Frankfurt am Main: Suhrkamp, 1969.

Hegel, Georg Wilhelm Friedrich. *Natural Law*. Translated by T.M. Knox. Philadelphia: University of Pennsylvania Press, 1975.

Hegel, Georg Wilhelm Friedrich. *Phenomenology of Spirit*. Translated by A.W. Miller. Oxford University Press, 1977.

Hegel, Georg Wilhelm Friedrich. "Über die wissenschaftliche Behandlungsart des Naturrechts, seine Stelle in der praktischen Philosophie und sein Verhältnis zu den positiven Rechtswissenschaften," IV, Absatz 3. In *Werkausgabe*, II. Frankfurt am Main: Suhrkamp, 1986.

Hegel, Georg Wilhelm Friedrich. *Hegel's Lectures on the Philosophy of Religion: The Lectures of 1827*. Translated by R. F. Brown, P. C. Hodgson, and J. M. Stewart, with H. S. Harris. Berkeley: University of California Press, 1988.

Hegel, Georg Wilhelm Friedrich. *The Phenomenology of Spirit*. Translated by Peter Fuss and John Dobbins. Notre Dame, IN: University of Notre Dame Press, 2019.

von Hentig, Hartmut. "Fragmente einer zukünftigen Pädagogik." *Frankfurter Hefte*, 1984.

Hinske, Norbert. "Welche Eigenschaften braucht der Mensch? Überlegungen zur Tugendethik," in *Forschung und Lehre* 7/98, 348–350.

Horkheimer, Max. *Gesammelte Schriften*, Band 6: *"Zur Kritik der instrumentellen Vernunft" und "Notizen 1949-1969."* Frankfurt am M: Fischer, 1991.

Horkheimer, Max, and Adorno, Theodor W. *Dialectic of Enlightenment*. Translated by John Cumming. New York: Continuum/Seabury, 1972.

Humboldt, Wilhelm von. "Theory of Bildung." Translated by Horton-Krüger. In *Teaching as a Reflective Practice: The German Didaktik Tradition*, 57–61. London: Lawrence Erlbaum, 2000.

Ionesco, Eugène. *Tagebuch*, 2nd ed. Neuwied and Berlin, 1969.

Ionesco, Eugène. *Fragments of a Journal*. Translated by Jean Stewart. New York: Paragon House, 1990.

Jaspers, Karl. *Socrates, Buddha, Confucius, Jesus: The Paradigmatic Individuals*. Translated by Ralph Manheim. New York: Harcourt, Brace & World, 1962.

Joubert, Joseph. *Pensées, essais, maximes et correspondance de J. Joubert*. Paris: Le Normant, 1850.

Joubert, Joseph. *Joubert: A Selection from His Thoughts*. Translated by Katharine Lyttelton. New York: Dodd, Mead, and Co., 1899.

Kant, Immanuel. *Grundlegung zur Metaphysik der Sitten*, 1785.

Kant, Immanuel. *Groundwork of the Metaphysic of Morals*. Translation of *Grundlegung zur Metaphysik der Sitten* by H. J. Paton. New York: Harper Torchbooks, 1964.

Kant, Immanuel. *Anthropology from a Pragmatic Point of View*. Translated by Mary J. Gregor. The Hague: Martinus Nijhoff, 1974.

Kant, Immanuel. *Ethical Philosophy*. Translated by James W. Ellington. Indianapolis, IN: Hackett, 1983.

Kant, Immanuel. *The Conflict of the Faculties*. Translated by Mary J. Gregor. In *Religion and Rational Theology*, 233–328. Cambridge: Cambridge University Press, 1996.

Kant, Immanuel. *Critique of Pure Reason*. Edited and translated by Paul Guyer and Allen W. Wood. Cambridge: Cambridge University Press, 1998.

Kierkegaard, Søren. *Concluding Unscientific Postscript*. Translated by David F. Swanson and Walter Lowrie. Princeton, NJ: Princeton University Press, 1941.

Kierkegaard, Søren. *The Point of View for My Work as an Author* (1848). Reprinted in *A Kierkegaard Anthology*, edited by Robert Bretal. Princeton, NJ: Princeton University Press, 1946.

Kierkegaard, Søren. *Either-Or*, I. Translated by David F. Swenson and Lillian Marvin Swenson. Princeton, NJ: Princeton University Press, 1959.

Kierkegaard, Søren. *Either-Or*, II. Translated by Walter Lowrie. Revised by Howard A. Johnson. Princeton, NJ: Princeton University Press, 1959.

Kierkegaard, Søren. *Two Ages: The Age of Revolution and the Present Age. A Literary Review*. Edited and translated by Howard V. Hong and Edna H. Hong. Princeton, NJ: Princeton University Press, 1978.

Kierkegaard, Søren. *Either-Or*, I and II. Translated by Howard and Edna Hong. Princeton, NJ: Princeton University Press, 1987.

Kierkegaard, Søren. *The Concept of Irony with Continual Reference to Socrates.* Translated by Howard and Edna Hong. Princeton, NJ: Princeton University Press, 1989.

Kierkegaard, Søren. *Concluding Unscientific Postscript.* 2 vols. Edited and translated by Howard V. Hong and Edna H. Hong. Princeton, NJ: Princeton University Press, 1992.

Kierkegaard, Søren. *Upbuilding Discourses in Various Spirits.* Edited and translated by Howard V. Hong and Edna H. Hong. Princeton, NJ: Princeton University Press, 1993.

Koch, Richard. *Ärztliches Denken. Abhandlungen über die philosophischen Grundlagen der Medizin.* München: J. F. Bergmann, 1923.

Kolakowski, Leszek. *Gespräche mit dem Teufel. Acht Diskurse über das Böse.* Munich: Serie Piper, 1963.

Kudszus, Hans. *Jaworte, Neinworte. Aphorismen.* Frankfurt am Main: Suhrkamp, 1970.

Landmann, Michael. "Georg Simmel als Prügelknabe," in *Philosophische Rundschau,* 14, 1967.

La Rochefoucauld, Franois Duc. *Maximes et Reflections Diverses.* Paris: Librairie Larousse, 1971.

La Rochefoucauld, Franois Duc. *Reflections, or, Sentences and Moral Maxims.* Translation by J. W. Willis Bund and J. Hain Friswell. London: Simpson Low, Son, and Marston, 1871.

Lichtenberg, Georg Christoph. *Sudelbücher*, Heft J, 1756–1770.

Long, A. A., and Sedley, D. N. *The Hellenistic Philosophers*, I. Cambridge: Cambridge University Press, 1987.

Lübbe, Hermann. "Wozu Philosophie? Aspekte einer ärgerlichen Frage," in *Wozu Philosophie? Stellungnahmen eines Arbeitskreises.* Edited by H. Lübbe. Berlin-New York: 1978.

Lübbe, Hermann. "Tugend tut not," in *Die Zeit*, 37 (10/9/93), 44.

Luhmann, Niklas. *Theory of Society*, 2 vols. Translated by Rhodes Barrett of *Gesellschaft der Gesellschaft.* Frankfurt am Main: Suhrkamp, 2021. Stanford, CA: Stanford University Press, 2012/2013.

Luther, Martin. *Three Treatises.* (No translator named.) Philadelphia, PA: Fortress Press, 1960.

MacIntyre, Alasdair. *After Virtue: A Study in Moral Theory*, 3rd ed. Notre Dame, IN: Notre Dame Press, 2007.

Maio, Giovanni. *Auf den Menschen hören. Für eine Kultur der Aufmerksamkeit in der Medizin.* Freiburg-Basel-Vienna: Herder, 2017.

Maio, Giovanni. *Vertrauen in der Medizin. Annäherungen an ein Grundphänomen menschlicher Existenz.* Freiburg-Basel-Vienna: Herder, 2023.

Mann, Thomas. *Reflections of a Nonpolitical Man.* Translated by Walter D. Morris. New York: Frederick Ungar, 1983. Republished 2021 by the New York Review of Books.

Mann, Thomas. *Joseph and His Brothers.* Translated by John E. Woods. New York: Knopf Doubleday, 2005.

Marinoff, Lou. *Plato, Not Prozac! Applying Philosophy to Everyday Problems*. New York: HarperCollins 1999.

Marquard, Odo. "Praxis, Philosophische," in the *Historischen Wörterbuch der Philosophie*, edited Joachim Ritter et al., vol. VII, 1307, Basel, 1989. Accessible online at www.achenbach-pp.de/.

Marquard, Odo. Der Einzelne. *Vorlesungen zur Existenzphilosophie*. Stuttgart: Reclam, 2013.

de Montaigne, Michel. *The Complete Essays of Montaigne*. Translated by Charles Cotton, 1877.

de Montaigne, Michel. *The Complete Essays of Montaigne*. Translated by Donald Frame. Stanford, CA: Stanford University Press, 1958.

Müller, Adam. *Zwölf Reden über die Beredsamkeit und deren Verfall in Deutschland*. Leipzig: Georg Joachim Göschen, 1816.

Nietzsche, Friedrich. *The Will to Power*. Translated by W. Kaufmann and R. J. Hollingdale. New York: Vintage Books, 1968.

Nietzsche, Friedrich. *Thus Spoke Zarathustra*. Translated by R. J. Hollingdale. Hammondsworth: Penguin, 1969.

Nietzsche, Friedrich. *Human, All Too Human*. Translated by Marion Faber with Stephen Lehman. Lincoln and London: University of Nebraska Press, 1984.

Nietzsche, Friedrich. *Unfashionable Observations: The Complete Works of Friedrich Nietzsche*, II. Translated by Richard T. Gray. Stanford, CA: Stanford University Press, 1995.

Nietzsche, Friedrich. *Beyond Good and Evil*. Translated by Helen Zimmern. Mineola, NY: Dover, 1997.

Nietzsche, Friedrich. *On the Genealogy of Morality*. Revised student edition. Translated by Carol Diethe. Cambridge: Cambridge University Press, 2007.

Nietzsche, Friedrich. *The Will to Power*. Translated by R. Kevin Hill and Michael A. Scarpitti. Hammondsworth: Penguin, 2017.

Nietzsche, Friedrich. *Unpublished Fragments from the Period of Thus Spoke Zarathustra* (Summer 1882–Winter 1883/84), vol. 14 of *The Complete Works of Friedrick Nietzsche*. Translated by Paul S. Loeb and David F. Tinsley. Stanford, CA: Stanford University Press, 2019.

Nietzsche, Friedrich. *Thus Spoke Zarathustra*. Translated by Adrian Del Caro. Cambridge: Cambridge University Press, 2023.

Novalis. *Werke, Tagebücher und Briefe*, II. Edited by Mühl and Samuel. Darmstadt: Wissenschaftliche Buchgesellschaft, 1978.

Novalis. *Philosophical Writings*. Translated and edited by Margaret Mahony Stoljar. Albany: State University of New York Press, 1997.

Panaitios. "Die Ethik, Das Werk über die Pflichten, in Das Sittliche," in Stoa und Stoiker, *Die Gründer, Panaitios, Poseidonios*, Bd. 1 (Bibliothek der Alten Welt, Griechishe Reihe). Edited and translated by M. Pohlenz. Zurich: Artemis, 1950.

Pascal, Blaise. Pensées. Translated by W. F. Trotter. New York: E. P. Dutton, 1958.

Picard, Michael. "Bewusstsein Und Realität: Die Frage Des Idealismus in Der frühen Indischen Philosophie" [Consciousness and Reality: The Question of Idealism in the Early Indian Philosophy]. *Gesellschaft für Philosophische Praxis* (GPP), 2019. Print available online at https://dc.arcabc.ca/islandora/object/dc%3A43806.

Picard, Michael. *How to Play Philosophy*. Lanham, MD: Hamilton, 2022.

Picht, Georg. "Enzyklopädie und Bildung." In *Merkur* 25 (279), 1971, 633.

Pieper, Josef. *Über das christliche Menschenbild*, 4th ed. Freiburg: Johannes Verlag Einsiedeln, 2018.

Pigliucci, Massimo. *How to Be a Stoic: Using Ancient Philosophy to Live a Modern Life*. New York: Basic Books, 2018.

Plato. *Complete Works*. Edited by John M. Cooper. Indianapolis, IN: Hackett, 1997.

Plato and Xenophon. *Apologies*. Translated by Mark Kremer. Newbury, MA: Focus Publishing/R. Pullins, 2006.

Plessner, Helmuth. *Die Stufen des Organischen und der Mensch*. Berlin/New York: de Gruyter, 1975.

Plutarch. *Lives of the Ten Orators* (832B–834B). In *The Older Sophists*, edited by Rosamond Kent Sprague. Columbia: University of South Carolina Press, 1972.

Plutarch. *Essays*. Translated by Robin Wakefield. Hammondsworth: Penguin, 1992.

Pohlenz, Max, (ed.). *Stoa und Stoiker, Die Gründer, Panaitios, Poseidonios*. Translated by Max Pohlenz. Zurich: Artemis, 1950.

Popper, Karl R. *Conjectures and Refutations: The Growth of Scientific Knowledge*. London: Routledge, 1963.

Popper, Karl. *Objective Knowledge: An Evolutionary Approach*. Oxford: Oxford University Press, 1972.

Popper, Karl. *Objektive Erkenntnis. Ein evolutionärer Entwurf*. Hamburg: Hoffmann Und Campe Verlag, 1973.

Putnam, Hilary. *Pragmatism: An Open Question*. Oxford: Blackwell, 1995.

Ricœur, Paul. "Philosopher après Kierkegaard," in *Revie de Théologie et de Philosophie*, 13. (1963). Accessed online at https://doi.org/10.5169/seals-380798.

Ricœur, Paul. "Philosophieren nach Kierkegaard," in *Materialien zur Philosophie Søren Kierkegaards*. Edited by Michael Theunissen und Wilfried Greve. Frankfurt am Main: Suhrkamp, 1979.

Robertson, Donald. *Stoicism and the Art of Happiness: Practical Wisdom for Everyday Life*, 2nd ed. London: Quercus, 2018.

Rosenzweig, Franz. Letter to Friedrich Meinecke. In *Das Buchlein vom gesunden und kranken Menschenverstand*. Düsseldorf: Melzer Verlag, 1964.

Rosenzweig, Franz. *Understanding the Sick and the Healthy: A View of World, Man, and God*. Translated by Nahum Norbert Galtzer. Boston, MA: Harvard University Press, 1999.

de Rougemont, Denis. *The Devil's Share: An Essay on the Diabolic in Modern Society*. Translated by Haakon Chevalier. New York: Pantheon Books, 1944.

de Rougemont, Denis. *Der Anteil des Teufels*. Munich: Matthes und Seitz Verlag, 1999.

Russell, Bertrand. *The Problems of Philosophy*. Oxford: Oxford University Press, 1912.

Schefczyk, Michael. "Philosophische und psychologische Individualberatung." *AGORA*, No. 10/11. 1991.

Scheler, Max. *Reue und Wiedergeburt, in Vom Ewigen im Menschen*, 3rd ed. Berlin: Der neue Geist Verlag, 1933.

Scheler, Max. "Das Ressentiment im Aufbau der Moralen," in *Gesammelte Werke,* III. Bern: Francke-Verlag, 1955.

Scheler, Max. *Ressentiment.* Translated by Lewis B. Coser of *Das Ressentiment im Aufbau der Morallen* (from the German text of 1915). Milwaukee, WI: Marquette University Press, 1994.

Schelling, Friedrich Wilhelm Joseph. *Erste Vorlesung in München vom 26.* November 1827, *Ausgewählte Werke, Schriften von 1813–1830.* Darmstadt: Wissenschaftliche Buchgesellschaft, 1976.

Schleiermacher, Friedrich Daniel Ernst. *On Religion: Speeches to Its Cultured Despisers*. Translated and edited by Richard Crouter. Cambridge University Press, 1988. Uber Religion. Reden an die gebildeten unter ihren Verächtern [1799].

Schleiermacher, Friedrich Daniel Ernst. "Das eigentliche Gespräch." From *Einleitung in die Dialektik.* In Friedrich Schleiermachers Dialektik. Edited by Rudolf Odebrecht. Leipzig: J. C. Hinrichs, 1942; Darmstadt: Wissenschaftliche Buchgesellschaft, 1976.

Schleiermacher, Friedrich Daniel Ernst. *Dialectic or The Art of Doing Philosophy.* Edited by Terrence N. Tice. Atlanta, GA: Scholars Press, 1996.

Schnädelbach, Herbert. "Das Gespräch der Philosophie." Farewell lecture at the Humboldt University, June 18, 2002.

Schopenhauer, Arthur. *Sämtliche Werke.* Edited by Angelika Hübscher. Manheim: Brockhaus, 1988.

Schopenhauer, Arthur. *On the Basis of Morality.* Translated by E. F. J. Payne. Indianapolis: Hackett, 1995.

Schopenhauer, Arthur. *The World as Will and Representation*, I. Translated by Judith Norman, Alistair Welchman, and Christopher Janaway. Cambridge: Cambridge University Press, 2010.

Schopenhauer, Arthur. *Parerga and Paralipomena: Short Philosophical Essays*, I. Translated by Sabine Roehr and Christopher Janaway. Cambridge: Cambridge University Press, 2014.

Schopenhauer, Arthur. *Parerga and Paralipomena: Short Philosophical Essays*, II. Translated by Adrian Del Caro and Christopher Janaway. Cambridge: Cambridge University Press, 2015.

Schopenhauer, Arthur. *The World as Will and Representation*, II. Translated by Judith Norman, Alistair Welchman, and Christopher Janaway. Cambridge: Cambridge University Press, 2018.

Schulz, Walter. "Philosophie als Beruf," in *Philosophie als Beruf.* Edited by J. Schickel. Frankfurt am Main: Fischer-Taschenbuch, 1982.

Seneca, *Letters from a Stoic*, Letter XVI to Lucilius. Translated by Robin Campbell. London: Penguin, 1969.

Seuse, Heinrich. *Henry Suso: The Exemplar, with Two German Sermons.* The Classics of Western Spirituality. Edited by Frank J. Tobin. New York: Paulist Press, 1989.

Sloterdijk, Peter. *Critique of Cynical Reason.* Translated by Michael Eldred. Minneapolis: University of Minnesota Press, 1987.

Sloterdijk, Peter. *Zur Welt kommen—Zur Sprache kommen.* Frankfurt am Main: Suhrkamp, 1988.

Sloterdijk, Peter. *God's Zeal: The Battle of the Three Monotheisms.* Translated by Wieland Hoban. Cambridge, UK: Polity, 2009.

Spaemann, Robert. "Die zwei Grundbegriffe der Moral." In *Grenzen. Zur ethischen Dimension des Handelns.* Stuttgart: Klett-Cotta, 2001.

Spaemann, Robert. "Wer ist ein gebildeter Mensch?" In *Grenzen. Zur ethischen Dimension des Handelns*. Stuttgart: Klett-Cotta, 2001.

Sprague, Rosamond Kent (ed.). *The Older Sophists*. Columbia: University of South Carolina Press, 1972.

Stöcklein, Paul. *Wege zum späten Goethe*. Darmstadt: Wissenschaftliche Buchgesellschaft, 1973.

Strauss, Botho. "Allein mit allen." In *Gedankenbuch*. München: Carl Hanser Verlag, 2014.

Tarnero-Pansart, Marie-Claude. "Der Patient als Dulder," in *Geduld: Die Kunst des Wartens.* Edited by Ruthard Stäblein. Darmstadt: Bühl-Moos/Elster, 1994.

Tauler, John. *The Sermons and Spiritual Conferences of John Tauler, the Illuminated Doctor*. Translated by Walter Elliot. Washington, DC: Apostolic Mission House, 1910.

Thibon, Gustave. *Nietzsche und Johannes vom Kreuz*. Paderborn: Ferdinand Schöningh, 1957.

Watzlawick, Paul. *Die Möglichkeit des Andersseins*. Bern-Stuttgart-Vienna: Huber, 1978.

Wilde, Oscar. *The Plays of Oscar Wilde*. Stansted, UK: Wordsworth Editions, 2000.

Wittgenstein, Ludwig. *Philosophical Investigations*. Oxford: Basil Blackwell, 1958.

Xenophon. *Conversations of Socrates*, rev. ed. Edited by Robin H. Waterfield, translated by Hugh Tredinnick and Robin H. Waterfield. London: Penguin Classics, 1990.

Zuckmayer, Carl. *Als wär's ein Stück von mir: Horen der Freundschaft. Werkausgabe in 10 Bänden*, II. Frankfurt am Main: Fischer, 1966.

Name Index

Subject Index

About the Author and Translator

AUTHOR

Dr. Gerd B. Achenbach was born 1947 in Hameln, Germany, and is the founder of the Philosophical Praxis as well as the founder and chairman of the first Society of Philosophical Praxis (GPP e.V., 1982). He is author of several books (*Die reine und die praktische Philosophie*, *Das Prinzip Heilung*, *Vom Richtigen im Falschen*, *Lebenskönnerschaft*, *Liebe—der göttliche Wahn*, *Das kleine Buch der inneren Ruhe*, *Philosophie der Philosophischen Praxis*), taught at numerous universities, and has been a keynote speaker on various international congresses.

TRANSLATOR

Michael Picard teaches philosophy at Douglas College in Vancouver, Canada. He holds an MSc and PhD in philosophy from Massachusetts Institute of Technology and is a longtime animator of public participatory philosophy, as well as creator of the web app and game Tug of Logic. Picard is author of *This Is Not a Book* (2007) and *How to Play Philosophy* (2022).

www.ingramcontent.com/pod-product-compliance
Lightning Source LLC
LaVergne TN
LVHW091530200926
848483LV00002B/353
* 9 7 8 1 7 9 3 6 5 1 1 3 6 *